COLORADO
Historical Tour Guide

pu   ites on
do   Colora-
da   GORDON C   ER   H LIBRARY   early-
wa   76 S   th 4th S   ncient
di   Carbonda   olorado   623   Where
th   known,
za   civili-
ab   ndians
pi   doned

The Story Behind the Legend

The story we relate here is adapted from an account by Russell Lopez of the Ute Mountain Ute Indian Tribe. It is a story that dates back to the early Utes and the legend about these strange mountains that rise on their lands.

In the very old days, Sleeping Ute Mountain was a Great Warrior God. He came to help fight against the Evil Ones who were causing much trouble. A tremendous battle between the Great Warrior God and the Evil Ones followed. As they stepped hard upon the earth and braced themselves to fight, their feet pushed the land into mountains and valleys. This is the way the country of this region came to be as it is today.

The Great Warrior God was hurt, so he lay down to rest and fell into a deep sleep. The blood from his wounds turned into living water for all creatures to drink. When fog or clouds settled over the sleeping Warrior God, it was a sign that he was changing his blankets of which he had four. When the Indians saw the light green blanket over their God, they knew it was spring. The dark green blanket was summer, the yellow and red one was fall, and the white was winter.

The Indians believed when clouds gather on the highest peak, the Warrior God was pleased with his people and let rain clouds slip from his pockets. Even today, Sleeping Ute Mountain is used by the people in the area to forecast the weather.

The Indians believed that the Great Warrior God would rise again to help them in their fight against their enemies.

Legend of the Sleeping Ute

From almost anywhere in the Cortez-Mesa Verde Area, the Sleeping Ute Mountain is clearly visible on the southwestern horizon. At first glance, this small isolated range of peaks and hills seems like nothing more than it is. But look again! Etched against the sky is the image of a giant man lying on his back. A feathered headdress streams outward from his reclining head; arms are folded carefully across his chest, thighs, knees, feet, and even toes—are all unmistakably clear. See the drawing over the photo and compare them.

Dedicated to Mrs. Geraldine Porter
Born in the 19th century but definitely a 20th century woman
One of the last of her breed.

Author D. Ray Wilson
COLORADO HISTORICAL TOUR GUIDE

First Edition, 1990

Published by Crossroads Communications
Carpentersville, IL 60110-0007
Manufactured in the United States of America

Library of Congress Catalog Number: 90-80022
International Standard Book Number: 0-916445-26-7

OTHER TOUR GUIDES BY D. RAY WILSON
"Nebraska Historical Tour Guide," 2nd edition
"Wyoming Historical Tour Guide," 2nd edition
"Iowa Historical Tour Guide"
"Kansas Historical Tour Guide," 2nd edition
"Missouri Historical Tour Guide"
"Greater Chicago Historical Tour Guide"

ABOUT THE AUTHOR

D. Ray Wilson, a native Californian, has been a journalist for more than 40 years and has served on newspapers in Nebraska, Kansas, California, Arizona, and Illinois. He is author of *"The Folks," "Fort Kearny on the Platte,"* and *"Episode on Hill 616"* in addition to his series of historical tour guides. Wilson, who received his journalism degree from Northern Illinois University, is publisher and editor of two Illinois daily newspapers and several weeklies. In 1985, he received an honorary Doctor of Letters degree from Judson College, Elgin, IL. He is listed in several editions of "Who's Who" and is founder and chairman of the board of the DuPage Heritage Gallery.

Table of Contents

Introduction

This book is written for those persons who appreciate the uniqueness of American history and are interested specifically in the State of Colorado's colorful past.

Colorado, the "Centennial State," has a unique history. Over 1400 years ago the Anasazi, a Navajo word meaning "the Ancient Ones," began building their cliff dwellings in Mesa Verde and over a 700 year period built five major such dwellings and numerous mesa top villages. Their origin and destination after abandoning the area remain a mystery to this day despite decades of research by archaeologists, anthropologists, and other specialists.

The discovery of gold in 1859 brought thousands of people to the territory and towns were established. Large cattle drives found their way through Colorado to the expansive Wyoming ranges. Then came the railroaders as the need for transportation arose quickly as the territory began to develop. While Promontory Point, Utah, looms large in transportation history, it connected rail service only between Omaha and Sacramento. Rail service from coast-to-coast, through the first continuous chain of railroads, did not become a reality until 1870 when East and West met at Comanche Crossing (at Strasburg), east of Denver.

When the great gold fields seemed to be played out, another rich ore was discovered—silver—creating another group of millionaires and many more disappointments.

There were Indian fights—the Sand Creek Massacre, the Battle of Summit Springs, the Battle of Beecher Island, and many others. There are numerous Indian tribes whose heritage is interwoven with Colorado's past.

The natural wonders of Colorado are well-known.

Many of the early-day explorers—Zebulon Pike, Stephen Long, James Pattie, and Charles Fremont—found their way through Colorado as they searched for routes to the West Coast. One of the many famous early-day trading posts was Bent's Fort, established by Charles Bent and Ceran St. Vrain, near today's La Junta. A section of the well-known Santa Fe Trail found its way through the southeastern part of Colorado.

Many famous names are associated with the "Centennial State." Among some of these are Kit Carson, Chief Ouray,

1

Charles Goodnight, John W. Iliff, Henry M. Teller, Otto Mears, Horace A. W. Tabor, Baby Doe, "Unsinkable Molly" Brown, "Buffalo Bill" Cody, George W. Swink, David H. Moffat, and Scott Carpenter. There were also the infamous—persons such as John Chivington and Alferd Packer for example. We could go on and on. There are many stories about people, places and things.

There is much to see and enjoy in the "Centennial State." This book is written as much for the natives as for the visitors to the state. We have crisscrossed it many times during our research and have come to appreciate the state more on each visit.

We could have continued the research but all of these projects must come to an end if they are ever to be published. During some of our research we found conflicting or differing stories. After careful research we have picked out those stories and accounts we felt most comfortable with.

The people here are friendly and most helpful. We received assistance from literally hundreds of persons connected with county historical societies and chambers of commerce. Several other interested individuals were also helpful.

My special thanks to Alice McCoy who assisted in every step of the research and played a major role in the production of this work. My thanks, too, to Jeri Salzmann for proofreading and copy editing. My thanks also to my wife, Bea, and my daughters for their forebearance and encouragement. Bea and I first met in Denver and this great city holds a special place in our lives. Just after World War II she was going to school there and I was stationed at Lowry Field, assigned to the Air Training Command.

While maps are included in the book, it would be well to have a good state map in hand on any tour.

Please slow up a bit next time you are in the "Centennial State" and enjoy some of its many offerings. We hope you enjoy this book and find it helpful.

D. Ray Wilson
Sleepy Hollow, IL

2

Chapter 1
An Overview

A look at the happenings and the people involved in the rich history of the Centennial State.

Tyrannosaurus Rex greets the visitor to the Denver Museum of Natural History, the seventh largest museum in the United States. Dinosaurs lived in the Colorado region over 100 million years ago.

Chapter 1
An Overview

Colorado, the Centennial State, was admitted as the 38th state to the Union, August 1, 1876. The natural beauty of the state is reflected in its name. "Colorado" is the Spanish word for "colored red." It is also believed the name may have been derived from the word "coloreado" which means "many colors together." The state also boasts of the Colorado River which flows through majestic canyons of red stone.

Evidence indicates that the history of the area extends as far back as 100 million years ago. Dinosaur remains from that period have been found in Fremont County.

The earliest inhabitants of Colorado are believed to have been the **Clovis people** who were here 11,600 and 10,900 B.C. **Clovis man** hunted mammoths and was followed by **Folsom man** who hunted giant bison here. Paleo Indian hunter kill sites and camps have been found in the area.

The Indians called **Basket Makers** established permanent residences on Mesa Verde, in the southwest corner of the state, as early as 500 or 600 B.C. By 1000 A.D. **Anasazi** and **Fremont people** had settled in western and southwestern Colorado.

By the 1300s, the Apaches were living on the Colorado plains where they grew corn, beans and squash. By 1700, the Utes were living in the Colorado mountains. Following contact with Europeans, the Indians began to acquire horses, guns and metal tools and equipment which greatly changed their lives.

Later, the Comanches moved onto the plains forcing the Apaches to move south. The Comanches were able to dominate the plains for the next century for several reasons. The vast buffalo herds provided them with food, the horse increased their mobility, and their friends supplied them with guns. In addition to the Apaches, Utes and Comanches, early explorers found several other Indian tribes in the area including the Arapaho, Cheyenne, Kiowa and Pawnee.

Mexican influences began early in the state's history. **Juan de Onate**, a Mexican gold seeker, ventured as far north as the present day site of **Denver** in 1601. **Silvestre Velez de Escalante** and **Francisco Atanasio Dominquez**, Franciscan friars,

Over 1400 years ago, a group of Indians, the Anasazi, living in the Four Corners region chose Mesa Verde for their home. For over 700 years their descendants lived and flourished here and then suddenly disappeared. This diorama of the Balcony House in Mesa Verde is on display at the Colorado History Museum in Denver.

explored southern Colorado while searching for a shorter route from New Mexico to the California missions in 1776.

Many claims were made on this colorful country. In 1682, the explorer La Salle claimed for France an area that included what is today eastern Colorado. In 1706, **Juan de Ulibarri** claimed the region for Spain. The eastern part of what is Colorado today was included in the Louisiana Purchase in 1803.

In 1806-07 **Lt. Zebulon Pike** reached the headwaters of the Arkansas River and then crossed the Sangre de Cristo Range to the Conejos River in the San Luis Valley during his explorations. Spanish dragoons captured Pike and his expedition in the Valley and took them to Santa Fe. They were released several months later. Pike first sighted the peak bearing his name from at least 150 miles out on the plains in 1806.

The most famous mountain peak in Colorado is 14,110-foot **Pikes Peak** near **Colorado Springs**. The highest mountain peak is **Mt. Elbert** that is 14,433 feet above sea level. It is located west of US 24 between **Leadville** and **Buena Vista** There are 54 peaks in the Colorado Rockies with elevations in excess of 14,000 feet. In the Sawatch Range alone, named by the Ute Indians and meaning "blue earth," there are 15 peaks of

6

14,000 feet or more. The state has 830 additional peaks over 11,000 feet.

One of the state's most spectacular drives is the road to the top of 14,264 foot **Mt. Evans**—the highest paved road in North America. At the summit of **Mt. Evans** are the remains of the historic **Crest House**, a gift shop and retreat for visitors. This building stood for 39 years. It was destroyed by fire in 1979.

Major Stephen H. Long explored the region in 1820. Members of Long's expedition were the first to climb **Pikes Peak**. **Longs Peak** (14,256 feet), in **Rocky Mountain National Park**, was named for Major Long.

In 1811, **Don Jose Rafael Serracino** led an expedition north of Santa Fe in search of a mysterious Spanish settlement. The next year, three Americans were imprisoned by the Spanish for attempting to open Santa Fe trade.

Mauricio Raze Lagos Garcia traveled through present-day western Colorado in 1813.

Trapping became a lucrative enterprise for many. **Auguste Chouteau** and **Julius de Munn**, with 45 men, trapped for furs in the Central Rockies in 1816-17.

In 1820, **Jean Baptiste Chalifoux** went on a fur trapping expedition in present northern Colorado.

Among the early trappers were the mountain men including such names as **William H. Ashley, James Bridger, Jedediah S. Smith, Kit Carson**, and the **Bent brothers—Charles and William**, the most noted of seven brothers. These men were drawn to the mountains by the beaver trade which lasted only from about 1820 to the early 1840s.

In 1821-22, **Hugh Glenn** and **Jacob Fowler** and 18 men trapped furs in the southern Central Rockies. There are records to indicate that they built a log hut near Pueblo.

Meanwhile the Arapaho and Cheyenne, living on the eastern plains, came into greater contact with the American explorers and trappers. The discovery of gold, the influx of settlers, railroad construction, and the destruction of the buffalo soon ended their traditional way of life.

Mexico gained control of western Colorado from Spain in 1821. The first wave of settlers to reach Colorado arrived from the south. They came to take possession of vast tracts of lands granted by the Mexican government. For the most part they were mestizos, people of both Mexican and Indian ancestry. The first permanent settlements were established in the 1840s

7

in the San Luis Valley and along the Purgatoire River.

James Ohio Pattie explored the Colorado Rockies between 1824-30.

In 1828, **Antoine Robidoux** built **Fort Uncompahgre**, a trading post, on the Gunnison River.

Charles Bent and **Ceran St. Vrain** formed a partnership to trade with the Indians on the Upper Arkansas River in 1830.

Bent's Fort, near the site of present day **La Junta**, was the first American settlement in the area. It was established in 1833 by the **Bent and St. Vrain Fur Company** and was used as a base by Kit Carson and other famous frontiersmen.

The Cheyenne defeated the Kiowas near present day Denver in 1833. That same year great meteorite showers created panic among the Plains Indians.

In 1835, **Luis Vasquez** and **Andrew Sublette** built a trading post they called **Fort Vasquez**. That same year, **Col. Henry Dodge** led U.S. dragoons on a peace mission to quell intertribal warfare.

Fort Lupton, a trading post, was established in 1836. In 1837, two forts were established. **Fort Davy Crockett** was established at **Brown's Hole** and **Bent, St. Vrain and Company** established **Fort St. Vrain**. Both were commercial trading posts.

A smallpox epidemic swept among the Kiowas and Comanches in 1839. That same year, the expedition of German scientist **F. A. Wislizenus** reached **Brown's Hole**.

Charles F. Fremont led his first expedition through the Rockies in 1842; his second in 1843. Fremont's third expedition through the Colorado Rockies was in 1845. In 1848, he led his disasterous winter expedition in the San Juan Mountains while in search of a railroad route through the area. Eleven of the 33 men in his party perished in a snowstorm during this expedition. Fremont's fifth and final expedition through the Rockies occurred in 1854.

Christopher "Kit" Carson (1809-1868) gained national prominence as a guide for Fremont on his western expeditions. He had worked as a trapper from 1829 to 1841 and was involved in several fights with the Indians. Carson went to California with Fremont at the outbreak of the Mexican War and later served with **Brig. Gen. Stephen Kearny** and the **Army of the West** during that war. At the outbreak of the Civil War he was made a colonel of the New Mexico Volunteer Regiment and fought both the Confederates and Indians during the war. Carson died at **Fort Lyon** in 1868.

The U.S. gained control of the territory during the Mexican War of 1846-48 and obtained the land under the terms of the treaty that followed that war. The mestizos settlers, who had come earlier at the invitation of the Mexicans, became new Americans.

Gen. Stephen W. Kearny, commanding the Army of the West that included the Mormon Battalion recruited at Omaha, Neb., traveled through the southeastern part of Colorado on the Santa Fe Trail during the Mexican War enroute to San Diego, Calif., in 1846. Kearny and his troops occupied New Mexico, held by the Mexicans, enroute to the West Coast.

Bent and St. Vrain ended their partnership; Bent's Fort was burned in 1849. In 1852 Bent established a new trading post on the Arkansas River. A cholera epidemic swept among the Comanches and Cheyennes.

Fort Massachusetts (1852-58) was the first Army post established in Colorado. The post was established June 22, 1852, on Ute Creek at the opening into the San Luis Valley as a defense against the Utes and Apaches. The post was garrisoned until June 24, 1858, when the troops were transferred to a new post, **Fort Garland**, a few miles to the south. The new post was established to protect settlers against Indians. **Brig. Gen. Kit Carson** was the commanding officer at the fort in 1866-67. The fort was abandoned on November 30, 1883.

The first Catholic mass was celebrated in the San Luis Valley in 1856. **Our Lady of Guadalupe** in **Conejos** was the first church built in Colorado.

Denver City Company was founded in 1858.

Denver was established with the merger of **Auraria**, organized by a group led by **William Green Russell**, and **Denver City**, organized by a group led by **William Larimer**. Auraria was established on the south bank of the Cherry Creek November 1, 1858 and Denver City across the creek a week later. The two towns merged April 5, 1860.

The new territory remained sparsely settled until the late 1850s. Gold was discovered at Cherry Creek near Denver, in 1858. **George A. Jackson** made his strike along the south fork of Chicago Creek on the present site of **Idaho Springs** on Janu-

9

ary 6, 1859; **John Gregory** struck gold on North Clear Creek near **Central City** in May. Silver was discovered at **Leadville** in 1877. These discoveries, and others, brought a rush of prospectors to the region.

An attempt was made in 1859 to organize the region into a territory that was to be called **Jefferson Territory**. This petition was denied by the Congress and official status as **Colorado Territory**, came February 28, 1861. **William Gilpin** was appointed the first territorial governor. **Henry M. Teller** and **Jerome B. Chaffee** were appointed as U.S. Senators representing the territory.

The *Rocky Mountain News*, established by **William N. Byers** in Denver on April 22, 1859, is the state's oldest newspaper. **KFKA** in **Greeley** was the state's first commercial radio station and went on the air in 1921. **KFEL-TV** (now **KWGN-TV**) in Denver became the state's first television station when it went on the air in 1952.

Fort Lyon was established on August 29, 1860, near Bent's Fort on the Arkansas River near present-day **Lamar**. First known as **Fort Wise**, for Virginia governor **Henry A. Wise**, the post was designated **Fort Lyon**, June 25, 1862. The fort was renamed for **Brig. Gen. Nathaniel Lyon**, who was killed leading the Union forces in the Battle of Wilson Creek, Mo., August 10, 1861. In June, 1867, this post was abandoned and new Fort Lyon was established 20 miles upstream. It was abandoned August 31, 1889.

Colorado contributed 4,903 men to the Union cause in the Civil War. **Camp Weld** was established two miles south of Denver on the east bank of the South Platte River as a staging area for Colorado troops during the war. It was closed in 1865. Three regiments and two smaller units were organized in the state. The **1st Colorado Infantry**, later designated the **1st Colorado Cavalry**, was commanded by **Col. John P. Slough** and **Col. John Chivington**. The **2nd Colorado Infantry**, commanded by **Col. Jesse Leavenworth**, and the **3rd Colorado Infantry**, commanded by **Col. James Fox**, were consolidated to form the **2nd Colorado Cavalry**. The **3rd Colorado Cavalry** was commanded by **Col. George Shoup**. The other two units were **McLain's Independent Battery** and **Captain Tyler's Mounted Rangers**. The regiments saw action in New Mexico and Missouri.

10

Dr. John Evans, who helped organize the Republican Party which nominated Abraham Lincoln, was offered the governorship of Colorado Territory. He had been instrumental in the founding of Northwestern University in Illinois and the Illinois town of Evanston is named in his honor. He made numerous contributions to his adopted state of Colorado.

Col. John Chivington commanded the 3rd Colorado Regiment, the "Bloody Third," at the Sand Creek Massacre in late 1864. In the massacre, 123 Indians were killed, a majority of whom were women and children. The event incited the Indians to go on the warpath, seeking revenge for what they believed was white treachery. For months they raided the major trails in Nebraska, Kansas, Colorado and Wyoming. Peace did not come until 1867 when treaties were signed and the Indians moved on a reservation in Oklahoma Territory.

The Confederacy had hoped to conquer Colorado and New Mexico to obtain a route to the Pacific and divert the mineral wealth of Colorado, Nevada, and California to bolster its treasury. While no Civil War battles were fought in Colorado, troops raised by **Territorial Governor William Gilpin** stopped the advance of **Brig. Gen. Henry H. Sibley** and his Confederate troops at Glorietta Pass, New Mexico, in 1862.

In 1863, Denver was hard-hit by a disasterous fire that destroyed 70 buildings. Thirteen months later, eight persons were killed and heavy property losses were sustained in the Cherry Creek flood. Indian trouble developed as settlers, traders and explorers continued to pour into their hunting lands. There were many small clashes and several important battles between the two.

The Army established **Camp Collins** in the fall of 1863 on the Cache la Poudre River at **Laporte** to protect the overland stage route, emigrant trains, and settlers from marauding Indians. The post was moved in August, 1864, to the site of present day **Fort Collins**. Fort Collins was established to guard the main wagon route in northern Colorado Territory. The freighters on this route, from Julesburg to Denver, ran through the hunting grounds of the Utes, Cheyenne, and Arapahoes and often came under attack during the uprisings of 1864-65. The Army abandoned the fort in the spring of 1867.

In the summer of 1864, the Sioux, with their Cheyenne and Arapaho allies, struck the Oregon Trail from the Little Blue in south central Nebraska to eastern Wyoming and northeastern Colorado. Travel on some 400 miles of the Oregon Trail came to a halt for several weeks. Scores of persons were killed in these raids and property losses were heavy. By late October, 1864, the raids had subsided and mail, freighting and immigrant wagon service was resumed on a limited basis.

The **Hungate Massacre** of June 11, 1864, created panic in Denver about the time of other major Indian uprisings on the Great Plains.

Several temporary military outposts were established to meet the Indian menace. **Camp Evans** came into existence c. 1864 2.5 miles northeast of Denver while **Camp Wheeler** was set up in Denver's Lincoln Park about the same time. **Denver Depot** was established c. 1863. **Fort Latham** was established six miles south of **Kersey** in 1864 as was **Fort Lincoln** at **Hunts-**

ville and the **Station at Gray's Ranch.**

The Indians rose up again after the **Sand Creek Massacre,** north of Bent's Fort, in the Colorado Territory. Here, November 29, 1864, **Col. John M. Chivington** and the "Bloody Third" **(3rd Colorado Regiment)** attacked the Sand Creek camp of Cheyenne **Chief Black Kettle,** who believed there had been an armistice. In the early morning attack, 123 Cheyennes were massacred, including 98 women and children. There were countless wounded. Chivington's forces lost nine troopers and suffered 38 wounded.

Indian raiders came out in full force in retaliation for the Sand Creek treachery.

The Indian uprisings on the Plains in 1864 created the need for an Army post on the overland trail junction near **Julesburg. Camp Rankin** was established on May 19, 1864, on the south bank of the South Platte River, opposite the mouth of Lodgepole Creek. The name was changed to **Fort Sedgwick,** September 27, 1865. The fort was abandoned on May 31, 1871.

The morning of January 6, 1865, a band of Indians swooped down on a wagon train outside of Julesburg and killed four men. The next morning, Indians appeared in large numbers surrounding Camp Rankin, just outside of Julesburg. About mid-morning, a small group of Indians approached the fort as decoys and drew out a force of 37 troopers of Co. F, 7th Iowa Cavalry, under the command of **Capt. Nicholas O'Brien.**

When the troopers were in the open, the full force of Indians attacked, driving the cavalrymen back into the fort but not before 14 soldiers were killed. In early February the Indians returned and burned Julesburg. Captain O'Brien and his company of the 7th Iowa Cavalry had established the post the previous fall.

In September, 1868, a large force of Indians, led by **Roman Nose,** attacked 50 Army Scouts led by **Col. George A. Forsyth** on the Arikaree River in Yuma County in eastern Colorado. The scouts fought for several days on **Beecher Island,** named for **Lt. Fred Beecher,** one of those killed in the battle. The small force was rescued by troops from Fort Wallace in Kansas.

Major (Bvt. Major General) Eugene Carr, commanding the **5th U.S. Cavalry,** and the **Pawnee Scouts,** led by **Major Frank North,** tracked down rampaging Cheyenne Dog Soldiers at **Summit Springs** on the northeastern Colorado plains after a 300 mile march in the summer of 1869. The Cheyennes were defeated and dispersed in the **Battle of Summit Springs**. This ended the Indian-white conflict on the plains.

The last major Indian battle in the state was the **Meeker Massacre** in the fall of 1879. In this fight, the Ute Indians killed their reservation agent, **Nathan C. Meeker** and 10 government employees. Three women, including Mrs. Meeker and her 19-year old daughter, Josephine, and two small children were abducted by the Utes.

Troops from Fort Steele and Fort Russell, Wyoming Territory, were dispatched to put down this uprising. **Major Thomas Thornburgh**, commander of Fort Steele, and 12 of his troopers were killed and 23 wounded September 29—October 5 enroute to the agency to put down the uprising. The Wyoming troops were pinned down by the Indians for five days.

To protect the stage line between the Missouri River and Denver, **Camp Wardwell** was established on July 1, 1865, and designated **Fort Morgan** on June 23, 1866. The fort was abandoned on May 18, 1868.

Fort Reynolds was established on July 3, 1867, on the Arkansas River, 20 miles east of **Pueblo**. It was abandoned July 15, 1872.

The **Goodnight-Loving Trail**, from Texas to Cheyenne through Colorado, was opened in 1866. The Texas cattlemen drove 2,000 head of cattle up this route. **Charles Goodnight** and **Oliver Loving** sold all of their steers at Fort Sumner and then Loving drove the cows and calves to Denver where he sold this part of their herd to **John Wesley Iliff**. That same year sugar beets were introduced in the Platte Valley by **Peter Magnes**.

Merino sheep were introduced into Colorado Territory in 1869.

The railroad, the Denver Pacific, linked Denver with the Union Pacific in Cheyenne and the East in 1870. A short time later that year, the Kansas Pacific reached Denver.

The territorial prison was built and opened in **Canon City** in 1871. The first person to be executed by the State of Colorado was **Noverto Griego**. He was convicted of murdering a man in **Trinidad** in 1890. **John Docherty** was the first man to be imprisoned in Colorado for practicing abortion. The youngest person to be imprisoned by the state was 11-year old **Antone**

Woode, convicted in 1893 for murdering a neighbor. He served 12 years of a 25 year sentence.

Territorial Governor John L. Routt was elected as the first state governor in 1876. Colorado became the 38th state on August 1.

An important figure in Colorado's history was **Henry Moore Teller** (1830-1914). Teller, originally a Republican, served five terms in the United States Senate. He was elected to his first term in 1876 but resigned in 1882 to become Secretary of the Interior under President Chester A. Arthur. He was elected to the Senate again in 1885 and 1891. In 1896, he withdrew from the Republican party because its platform called for a monetary system based on the gold standard and Teller favored the free coinage of silver because it would benefit Colorado. He was elected to the Senate in 1897 as a Silver Republican party candidate and was reelected in 1903 as a Democrat.

A new mining boom, through silver discoveries extracted from carbonates discarded at the gold mines, brought new wealth and more people in the early days of statehood. **Leadville** and **Aspen** became silver centers. One of the most colorful characters to emerge during this period was **Horace A. W. Tabor,** who became known as the "Silver King." With his silver fortune he built several of the most prominent buildings in Leadville and Denver. His investments in Denver helped the city to become a business and financial center. He became a U.S. Senator and President Chester A. Arthur attended his wedding to **Elizabeth "Baby" Doe.**

Nathan C. Meeker, sponsored by *New York Tribune* Editor **Horace Greeley,** founded **Union Colony** in 1870, a cooperative agricultural community in the South Platte Valley. The town that grew out of it, north of Denver, was named for **Greeley.** Meeker was killed on the Ute Indian reservation in an uprising in 1879.

A grasshopper plague hit Colorado in 1875.

Silver was found near present-day Leadville in 1877 and the silver rush was on early the next year. The silver and lead taken from the old gold mines soon exceeded the output of the gold output. But with these new developments came another kind of crisis. By 1880 labor problems developed at the mines and the first major strike was called in Leadville. The so-called **Royal Gorge War,** between the Atchison, Topeka & Santa Fe and

Elizabeth McCourt married Harvey Doe in Oshkosh, Wisconsin, and the two went to Central City hoping to strike it rich. Instead the two separated, and Baby Doe, as she became known, met the wealthy H.A.W. Tabor. They fell in love and were married in a lavish Washington, D. C., wedding after divorcing their spouses. Tabor lost his fortune in the silver crash of 1893 and on his deathbed implored Baby Doe to hang on to the Matchless Mine in Leadville. She spent 30 years at the unproductive mine and died in poverty.

Horace Austin Warner Tabor struck it rich by staking two miners in Central City for a third interest in the Little Pittsburgh. He divorced his wife, Augusta, shortly after meeting the beautiful Baby Doe. Tabor was one of Central City's and Denver's benefactors. Augusta, the rejected wife, died a wealthy and respected woman. He became postmaster in Denver and died in rather poor financial circumstances at the age of 69.

Denver & Rio Grande railroads, lasted from 1878 to 1880. Ultimately, the Rio Grande won the route to Leadville; the Santa Fe took the route to New Mexico.

On October 15, 1878, an Army post was established on the San Juan River at **Pagosa Springs** to guard the Ute Indian Reservation. It was named **Camp Lewis** and in December became **Fort Lewis**. The post was ordered to a new site on the La Plata River, 12 miles west of **Durango**. The original post was renamed **Cantonment Pagosa** and was abandoned after a brief period. The new **Fort Lewis** was abandoned on October 15, 1891.

After the Indian uprising in 1879, a post, **Cantonment on the Uncompahgre**, was established eight miles south of present day **Montrose** in June, 1880. The post was renamed **Fort Crawford** on December 15, 1886. It was abandoned on September 23, 1890.

In 1884, 59 miners were killed in a coal mine explosion at **Crested Butte**.

Fort Logan, originally called the **Post at Denver**, was established in October, 1887, as one of several troop centers. It was designated **Fort Logan** on April 5, 1889. It was closed after World War II.

The **Homestead Act** was amended in 1887 to include an additional 160 acres to encourage planting of trees on the plains. This amendment was referred to as a timber claim. **George Washington Swink**, who had come to Colorado in 1871 from Illinois, filed a homestead claim and a timber claim about three miles north and west of Rocky Ford. His claim, filed under the timber claim amendment, was the first issued. He received Patent No. 1, dated November 3, 1887, signed by President Grover Cleveland. Swink became the father of the Rocky Ford melon industry and was well known for his varieties of cantaloupes.

In 1888, two cowboys from the **Alamo Ranch** discovered the now well known Indian ruins at Mesa Verde.

The discovery of gold at **Cripple Creek** in 1891 set off one of the world's greatest gold rushes. Serious disputes between mine owners and the **Western Federation of Miners**, a labor union, occurred the last decade of the 19th century.

In 1893, Colorado became the second state to extend women's suffrage.

Margaret "The Unsinkable Molly" Tobin Brown gained the sobriquet by her actions during the sinking of the Titanic Monday, April 15, 1912, off the coast of Newfoundland. She was purported to have saved the lives of several passengers. Her husband, James Brown, struck it rich in Leadville and Molly eventually persuaded him to move to Denver where she struggled to become recognized by the city's upper-crust. A musical has been written about the intrepid Mrs. Brown.

It was also in 1893 that **Katherine Lee Bates**, a visiting professor at **Colorado College** in **Colorado Springs**, made the trip up Pikes Peak and was so inspired by the view wrote the poem "America the Beautiful."

The state capital was completed in 1894. That year Russian thistles, also known as "tumbleweeds," infested Colorado farmlands and a severe drought affected the state.

The 1893 nationwide Depression and repeal of the **1890 Sherman Silver Purchase Act** caused a serious drop in silver prices and many of the mines were closed as a result. The Sherman Silver Purchase Act had not only required the U.S. government to purchase nearly twice as much silver as before, but also added substantially to the amount of money already in circulation. The gold discovery at Cripple Creek helped to soften the blow of the silver crash and the state's economy continued to show growth.

The National Guard broke the miners' strike in Leadville in

One of the most spectacular crimes in Denver in the 1920s was the robbery that occurred in front of the U.S. Mint in 1922. Four bandits held up a Federal Reserve Bank car in front of the Mint which attracted its employees who gave battle to the bandits who made good their escape. The headlines in the Denver Post issued December 22nd headlined the story that rocked the city.

William F. "Buffalo Bill" Cody became one of the West's legends. As a teenager he joined the ill-fated Pony Express at Julesburg. He later served as a scout for the Army and was on the expedition that led to the Battle of Summit Springs in eastern Colorado. He entered show business before he was 30 years old. He earned his reputation as a buffalo hunter when he killed over 4,000 of the shaggy animals for meat for a Kansas railroad construction crew. Cody is buried on Lookout Mountain overlooking Denver.

1896. That same year a fire destroyed the downtown area of Cripple Creek.

Violent strikes occurred in 1901 in the **Union and Smugglers mines** near **Telluride** and continued into 1902.

In 1903 striking miners and National Guardsmen battled in Cripple Creek as labor problems in the mines continued. The miners strike at **Victor** was broken in 1904.

The state's first sugar refinery opened in **Grand Junction** in 1899. The U.S. Mint in Denver began producing coins in 1906. That same year Congress established **Mesa Verde National Park.**

Hog cholera devastated pork production in the state in 1912.

The **Ludlow massacre of 1914** shocked the nation. This tragedy occurred April 20, 1914, when the militia opened fire on striking coal miners living in a tent city just outside the mining camp, killing 19 miners, two women and 11 children. The camp of some 275 tents, housing about 800 miners and their families, was razed.

Colorado has two National Parks—**Mesa Verde National Park**, near **Cortez** in the southwest, designated in 1906, covering 51,017 acres that centers on prehistoric cliff dwellings, and **Rocky Mountain National Park** in central Colorado, designated in 1915 and covering 256,468 acres that includes many snow-capped peaks over 10,000 feet.

There are six National Monuments in the state. These include: **Black Canyon of the Gunnison National Monument**, near **Montrose**, designated in 1933 and covering 12,033 acres that include the deep narrow canyons of the Gunnison River; **Colorado National Monument**, near **Grand Junction**, designated in 1911 and covering 17,606 acres with huge monoliths, curious products of erosion; **Dinosaur National Monument**, in the northwest, designated in 1915 and covering 184,913 acres rich in fossil quarries; **Hovenweep National Monument**, in the southwest, designated in 1923 and covering 505 acres with four groups of prehistoric Indian pueblos and cliff dwellings; **Great Sand Dunes National Monument**, southwest of **Alamosa**, designated in 1932 and covering 34,979 acres with large, huge dunes in the Sangre de Cristo mountains; and **Yucca House**, near **Cortez**, designated in 1919 and covering nine acres with the remains of a prehistoric Indian village.

Shadow Mountain National Recreation Area, near **Boulder**, was designated in 1952 and covers 15,540 acres.

By 1920, oil had become Colorado's most important mineral product as many new oil fields were discovered.

The height of the **Ku Klux Klan** influence on state politics was reached in 1924-25.

Moffat Tunnel, a railroad tunnel through the mountains 40 miles west of Denver, was completed in 1927. The tunnel, 6.23 miles long, is one of the longest railroad tunnels in the world. It is named for **David H. Moffat**, a banker and railroad builder. The tunnel shortened the distance between Denver and Salt Lake City by 176 miles. It was leased to the Denver & Salt Lake Railroad.

Striking coal miners and the Colorado National Guard battled near **Lafayette** in 1927.

A riot at the **Colorado State Penitentiary** on October 3, 1929, saw eight guards and six prisoners killed and 10 others wounded.

Colorado was hard-hit by the Great Depression of the 1930s. Much of eastern Colorado became part of the midwest's "Dust Bowl" during the 1932-38 period.

In 1936 **Governor Johnson** ordered the National Guard to prevent Mexican laborers from entering the state.

Two major military facilities were in existence in Denver before the outbreak of World War II. **Fitzsimons Army Medical Center**, which came into existence in 1918 as U.S. Army Hospital No. 21. **Lowry Field** was established by the U.S. Army Air Corps in 1937.

The state's economy boomed during World War II. The government established several military bases in the state. **Fort Carson**, near **Colorado Springs**, and an ordnance plant at **Pueblo** were opened. **Camp Hale** was established to train ski troops; **Rocky Mountain Arsenal** opened; **Buckley Army Air Field, Peterson Army Air Field, Pueblo Army Air Field,** and **La Junta Army Air Field** were built to train air crews.

By the 1950s several government offices and military installations were established. Among some of these large facilities were the **National Bureau of Standards laboratory**, moved from Washington to Boulder in 1954; the **U.S.A.F. world-wide financial center** in Denver; the **U.S. Air Force Academy** opened in Colorado Springs in 1958; and headquarters for the **North American Air Defense Command (NORAD)** were completed in 1966 near Colorado Springs.

22

The Garden of the Gods with its red rocks of various sizes and shapes, in Colorado Springs, draws thousands of visitors annually. It is one of Colorado's many natural wonders.

The Air Force Academy's Cadet Chapel, a national landmark, is a popular tourist attraction in the Colorado Springs area. The Chapel features a 1,200-seat Protestant nave, a 500-seat Catholic sanctuary and a 100-seat Jewish synagogue.

A total of 139,000 Coloradoans served in the Armed Forces during World War II; 2,700 were killed.

In 1942, a **Japanese Relocation Camp**, referred to as **Amache**, was established at **Granada** in the southeastern part of the state. Amache was the name of a daughter of **Chief One Eye**, of the Southern Cheyenne, killed in the **Sand Creek Massacre** of 1864. Ten thousand persons were housed here. A camp for German POWs was established at **Camp Hale** during World War II. POW camps were also established at Frazier and Fort Morgan.

A major disaster occurred in 1976 when the floodwaters of the Big Thompson River swept through Big Thompson Canyon, near **Loveland**, killing more than 135 persons in its wake.

The **Alva B. Adams Tunnel**, completed in 1947, carries water through the Rocky Mountains from western Colorado to the area east of the mountains. It is part of a project that irrigates farmland in the northeastern part of the state. The **Colorado-Big Thompson Project**, a series of dams, pumping stations, reservoirs, and tunnels, irrigates over 700,000 acres of farmland.

The **Eisenhower Memorial Tunnel**, west of Denver on I-70, is the highest tunnel for motor vehicles in the world. It extends 1.7 miles at an altitude of 11,000 feet.

Several authors have come from Colorado. Among these are Helen Hunt Jackson, Hamlin Garland, Arthur Chapman, Gene Fowler, Mary Chase, Damon Runyon, and Eugene Field. Field served as managing editor of the *Denver Tribune* from 1881-83. Runyon wrote two books while working on the staff of the *Denver Post*. Mary Chase was awarded the Pulitzer Prize for her play, "Harvey."

The state government is headed up by the governor, elected to a four year term. The other elected officials, who also serve four-year terms, are the Lieutenant Governor, Secretary of State, Treasurer, and Attorney General. The auditor is appointed by the legislature to a five-year term. The General Assembly, composed of the Senate and House of Representatives, is the legislature of Colorado. The General Assembly convenes annually on a designated day in early January. The Senate consists of 35 senators who are elected for four-year terms, with one-half being elected every two years. The House of Representatives consists of 65 members who are elected for two-year terms. The great molybdenum deposit at **Climax** and the tungsten mines near **Boulder** began to be developed in 1918. Vast deposits of coal, natural gas, petroleum, uranium, vanadium, and zinc also help support Colorado's economy.

Colorado is a major producer of cattle with beef cattle accounting for nearly two-thirds of the state's agricultural income. There are large feed lot operations, especially in the **Greeley** area, where cattle are fattened. Colorado is also a leading sheep producer. The major field crops are wheat, corn, and sugar beets.

Chapter 2
The Greater Denver Area

A brief history of Denver and Denver County as well as parts of Adams, Arapahoe, Jefferson and Douglas Counties. A listing of all museums and historical places is included.

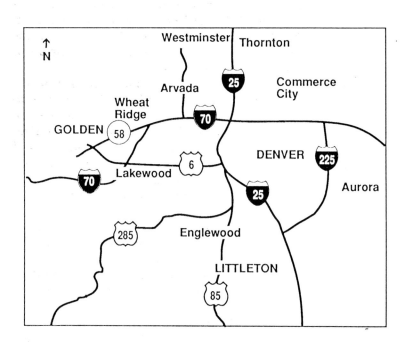

Chapter 2
The Greater Denver Area

Denver (pop. 514,678), capital of Colorado and county seat of Denver County, was settled in 1858 and incorporated in 1861. It was named for **James William Denver**, territorial governor of Kansas in 1858. As governor, Denver established order in the newly discovered Colorado gold mines and helped bring about the separation of Colorado from Kansas.

James Denver (1817-92), a Virginian, commanded a company of Missouri volunteers in the Mexican War. In 1850 he went to California where he served as a state senator and Secretary of State before being elected to the U.S. House of Representatives in 1855. President Buchanan appointed him Commissioner of Indian Affairs in 1857 and territorial governor of troubled Kansas the following year. He served as a brigadier general of volunteers during the Civil War. After the war, he practiced law in Washington, D.C.

The first Territorial Legislative Assembly met in Denver on September 9, 1861. **Colorado City**, now part of **Colorado Springs**, was designated the first Territorial capital. In 1862, the capital was transferred to **Golden City**, and finally, in 1867, Denver was selected as the permanent seat of Colorado government.

The city has a colorful past and was born out of the great "Pikes Peak or Bust" gold rush of 1859. While gold was discovered on **Cherry Creek**, where Denver began, the big strikes were found in the mountains to the west—in places like **Central City**. Denver became a distribution center for the miners and later became the social and recreational center for those who hit it big.

Green Russell and a party of Georgians arrived in the summer of 1858 at the diggings of Cherry Creek. They settled at a point where Speer Boulevard crosses Larimer Street today and called their camp **Auraria**. Another group arrived a short time later and set up town stakes across the creek and called their settlement **St. Charles**. Most of the second group returned to Leavenworth, Kansas, to register their townsite. As this group left another group from Kansas, under the leadership of **Gen.**

William Larimer arrived at St. Charles and liked what they saw. Larimer sent representatives back to Leavenworth immediately and they were able to file on St. Charles before the original group. Larimer and his group were responsible for naming the new town for James Denver.

The area grew quickly and soon required and enjoyed the amenities of civilized living. The first school was opened in the Cherry Creek area in 1859 by **O.J. Goldrick**. He opened Union School on Blake Street in Auraria, October 3, 1859, with 13 children in attendance on opening day. The first public library was established in Denver in 1860. The first stage performance held in Denver City was on October 3, 1859.

Two performances were presented that evening in Apollo Hall, above a saloon on Larimer Street. The titles of the plays performed were "The Cross of Gold" and "The Two Gregories."

James Pierson Beckwourth, the famed black mountain man, worked in Denver for seven years as a storekeeper for **Louis Vasquez** at a shop on what is 11th Street in downtown Denver today. At that time he lived in a cabin on the east bank of the South Platte River off US 285. Beckwourth (1798-1867?) came west into the Rocky Mountains with the fur traders in the 1820s. From 1826 to 1837 he lived with the Crow Indians, becoming a chief. He served as an Army scout for **Col. John Chivington** and the "Bloody Third" (**3rd Colorado Regiment**) and was involved with the **Sand Creek Massacre**. Later he operated trading posts in the mountains and ultimately settled in the California area named after him, **Beckwourth Valley**. Around the 1850s he discovered the pass through the Sierra Nevadas that opened the Sacramento Valley in California. This pass is known as the **Beckwourth Pass**. It was during this time that gold was discovered in Colorado. Beckwourth died when he ate poisoned meat served by the Crow Indians, who killed him because he would not return to their tribe.

Denver was served by the **Central Overland & Pikes Peak Express stage** in 1859 off the Oregon Trail. In 1860, the **Leavenworth & Pikes Express Company** stage reached the frontier town. **David Butterfield's Overland Despatch**, from Atchison and Leavenworth, also served Denver during the Civil War.

Early Denver had its share of unfortunate incidents. A disasterous fire in April 1863, destroyed 70 buildings in Denver. The fire started April 19 in a trash pile behind the Cherokee House

Hotel. Thirteen months later, May 19, 1864, eight persons lost their lives in the Cherry Creek flood. Property losses totaled several hundreds of thousands of dollars. Since the telegraph had reached Denver in '63, news spread east quickly.

June 11, 1864, Denverites were outraged by an atrocity committed by a small band of Indian raiders in a remote, desolate spot on Running Creek, 30 miles southeast of the town. Twenty-nine year old **Nathan W. Hungate**, his wife Ellen, and two daughters, three year old Laura and five-month old Florence, were massacred at the I. P. Van Wormer ranch. The Hungates' bodies had been mutilated. Only a German ranch hand survived and sounded the alarm in Denver. The bodies were returned to Denver and put on public display as the story of the massacre spread like wildfire from one settlement to another.

The settlers had been edgy since the April 12 battle at **Fremont Orchard Station**, 84 miles northeast of Denver. A small detail of troops of the **1st Colorado Cavalry** finally charged a camp of 200 Indians there. Two troopers lost their lives in the battle; two others were wounded.

About the same time, the **Independent Battery of Colorado Volunteer Artillery** was sent out from **Camp Weld**, two miles from Denver, to recover a stolen herd of cattle belonging to government contractors.

Camp Weld was opened during the Civil War as a staging area for Colorado troops. It was named for Colorado Territory's first lieutenant governor, **Lewis L. Weld**. He served with territorial governor **William Gilpin** in offices in the New York Store at Larimer and 14th Streets. Weld went on in 1863 to serve in the Union Army where he commanded black troops. He died in January, 1865 of a fever he had contracted at Appomattox.

Governor Gilpin acted promptly at the outbreak of the war to purchase firearms, recruit troops and to establish Camp Weld. He issued drafts totalling $375,000 which the War Department refused to honor because he had acted without federal authority. He was sacked by President Lincoln for his rashness and replaced by **John Evans** as governor, March 24, 1862. (The government eventually had to honor the drafts issued by Gilpin.)

The first cattle drive to Denver was up the **Goodnight-Loving Trail** (from Texas to Cheyenne) in 1866. **Charles Goodnight** and **Oliver Loving**, with 18 riders, drove 2,000 head of cattle from Texas to Fort Sumner, N.M., where they sold the steers. Loving took the cows and calves on to Denver where he sold them to **John Wesley Iliff**, an early day cattle baron. Iliff left a large part of his estate to the founding of the **Iliff School of Theology** in Denver.

Rail service reached Denver in 1870. The Denver Pacific connected with the main line Union Pacific at Cheyenne June 24th. The Kansas Pacific also arrived that year, August 15th, to provide service to Kansas City and the east.

Telephone service was established in Denver in 1879. In 1880 Denver was the fourth city in the world to adopt electric street lighting.

The **Denver Union Stockyard Company** was established in 1886.

The state capitol building was occupied in 1894, however, it actually took 22 years to complete the project. Construction of the building began July 5, 1886. Designed on an axis in the form of a Greek cross measuring 383 feet long by 315 feet wide, the capitol resembles the basic design of the nation's capitol in Washington, D. C.

By 1902, Denverites boasted a total of 200 automobiles, thus the 20th century was off to a running start.

Eight universities and colleges are located in Denver. These include **Colorado Women's College**, founded in 1888; **Conservative Baptist Theological Seminary**, 1950; the **University of Denver**, 1864; **Iliff School of Theology**, 1892; **Loretto Heights College**, 1918; **Metropolitan State College**, 1967; **Regis College**, 1887; and **St. Thomas Seminary**, 1906.

The Democratic National Convention was held in Denver in 1908. The Democrats nominated **William Jennings Bryan** as their presidential candidate. His running mate was **John W. Kern**.

Emily Griffith opened her **Emily Griffith Opportunity School** in Denver, September 7, 1916. The purpose of the school was to teach foreigners and disadvantaged students, ranging in age from 16 to 75. The school is located at 1250 Welton Street. Unfortunately, Miss Griffith and her sister Florence were found murdered in a remote cabin in June, 1947.

The longest street currently in Denver is Colfax Avenue, 26 miles in length. It is named for Schuyler Colfax (1823-85), a member of the House of Representatives for 14 years (1855-69) and then Vice President during President Grant's first term.

J. K. Mullen and Stephen Knight presented this sculpture, "Broncho Buster," to the City of Denver in 1920. The sculpture was placed in Capitol Park, between the state capitol and Denver's city hall (to the right in the photo).

The first issue of what was to become the *Rocky Mountain News* was published April 23, 1859 by **William N. Byers**, who moonlighted as a land agent. One of the first stores, built of hewn logs, in Denver was built by **Richens L. "Uncle Dick" Wootton**, a colorful figure in the early West, and it was upstairs in this store that Byers printed his early editions of the News. The *Rocky Mountain News* is the state's oldest newspaper. Uncle Dick Wootton remained in Denver for less than a half dozen years.

Caroline Churchill, an early-day feminist, launched the monthly *Colorado Antelope* in 1879, in Denver. By 1882, the newspaper was published weekly and had been renamed *Queen Bee*. Miss Churchill was an outspoken advocate of equal rights for women.

Since many people didn't own cars yet, they relied on the tramway system in Denver. In 1920, there was a tramway workers' strike which temporarily interrupted transportation services.

Although Denver's first airplane flight was in 1910, an airport was not opened until October of 1929, two weeks before the Wall Street Crash. Originally called the Denver Airport, it was renamed for the late mayor, **Ben Stapleton**, in 1944.

Frederick Gilmer Bonfils (1860-1933), a native of Troy, Missouri, and **Harry H. Tammen** bought the *Denver Post* in 1895 for $12,500. They soon expanded the newspaper's circulation rapidly with sensationalism of the news and such devices as "red banner headlines." They exposed the infamous Teapot Dome scandal of the 1920s.

Two very colorful women associated with Denver were **Elizabeth "Baby Doe" Tabor**, the second wife of **Horace Austin Warner Tabor**, and **Molly Brown**, who became famous in a sense, with the sinking of the Titanic in April 1912. Both married wealthy men and attempted to become part of Denver's elite social set.

Baby Doe and Horace Tabor, who gained his fortune in Leadville, were married in an elaborate Washington ceremony in 1883 attended by President Chester Arthur during the brief period Tabor served in the U.S. Senate. The very wealthy Tabors were scorned by Denver society because of their ostentatiousness. By 1893 he had lost his vast fortune and only held the **Matchless Mine** in **Leadville** by 1898. He was appointed the postmaster at Denver and died in 1899. Baby Doe returned to Leadville and lived out the next 36 years as a recluse in the cabin beside the Matchless. She was found frozen to death in March, 1935. They are buried in Mt. Olivet Cemetery in Denver.

Molly Tobin married **Jimmy J. Brown**, who struck it rich in the Little Jonny mine in Leadville. They moved to Denver and purchased the mansion called **House of Lions**. She was determined to crash Denver's high society but was a little too pretentious for the ladies of the city. Later, she went to New York and traveled widely. She booked passage on the maiden voyage of the ill-fated Titanic in 1912. Late in the night of April 14, the Titanic struck an iceberg and began to sink. Women and children were rushed to lifeboats and Molly took charge of her boat. They were rescued the next day. Upon arriving in New York, Molly, found she was a heroine. When asked by reporters, "Mrs. Brown, how did it happen you didn't sink?" she replied, "Hell, I'm unsinkable" thus beginning the legend of "The Unsinkable Molly Brown."

Douglas Fairbanks Sr. (1883-1939), one of the most popular actors of his day, was born in Denver. He and his second wife, **Mary Pickford**, were called the "King and Queen of Movieland." Fairbanks acted on the New York stage until he entered the movies in 1915. He is especially remembered for his roles in "Robin Hood" and "The Thief of Baghdad." His son, **Douglas Fairbanks Jr.**, also won acclaim for his acting abilities.

Paul Whiteman (1890-1967), the "King of Jazz," was born in Denver and played first viola in the Denver Symphony Orchestra while still in his teens. He introduced the first "symphonic jazz" in 1919, formed his own orchestra and toured the U.S. and Europe. In 1943, he became musical director of the Blue Radio Network, forerunner of the American Broadcasting Company.

The Congressional Medal of Honor recipients from the Denver area include **Capt. Marcellus H. Chiles**, 356th Infantry, 89th Infantry Division, near Le Champy Bas, France, November 3, 1918; **Pvt. Elmer E. Fryar**, 511th Parachute Infantry, 11th Airborne Division, Leyte, Philippines, December 8, 1944; **Lt. Col. William R. Grove**, 36th Infantry U.S. Volunteers, near Porac, Luzon, Philippines, September 9, 1899; **2nd Lt. George W. Wallace**, 9th U.S. Infantry, Tinuba, Luzon, Philippines, March 4, 1900; **2nd Lt. J. Hunter Wickersham**, 353rd

Fitzsimons Army Medical Center was established in Denver in 1918 and has served as an Army hospital continuously since then. It was named in honor of an Army doctor killed in France in World War I.

Infantry, 89th Infantry Division, near Limey, France, September 12, 1918; and **Cmdr. Bruce McCandless**, on the *U.S.S. San Francisco*, in the battle off Savo Island, November 12-13, 1942.

Fort Logan was established southwest of Denver in 1889 and was not closed until 1946. The Fort Logan National Cemetery was established here.

Fitzsimons Army Medical Center had its beginnings following World War I. The center, then known as **U.S. Army Hospital No. 21**, was started in April, 1918, to treat the influx of veterans returning from the war, many of whom suffered from respiratory diseases. By 1919, the 73-building hospital was treating an average of 1,400 patients daily. In 1920, the facility was renamed **Fitzsimons General Hospital** in honor of **1st Lt. (Dr.) William Thomas Fitzsimons**, a native of Burlington, Kansas, who was killed near Dannes-Camiers, France, in a bombing attack, September 4, 1917. The hospital was expanded and the new art-deco style building was dedicated on December 3, 1941. During World War II, several "semi-permanent" buildings, including a POW internment camp, were constructed to handle more than 4,000 patients daily. For several weeks in 1955, **President Dwight D. Eisenhower** was hospitalized here while recovering from a heart attack suffered during a visit

36

to Colorado. In March, 1973, the facility was renamed Fitzsimons Army Medical Center.

Lowry Air Force Base began with the raising of the flag over an old sanitarium in September, 1937. The airfield, named for **Lt. Francis B. Lowry**, a Denver aviator killed in World War I, was selected for the excellent flying weather and Denver's promise of a bombing range. The bombing range is located about 25 miles east of the airfield. Among its several missions during World War II was the training of flight crews for B-24 and B-29 bombers. President Dwight D. Eisenhower used the airbase for his "Summer White House" and it also served as an interim site for the **U.S. Air Force Academy**. In the 1960s Lowry became the headquarters for Titan I Missile operations. In the 1980s, Lowry AFB had become one of the major technical training centers in the world. Major areas of training include: avionics, space operations, air intelligence, logistics, munitions, and audiovisual. Flight training ended in the 1960s.

Buckley Air National Guard Base began early in World War II as **Buckley Field**, named in honor of **1st Lt. John Harold Buckley**, of **Longmont**, Colorado. Buckley, a World War I pilot, was killed when he was shot down over France, September 17, 1918, behind German lines during the Argonne offensive. Construction of the airfield began in May, 1942, and two months later the **Army Air Corps Technical School** was opened to train B-17 and B-24 bombardiers and armorers. The **Arctic Training Command** transferred to Buckley Field in 1943. When the war ended, Buckley Field became an auxiliary field for Lowry, who turned it over to the Colorado Air National Guard in 1946. In 1947, the Navy took charge of the airfield and designated it **Naval Air Station-Denver**. It was operated as a naval air station until June 30, 1959, when it was decommissioned and returned to the Air Force. In 1960, it became Buckley Air National Guard, the first ANG base in the nation.

The **Rocky Mountain Arsenal**, established here in 1942, produced lethal nerve gas for the U.S. Army. The Arsenal, located north of Stapleton International Airport, has recently been deactivated.

The Titan rocket, used in the early space shots, was manufactured by Martin-Marietta in this area. The Viking Lander, used to test soil on Mars in 1976, was also developed here.

There are over 150 buildings in Denver listed on the National

Colorado's State Capitol was completed in 1908. Construction began in 1886 and took 22 years to complete.

Register of Historic Places. The latest list available appears at the back of this chapter.

Among the tourist attractions:

COLORADO STATE CAPITOL, Broadway and Colfax, is located on 10-acres offered to the Territorial Legislature in 1874 by Henry C. Brown. Construction of the capitol building began in 1886, almost 10 years following Colorado's statehood. Although it took more than 22 years to complete the offices were occupied in 1894. The building materials include Gunnison granite for the outer walls, sandstone from Fort Collins for the foundations, marble for floors and stairs from the town of Marble, and wainscoting of exquisite rose onyx from Beulah. Only the ornamental brass, steel girders, and white oak woodwork were shipped from out-of-state. When the capitol was under construction, copper was used to cover the 272 foot dome. The citizenry objected because copper was not a primary metal in Colorado. It was decided to use gold instead and Colorado miners contributed 200 ounces to produce the thinner-than-paper sheets of gold leaf. A second coating of gold leaf was applied in 1950. Near the top of the dome is the Colorado Hall of Fame, made up of stained glass portraits of 16 pioneers. Descriptive biographies of each person are found in the Inside Observation Gallery. Included in the Hall of Fame are **William N. Byers**, Newspaperman, *Rocky Mountain News*; **William Gilpin**, first Colorado Territorial Governor; **J. W. Denver**, Governor of Kansas Territory (part of which became Colorado) when gold was discovered; **John Evans**, second Governor of Colorado; **Casimero Barela**, State Senator and stockman; **Nathaniel P. Hill**, U.S. Senator and mining man; **Kit Carson**, Colorado pioneer, helped open the West; **Alexander Majors**, Pony Express organizer; **General Bela M. Hughes**, who originated the Overland Stage Coach Company; **R. G. Buckingham, M.D.**, public spirited physician who aided in educational development; **John L. Dyer**, famous as the "snow-shoe preacher"; **Ouray**, Chief of the Utes, peace-maker with the U.S. Government; **William J. Palmer**, railroad builder; **Frances Wisbart Jacobs** (the only woman), who founded many charities in Colorado began free kindergarten; **Jim Baker**, famous early frontiersman; and **Benjamin H. Eaton**, developer of irrigation systems.

There are two "Mile High" markers on the front steps of the

Denver is renowned as the "Mile High City" and the granite step on the west side of the building boasts "One Mile Above Sea Level." In 1969, this step was found in error by engineering students from Colorado State University. As a result a geodetic survey plug was imbedded three steps above the original marker providing a double "Mile High" marking.

capitol. Engraved in one of the granite steps on the west side of the building is "ONE MILE ABOVE SEA LEVEL." In 1969 this step was found to be in error by students from the engineering school of Colorado State University and today a geodetic plug is embedded three steps above the original marker marking the actual 5,280 feet level.

Two statues at the west and east entrances of the capitol are noteworthy. On the west side is a Civil War monument listing the regiments and units organized for the Union in the Colorado Territory and lists the battles these units participated in. On the east lawn is "The Closing Era," representing an Indian hunter examining his prey, a dying buffalo.

The Colorado Historical Society operates several museums and historic sites including the **Colorado History Museum, Grant-Humphreys Mansion, Pearce-McAllister Cottage,** and **Byers-Evans House,** all in Denver; **Bloom House, Baca House,** and **Pioneer Museum,** all in Trinidad; **Fort Garland,** 25 miles east of Alamosa; **Fort Vasquez,** south of Platteville;

Colorado's diverse history is portrayed in the Colorado History Museum. It also houses the Colorado Historical Society's collections of manuscripts, books, newspapers, and photographs.

El Pueblo Museum, Pueblo; **Ute Indian Museum,** Montrose; **Healy House and Dexter Cabin,** both in Leadville; and **Georgetown Loop Historic Mining and Railroad Park,** Georgetown/Silver Plume. The Colorado Historical Society is headquartered at 13th and Broadway in Denver. The telephone number is (303) 866-3682.

COLORADO HISTORY MUSEUM, 13th and Broadway, includes permanent and changing exhibitions that trace the lives, history, and diversity of Colorado's people. It includes collections of Indian artifacts, the state's mining heritage, dioramas, and a unique "time line" that spans 150 years of Colorado's history. There are also regular changing exhibits. This excellent museum is open 10 a.m. to 4:30 p.m. Monday through Saturday and 12 noon to 4:30 p.m. Sunday. An admission is charged. The library provides access to the Colorado Historical Society's collections of manuscripts, books, newspapers, and photographs. The library is open 10 a.m. to 4:30 p.m. Tuesday through Saturday. Admission is free.

GRANT-HUMPHREYS MANSION MUSEUM, 770 Pennsylvania St., was built at the turn-of-the-century for **James B. Grant,** governor of Colorado from 1883 to 1885. The richly decorated and elegantly furnished mansion is in the Beaux-Arts style. The 30-room mansion was completed in 1902 at a cost of

These dioramas exhibited in the Colorado History Museum in Denver feature (top) Bent's Fort and (below) early day fur trappers.

Visitors enjoy the time line, "Colorado Chronicle," at the Colorado History Museum in Denver.

The "Colorado Scrapbook" exhibit at the Colorado History Museum in Denver offers a personal look at history in the state.

This diorama shows Denver as it appeared in 1859 and is displayed in the Colorado History Museum.

$35,000. When James Grant died in 1911 his widow, Mary, sold the mansion in 1917 to **Albert E. Humphreys** and his wife, Alice Boyd Humphreys. Humphreys had made and lost two fortunes before amassing a third through oil speculations in Oklahoma, Texas, and Wyoming. The mansion is listed on the National Register of Historic Places and has been designated a Denver Landmark. It is open year-round from 10 a.m. to 2 p.m., Tuesday through Friday. An admission is charged.

THE MOLLY BROWN HOUSE MUSEUM, 1340 Pennsylvania St., was the lavishly decorated home of "The Unsinkable Molly Brown." Molly was born **Margaret Tobin** on July 18, 1867, in Hannibal, Missouri. When she was 18 she followed her older brother to Leadville where she met her future husband, **James Joseph Brown**, born September 27, 1854. They were married at the Church of the Annunciation on September 1, 1886 and lived in Leadville until 1894 when she persuaded her husband to move to Denver. The Browns legally separated in

The Governor's Mansion is located at 8th St. and Logan Ave. and is open for public tours on Thursdays.

The Grant-Humphreys Mansion, listed on the National Register of Historic Places, houses a museum today. The home was built for a former governor of Colorado.

The Unsinkable Molly Brown once lived in this Denver home, guarded by lion statues. The House of Lions cost Molly and her husband $30,000.

1909 and Molly began traveling. Molly became a national heroine in 1912, after surviving the sinking of the *Titanic*. In 1930, Molly purchased the poet Eugene Field's home and gave it to Denver as a memorial. She died in New York in 1932. The mansion today is furnished in the style of an upper middle-class home of the late 19th and early 20th centuries. The collection includes furnishings and decorative art objects which were possessions of the Brown family. It is open 10 a.m. to 4 p.m. Tuesday through Saturday and 12 noon to 4 p.m. Sundays, April through September, and until 3 p.m. from October through March. It is also opened 10 a.m. to 4 p.m. Mondays, June through August. It is closed on Easter Sunday, Memorial Day, July 4th, Labor Day, Thanksgiving, Christmas Eve and Day, and New Year's Eve and Day. An admission is charged. The mansion is listed on the National Register of Historic Places.

UNITED STATES MINT, W. Colfax at Delaware St., began producing coins in 1906. The Denver Mint opened for business in 1863 as an U.S. Assay Office. The government acquired Clark, Gruber & Company, a private mint, at 16th and Market Streets for this operation. The government did not begin coinage of gold here as first intended because of Indian problems and the Civil War. The U.S. Assay Office accepted gold brought in by miners from the surrounding area for melting, assaying, and stamping of cast gold bars. The bars were returned to the depositors as unparted bars stamped with weight and fineness of the gold. Hope was revived for branch mint status in the early 1890s. The site for the new mint at West Colfax and Delaware Streets was purchased in 1896 and construction began the next year. The new building was not completed until 1904. Coinage operations began in February, 1906.

One of the biggest robberies in Denver history up to that time occurred in front of the Mint in 1922. At 10:30 a.m. Monday, December 22, four bandits held up a Federal Reserve Bank car in front of the Mint. Two of the bandits, armed with sawed-off shotguns, leaped from their car and bombarded the front door. Fifty Mint employees were summoned by an alarm and grabbed shotguns to battle the attackers. At the outset of the gunfight that followed, **Charles L. Linton**, a Federal Reserve guard and well-known political figure, was fatally wounded. He died that afternoon in the county hospital. One of the bandits was shot in the jaw but was loaded into the getaway car by his companions.

The U.S. Mint in Denver began producing coins in 1906.

It took the bandits five minutes to steal $200,000 in five dollar bills. The bandits escaped and were never caught.

The second largest gold depository in the United States, the Mint produces coins from the penny to the dollar. Numismatic items and coin sets are on sale at the Mint. Tours of the Mint are available 8 a.m. to 3 p.m. weekdays during the summer months and 8:30 a.m. to 3 p.m. during the winter months. It is closed on all holidays. Admission is free.

DENVER FIREFIGHTERS MUSEUM, 1326 Tremont Pl., a block from the U.S. Mint, is located in Fire House No. 1 and listed on the National Register of Historic Places. The museum is housed on two floors of the Old Fire House No. 1, built in 1909. The museum presents a well-preserved collection of Denver's original hand drawn firefighting equipment as well as two American LaFrance fire engines from the 1920s. The museum and restaurant is open 11 a.m. to 2 p.m. weekdays. An admission to the museum is charged.

DENVER ART MUSEUM, 100 W. 14th Ave. Parkway, across from the Civic Center, has over 40,000 art objects on seven floors representing Western, Asian, European, New World, Native American, contemporary and textiles collections. It also features touring exhibits. Its Native American collection represents nearly every U.S. and Canadian Indian tribe. Included are one-of-a-kind masterpieces such as traditional clothing, masks, ceremonial pipes, metal jewelry, rugs, baskets, and

The unique Denver Art Museum.

Denver's Firefighters Museum.

The Museum of Western Art is housed in this former Denver brothel and gambling hall.

pottery. The museum is open 10 a.m. to 5 p.m. Tuesday through Saturday, noon to 5 p.m. Sunday. It is closed on Monday and major holidays. An admission is charged. (The museum is free of charge all day Saturday.)

MUSEUM OF WESTERN ART, 1727 Tremont Pl., was founded in 1983 as an international showcase for the art of Western America. The core of the museum's collection features masterworks of Bierstadt, Moran, Farny, Russell, Remington, Blumenschein, O'Keeffe and 50 other artists who lived or trav-

The Pearce-McAllister Cottage houses the Denver Museum of Miniatures.

eled extensively in the West between the Civil War and World War II. The museum is located in the "Old Navarre" building, that once housed a gambling hall and bordello. It is open 10 a.m. to 4:30 p.m. Tuesday through Saturday. Closed on Sunday and Monday and on Thanksgiving, Christmas and New Year's Day. An admission is charged. Guided and unguided group tours are available, as well as foreign language tours. The museum offers handicapped access, benches in the galleries, and restrooms in the lower level.

PEARCE-McALLISTER COTTAGE, 1880 Gaylord St., was built in 1899 for **Harold V. Pearce** and his wife, **Cara Rowena Pearce**. It is an outstanding example of the Colonial Revival movement, which shaped America's taste in architecture and interior furnishings between 1876 and the 1930s. The cottage was sold to **Henry McAllister**, an attorney, and his wife, Phoebe, in 1908. The cottage has been designated an official Denver Landmark and is listed on the National Register of Historic Places. It is owned and operated by the Colorado Historical Society. The cottage also houses the DENVER MUSEUM OF MINIATURES, DOLLS AND TOYS, noted in Denver for

51

its charming exhibits of interest to all ages. Antique toys, dollhouses, Teddy bears, trains, toy soldiers and a vast collection of miniatures are exhibited according to themes in the galleries. The museum features a Southwestern gallery, antique and collectible dolls, and exact miniature dioramas. Of particular interest are the occasional special loans of fine collections owned by private collectors, not ordinarily exhibited. The museum gift shop is noted for unique and special items, many of which are designed by artists and craftsmen from all over the United States, as well as local artists. The museum and Pearce-McAllister house are open 10 a.m. to 4 p.m. year-round Wednesday through Saturday and noon to 4 p.m. Sunday. An admission is charged.

BYERS-EVANS HOUSE, 1310 Bannock St., was built in 1883 by **William N. Byers**, founder of the *Rocky Mountain News*. Byers is considered one of the prime builders of Denver. In 1889, **William Gray Evans**, son of Colorado's second territorial governor, John Evans, purchased the Byers house. The Evans family was instrumental in development of such Denver institutions as the Denver Tramway Co., the Denver Art Museum, and the University of Denver. Listed on the National Register of Historic Places, it is the newest museum of the Colorado Historical Society. It is open 11 a.m. to 3 p.m. daily except Tuesday for guided tours. An admission is charged.

DENVER MUSEUM OF NATURAL HISTORY, located in City Park at Colorado and Montview Blvds., is the seventh largest museum in the United States and is one of the great natural museums of the world. Thousands of objects of artifacts are displayed in three floors of museum galleries. On display are such exhibits as dinosaur remains, Indian artifacts, minerals and gems and many others. Also included is the **IMAX Theatre** and **Charles C. Gates Planetarium.** The IMAX Theatre projects images on a movie screen four-and-a-half stories tall and six-and-a-half stories wide. Movies are presented daily. It is open 9 a.m. to 5 p.m. daily. Admissions are charged to both the museum and the IMAX Theatre.

LOWRY HERITAGE MUSEUM, located in Building 880 on Irvington Pl. at Lowry AFB, has as its mission the preservation and protection of the artifacts of Lowry AFB's colorful past. The museum building originally housed the offices of the Commandant of Cadets of the U.S. Air Force Academy and has been

An exterior shot of the Denver Museum of Natural History and one of the Indian exhibits displayed within.

Dinosaur exhibits in the Denver Museum of Natural History.

Indian exhibits in Denver's Museum of Natural History.

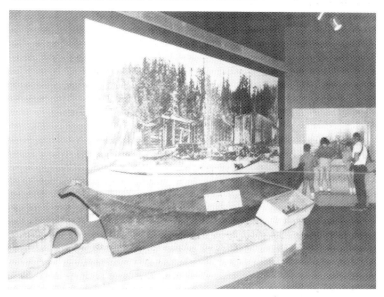

Lowry Heritage Museum is located on Lowry Air Force Base, which began in an old sanitarium in September, 1937. (Below) This U-3A Air Force aircraft (below) is one of several displays just outside the LAFB museum.

The *F-100-D Super Sabre (above) is also displayed just outside the Lowry AFB museum along with the T-33A jet trainer (below). These aircraft are in the park around the parking lot.*

Two other aircraft displayed just outside the Lowry AFB museum is this B-29 bomber (above) and an H-21B helicopter. These aircraft may be seen when the museum is not open.

The Ivy Chapel at the entrance of the Fairmount Cemetery where many of the state's prominent pioneeers are buried. The cemetery dates back to 1890.

identified as a historical site by the City of Aurora. The story of Lowry Technical Training Center is portrayed through exhibits that walk through Lowry's past. The museum's core exhibit on photography traces the history of military photography from the American Civil War to the present. The Academy Room houses memorabilia from the U.S. Air Force Academy. A gallery of temporary and changing exhibits completes the portrayal of the history of Lowry AFB. The museum's aircraft park gives visitors hands-on and closeup experiences with twenty Air Force aircraft. It is open 9 a.m. to 4:30 p.m. weekdays and from 10 a.m. to 4 p.m Saturday. It is closed on all holidays. Admission is free. Visitors should use the base's east gate entrance.

FAIRMOUNT CEMETERY, 430 S. Quebec St. (E. Alameda and Quebec Sts.), celebrated its 100th anniversary in 1990. The Cemetery contains graves of many of Colorado's most illustrious pioneers and prominent citizens and invites the public to enjoy self-guided historic tours and nature walks. Helpful booklets which explain these educational and pleasant activities are available at its Main Office. Fairmount also contains one of the largest community Mausoleums west of the Mississippi River and two registered Denver landmarks—the Gate Lodge and Ivy Chapel, each completed in 1890.

MIZEL MUSEUM OF JUDAICA, 560 S. Monaco Pkwy, features changing exhibits of international and local Jewish art and heritage. The museum was established in 1982 to honor the beauty of the Jewish heritage to young and old, to Jews and non-Jews throughout Colorado. Tours and lectures are available. It is open 10 a.m. to 4 p.m. Monday through Thursday and 10 a.m. to noon on Sunday.

Mizel Museum of Judaica, featuring Jewish heritage and culture, is located at 560 S. Monaco Parkway in Denver.

BLACK AMERICAN WEST MUSEUM AND HERITAGE CENTER, 608 26th St., is a unique museum, that through its exhibits and historical materials, provides information on the contributions and history of black cowboys. About one-third of the cowboys of the Old West were black. It is open 10 a.m. to 2 p.m. Wednesday through Friday, 10 a.m. to 5 p.m. Saturday, and 2 to 5 p.m. Sunday. An admission is charged.

FORNEY TRANSPORTATION MUSEUM, 1416 Platte (Exit 211 off I 25), overlooking the birthplace of Denver, is housed in one of Denver's historic landmarks. Over 400 cars, carriages, cutters, costumes, cycles, steam engines, rail coaches and airplanes are displayed. The world's largest steam locomotive, "Big Boy," is on display. Some of the museum's most famous autos include Amelia Earhart's "Gold Bug" Kissel, Prince Aly Kahn's Rolls Royce, the 25-foot wheel-based six wheel 1923 Hispano Suiza, an 1899 4 passenger Locomobile, and Teddy Roosevelt's parade car. It is open 10 a.m. to 5 p.m. weekdays and Saturday and 11 a.m. to 5 p.m. Sunday. An admission is charged.

FOUR MILE HISTORIC PARK, 715 S. Forest St., includes the oldest house in Denver, built on Cherry Creek in 1859. It

Forney Transportation Museum in Denver offers a wide range of exhibits relating to transportation.

61

Denver's Brown Palace Hotel is listed on the National Register of Historic Places.

has served as a stage coach stop, a tavern, and a farm house. It is open for tours 10 a.m. to 4 p.m. Wednesday through Sunday. Reservations are required for groups of 10 or more. Telephone (303) 399-1859 for other information. An admission is charged.

Historic Denver, Market Center, 1330 17th St., offers a number of walking and van tours from May through September. Among these are MANSIONS AND MILLIONS, a two-hour walking tour starting at the Molly Brown House Museum, 1340 Pennsylvania St.; THE HEART OF OLD DENVER, a two-hour walking tour of lower downtown, starting at Union Station, 1701 Wynkoop; QUEEN CITY: OLD AND NEW, a two hour walking tour focusing on historic buildings and their contemporary counterparts, starting at the Brown Palace Hotel; NINTH STREET HISTORIC PARK, a one-hour walking tour of Denver's oldest residential block that is still intact, from the Auraria campus; and CITY OF MANSIONS, a three-hour van tour of Denver's mansion area, departing from Union Station, 1701 Wynkoop. Also available are tours of The Molly Brown House Museum, 1340 Pennsylvania St., and Four Mile Historic Park, 715 S. Forest St. For information on times and prices of these tours, contact Historic Denver at 1330 17th St.

Aurora

Just east of Denver is **Aurora** (pop. 158,588), began as Fletcher in 1891 when it was first incorporated. The name was changed to Aurora in 1907.

AURORA HISTORY MUSEUM, 1633 Florence St., offers programs on local history and provides a reference library for historical research. It is open 9 a.m. to 4 p.m. Tuesday through Friday. Admission is free. (Beginning in 1991 this museum will be located at 15001 E. Alameda Dr., Aurora.)

DELANEY FARM, 170 S. Chambers Rd., was acquired by the City of Aurora in 1983 and is dedicated to open space and historic preservation. This 168-acre farm dates back to the 1870s. The Delaney Barn is listed on the National Register of Historic Places. In addition to the round frame barn and wood frame farmhouse the farm is the site of the Gully Homestead, listed on the National Register of Historic Places. This three-room house was built in 1871 by Thomas and Temperance Theresa Gully a mile south of its current location. It was moved here in 1983. The Gully Homestead House at the DeLaney Farm is open 10 a.m. to 1 p.m. Wednesday through Saturday during the summer months. Admission is free. Call (303) 360-8545 to arrange a visit at other times.

Two other sites in Aurora are listed on the National Register of Historic Places. These include the Melvin School, 4950 S. Laredo St., and the William Smith House, 412 Oswego Ct. Other sites listed on the National Register of Historic Places in Arapahoe County include the David W. Brown House, 412 Oswego Ct. in Englewood and the Seventeen Mile House, 8181 S. Parker Rd., in Parker.

Arvada

Just northwest of Denver is **Arvada** (pop. 84,576), incorporated in 1904. It can be reached off I-70.

ARVADA CENTER MUSEUM, located in the Arvada Center for the Arts and Humanities, 6901 Wadsworth Blvd., presents changing exhibits on Arvada and Colorado history, art history and humanities. It houses the Haines log house, the oldest remaining dwelling in Arvada and other permanent exhibits on Arvada's history. It is open 9 a.m. to 5 p.m. weekdays and Saturday, and 1 to 5 p.m. Sunday. Admission is free. Free docent led tours available by calling (303) 431-3080.

The Arvada Flour Mill, 5580 Wadsworth Blvd., and the Russell Graves House, 5605 Yukon St., in Arvada, are listed on the National Register of Historic Places.

Westminster

Just north of Arvada is **Westminster** (pop. 50,211). There are two sites here listed on the National Register of Historic Places. These include the Bowles House, 3924 W. 72nd Ave. and Westminster University/Belleview College, 3455 W. 83rd Ave.

Lakewood

Just west of Denver is **Lakewood**, founded in 1888 by W.A.H. Loveland, Miranda Loveland, and Charles Welch. The Spotswood McClellan stage route, following the Old Bradford Road, was established through Lakewood in 1873. The same year, Denver South Park & Pacific Railroad built its road across Lakewood. The Denver, Lakewood & Golden Railroad was established in 1890, later becoming the Colorado Central, and still later, the Denver & Intermountain Railroad.

In the early 1920s, one of the largest prohibition raids in the state took place in a Lakewood-area farmhouse. This farmhouse is now located at Lakewood's Historical Belmar Village. May Bonfils, local philanthropist and daughter of the founder of the

Two of the structures in the Belmar Museum in Lakewood, just west of
Denver. The ranchhouse (below) dates back to the 1870s.

The Wheat Ridge Sodhouse and Museum is listed on the National Register of Historic Places. The earliest building dates back to 1860.

Denver Post, built her mansion, a replica of Marie Antoinette's Trianon Palace in France, in the heart of today's Lakewood during the Depression of the 1930s.

The "Unsinkable Molly Brown" established her summer home, "Avoca Lodge," in this area. Her husband, J. J., enjoyed working his hay farm here.

LAKEWOOD'S HISTORICAL BELMAR VILLAGE, MUSEUM AND PARK, 797 S. Wadsworth Blvd., Lakewood, offers permanent and changing exhibits of art, history, archaeology, geology, natural history, and technology. It occupies 15 of the 127 acres of Belmar Park, the former estate of the late May Bonfils Stanton. Three historic buildings have been relocated here—the Ranch House, the Country School, and the Peterson House, all dating back to c. 1870. The Peterson House is listed on the National Register of Historic Places. The museum is open 10 a.m. to 4 p.m. weekdays and 1 to 5 p.m. Saturday. Admission is free.

The Tower of Memories, in Crown Hill Cemetery, 8500 W. 29th Ave.; the Stone House, south Lakewood off S. Wadsworth Blvd.; and the JCRS Historic District/American Medical Center, 6401 W. Colfax, in Lakewood, are also listed on the National Register of Historic Places.

Wheat Ridge

Another western suburb of Denver is **Wheat Ridge** (pop. 30,293). It is home of the WHEAT RIDGE SOD HOUSE AND MUSEUM, 4610 Robb St. The sod house dates back to the 1860s and the complex reflects the early-day agricultural heritage of the area. Featured are special demonstrations depicting life in the mid-19th century. It is listed on the National Register of Historic Places. It is open from 12 noon to 4 p.m. the second and fourth Saturday and by appointment. Admission is free.

The other Wheat Ridge site listed on the National Register of Historic Places is the Richards Mansion/Hart Estate, 5349 W. 27th Ave.

In Jefferson County

Southwest of Denver, in Jefferson County, is **Buffalo Creek** and **Evergreen**. The sites in Buffalo Creek and vicinity listed on the National Register of Historic Places include the Blue Jay Inn, CO 126; Green Mercantile Store, northwest of the town; Green Mountain Ranch, south on CO 126; and La Hacienda (John L. Jerome summer estate), on State Road off US 285. There are also four sites in the Evergreen area including Hiwan Homestead, Meadow Dr.; Humphrey House/Kinnikinnik Ranch, 620 S. Soda Creek Rd.; Everhardt Ranch/Herzman Ranch, Long Peak Dr. and Mountain Park Rd.; and Evergreen Conference District, Bear Creek and CO 74.

Golden

Further west of Denver is **Golden** (pop. 12,237), county seat of Jefferson County. It was founded as a camp in late 1858 by **Thomas L. Golden, James Saunders,** and **George Andrew Jackson**, all prospectors. The town that emerged was named for Tom Golden. Golden served as the second territorial capital from 1862 to 1867. The capital was located in the Loveland Building, built in 1861, at 12th and Washington Sts.

There are several historic buildings on 12th and 13th Sts., between Washington Ave. and Maple St. Among these are the Loveland building; the Astor House, 906 12th St., the oldest stone hotel west of the Mississippi, built in 1867; a brown stucco house built in 1879, at 906 12 St.; a two-story brick, Italianate house, 920 12th St., built in 1874 by Dr. James Kelly; a

Among several of Golden's historic buildings, the Astor House Hotel *(above)* and The Armory Building are listed on the National Register of Historic Places. The Armory is the largest cobblestone building in the U.S.

The Colorado Railroad Museum in Golden is the largest railroad museum in the Rockies.

red pressed brick home, 1000/1004 12th St., built as a double house in 1899; a one-and-a-half-story buff brick house built as a parsonage in 1872, 1006 12th St.; the home of George West, editor of the *Golden Transcript*, one of Colorado's oldest newspapers still in publication, 1018 12th St., built in 1872; a pink brick house, 1106 12th St., built in 1872 and remodeled in 1913; a two-story residence at 1123 12th St., built in 1874, for George Kimball, who had served as a captain in the Union Army during the Civil War; a brick cottage, 1105 12th St., built in 1874 for Charles Welch, a business associate of W. A. H. Loveland; the yellow brick residence, 1003 12th St., built in 1873; the Episcopal Church, at the corner of Arapahoe and 13th Sts., built in 1867; and the Armory Building, just across the street, built in 1913. The Armory is the largest cobblestone building in the U.S. and is listed on the National Register of Historic Places. The Astor House Hotel is also listed on the NRHP.

Other sites in Golden listed on the National Register of Historic Places include the Lorraine Lodge (Charles Boettcher Summer Home), 900 Colorow Rd on Lookout Mountain; the Magic Mountain site, on Heritage Square; the Mt. Vernon House/Robert W. Steele House, one mile south of Golden at I-70, CO 26 and Mt. Vernon Canyon Rd.; and the Rooney Ranch, intersection of Rooney Rd. and Alameda Pkway.

William A. H. Loveland, who founded the Colorado Central

*"Buffalo Bill" Cody's grave on top of Lookout Mountain. Cody had ex-
pected to be buried in Cody, Wyoming, but his wife, Louisa, chose this
spot on the mountain overlooking Denver. Cody died and was buried in
1917.*

& Pacific, made his home in Golden in the 1860s.

The **Colorado School of Mines**, the nation's largest and foremost school of mineral engineering, was founded in 1869.

COLORADO RAILROAD MUSEUM, 17155 W. 44th, Golden, is the largest railroad museum in the Rockies. To reach the museum, take Exit 265 off I-70 and follow the green and white signs. The museum building is a replica of an 1880-style masonry railroad depot. It houses rare old papers, photographs, and artifacts displayed to give the visitor an insight into the interesting histories of the various roads. It also features narrow-gauge mountain trains and cars. Open daily year-round 9 a.m. to 5 p.m. The summer hours (June through August) are from 9 a.m. to 6 p.m. An admission is charged.

BUFFALO BILL MEMORIAL MUSEUM AND GRAVE, on Lookout Mountain in Golden, can be reached off I-70, west of Denver, taking Exit 259 or Exit 256 to US 40 and then west to Lookout Mountain Road or Exit 254 to US 40 and then east to Lookout Mountain Road. It is three miles on Lookout Mountain Road. The Memorial Museum was completed in 1921 by Johnny Baker, a close friend of **William F. "Buffalo Bill" Cody** and a member of Cody's Wild West Show. Cody, born in Iowa, earned his reputation as buffalo hunter for a railroad construction crew in Kansas. During an 18-month period he killed over 4,200 buffalo. He became famous also as a scout and showman. While a young teenager he was one of the colorful riders for the short-lived Pony Express in 1860-61. Buffalo Bill's Wild West Show gave its first performance in 1883 and continued until after the turn of the century. Cody died in Denver at the home of his sister, Mary Cody Decker, 2932 Lafayette St., January 10, 1917. His wife, Louisa, had him buried on Lookout Mountain in a steel vault in a cement-lined grave carved in granite so the remains cannot be stolen. The museum hours are 9 a.m. to 4 p.m. November 1 through April 30 and 9 a.m. to 5 p.m. May 1 through October 31. An admission is charged.

MOTHER CABRINI SHRINE, on Lookout Mountain, Exit 259 off I-70, is dedicated to America's first citizen saint, **St. Frances Xavier Cabrini**. Saint Cabrini was the founder of the Order of the Missionary Sisters of the Sacred Heart, an orphanage, several schools and hospitals. Mother Cabrini was born in Italy in 1850 and because of her delicate health was unable to enter the religious life. Upon the request of the Bishop of Lodi in Italy she took charge of a home for orphans and was very suc-

71

The statue of the Sacred Heart of Jesus overlooks the Saint Frances Xavier Cabrini Shrine on Lookout Mountain west of Denver off I-70. She was canonized by Pope Pius XII on July 7, 1946.

cessful. After six years the situation being more than unbearable the bishop asked her to found a new religious congregation. She had hoped to do missionary work in China when Pope Leo XIII sent her to America. She made 25 trips across the Atlantic and traveled the length and breadth of the United States establishing schools and hospitals. She died in 1917 in Chicago but she was interred in New York. Pope Pius XI declared her Blessed, November 13, 1938 and on July 7, 1946 Pope Pius XII canonized her. In 1912, Mother Cabrini visited the site now known as The Mother Cabrini Shrine. The trip to the Mount of the Sacred Heart was made on a burro that refused to go any further. As she descended the hill, Mother Cabrini stopped where spring water is drawn today. She pointed to a rock with her staff and correctly told the sister accompanying her to dig and she would find water. The original grotto built in 1929 was replaced by a new chapel in 1954. The statue at the Shrine is 22 feet high and stands on an 11 foot base. It stands in front of a symbol of the Heart of Christ fashioned by Mother Cabrini in 1912 from the quartz rock found here. The shrine is open 7 a.m. to 7 p.m. daily. Admission is free.

GOLDEN D.A.R. PIONEER MUSEUM, 911 10th St. in the Municipal Building, is filled with memorabilia of the Golden area from the days of the first settlers who came seeking gold, through its Territorial Capitol Days and into the turn of the century to the period of the 1930s. It is open 11 a.m. to 4 p.m. Monday through Saturday, Memorial Day to Labor Day, and 12 noon to 4 p.m. Monday through Saturday the balance of the year. Admission is free.

ASTOR HOUSE HOTEL MUSEUM, 822 12th St., is a hotel museum built in 1867 by Seth Lake. It was the first stone hotel built west of St. Louis. Guided tours are available 10 a.m. to 3 p.m. weekdays and by arrangement on weekends.

COLORADO SCHOOL OF MINES GEOLOGY MUSEUM, at 16th and Maple, features exhibits that include mineralogy, fossils, rocks, gemstones, gold, silver, and mining. It is open 9 a.m. to 4 p.m. Monday through Saturday and 1 to 4 p.m. Sunday. Tours are available but the public is also welcome to drop by and browse at their leisure. Guided tours for larger groups should call (303) 273-3815 in advance. Admission is free.

U.S. GEOLOGICAL SURVEY, NATIONAL EARTH-QUAKE INFORMATION CENTER, 1711 Illinois on the CSM campus, records earthquakes throughout the world. The U.S. Geological Survey collects information and conducts research here. Pre-arranged tours may be taken of the facility. Admission is free.

ADOLPH COORS COMPANY, 13th and Ford, Golden, is the world's largest single brewery facility. This legendary brewery is open for tours daily and Saturdays. The tour takes half an hour and includes seeing the malting of the barley, the brewing and

One of the great rock formations in the Red Rocks Amphitheatre 12 miles west of Denver.

packaging of the beer. At the conclusion of the tour those of legal drinking age may sample complimentary glasses of Coors Light, Premium or George Killian's Irish Red Ale. All children must be accompanied by an adult. Tours are also available for the handicapped (hearing and mobility impaired) as well as foreign visitors (with advance reservations). Advance reservations are also necessary for groups of 14 or more. It is open 8:30 a.m. to 4:30 p.m. Monday through Saturday, June through August. It is closed Sundays and holidays. For the winter schedule call 277 BEER. Admission for the tours is free.

RED ROCKS PARK, south of Golden via the Morrison/Red Rocks Exit off I-70, is a must-see. In this world famous phenomenon of geology, roads wind between sandstone spires and ledges to Red Rocks theatre, a natural outdoor amphitheatre. Geographers once recognized Red Rocks as one of the Seven Wonders of the World. The gates are open from 8 a.m. to 11 p.m. daily unless a concert is scheduled. For information about performances here, call (303) 575-2638.

Littleton

Littleton (pop. 28,631), incorporated in 1890, is the county seat of Arapahoe County. It was named for **Richard S. Little** who was one of the early-day settlers here, arriving in 1858. The town was platted in 1872, a year after the Denver & Rio Grande Railroad arrived. The Littleton Town Hall, 2450 W. Main St., is listed on the National Register of Historic Places. Also listed is the Hildebrand Ranch, seven miles southwest of Littleton off Deer Creek Canyon Rd.

LITTLETON HISTORICAL MUSEUM, 6028 S. Gallup St., is located in the city's largest park complex, Gallup Park and Ketring Park. The main museum building houses a non-circulating reference library of materials on Littleton including a collection of over 3,000 photographs of business and community life. Changing exhibits in the museum's three galleries span the centuries with themes about people, events and things and their impact on times, past and present. Also on the grounds is an 1890s farm and blacksmith shop, an 1860s schoolhouse, a c. 1900 ice house, and an 1860s homestead. Costumed staff and volunteers act out their roles as blacksmith, schoolmaster, and members of a farm family to present a living history interpretation of life in early Littleton. The museum is open 8 a.m. to 5 p.m. weekdays, 10 a.m. to 5 p.m. Saturday, and 1 to 5 p.m. Sunday. It is closed on all holidays. Admission is free.

TINY TOWN, a miniature city built in 1915 as a play town for a businessman's daughter, has been reopened as an area tourist attraction. George Turner, who ran a moving company, built the first few buildings with its miniature replicas of Denver historical buildings in 1915 and by 1925 had created about 125 buildings. Twenty of the buildings today, most of which are little taller than an adult's waist, are the originals. At one time,

The 1860s homestead on the grounds of the Littleton Historical Museum and (below) one of the changing exhibits in the museum's main building.

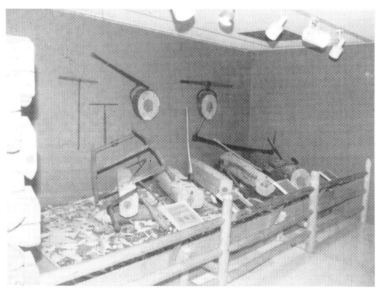

Four Mile Historic District contains many of Denver's historical buildings, including the oldest home built on Cherry Creek in 1859.

Tiny Town, five miles southwest of Denver, is a miniature city of historic buildings built 75 years ago by a Denver businessman as a play town for his daughter. It has been reopened as an area tourist attraction.

Tiny Town was one of the state's top three tourist attractions behind "Buffalo Bill" Cody's grave and Pikes Peak. The attraction reopened in 1988. It can be reached by driving west on US 285 (Hampden Ave.), then left on Turkey Creek Rd. (past mile marker 246). It is open weekends during the summer months. An admission is charged.

Morrison

Also in Jefferson County is the town of **Morrison** (pop. 478) with two buildings listed on the National Register of Historic Places. These include the Bradford House III, four miles south of Morrison, and the Morrison School House, 226 Spring St. The Morrison Historic District is located on CO 8.

In Douglas County

South of Denver is Douglas County and the county seat is **Castle Rock** (pop. 3,900). There are several sites in the county listed on the National Register of Historic Places. These include the Castle Rock Depot, 304 Elpert; Castle Rock Elementary School, 3rd and Cantril Sts., in Castle Rock; the Glen Grove School, north of Palmer Lake off Perry Park Rd.; the John Kinner House, 6694 Perry Park Rd.; and the Spring Valley School/The School House, Spring Valley and Lorraine Rds., in the Larkspur area; the Ben Quick Ranch and Fort, 6695 W. Plum Creek Rd., at Palmer Lake; the Ruth Memorial Methodist Episcopal Church, 19670 E. Main St., Parker; Church of St. Philip-in-the-Field/Bear Canon Cemetery, five miles south of Sedalia, and the Indian Park School, in Sedalia; the Roxborough State Park Archaeological District, in Waterton; and the Bear Canon Agricultural District, on both sides of CO 105 from CO 67 to Jarre Creek, south of Denver.

DENVER SITES ON THE NATIONAL REGISTER
OF HISTORIC PLACES

All Saints Episcopal Church/Chapel of Our Merciful Savior, 2222 W. 32nd Ave.

Arno Apartments, 325 E. 18th Ave.

Bailey House, 1600 Ogden St.

Bats Grocery Store, 4336 Clayton St.

Belcaro/Phipps House, 3400 Belcaro Dr.

Boston Building, 828 17th St.

Botanic Gardens House/Richard Crawford Campbell House, 909 York St.

Bouvier-Lathrop House, 1600 Emerson St.

Brinker Collegiate Institute/Old Navare, 1725-27 Tremont Pl.

J. S. Brown Mercantile, 1634 18th St.

Brown Palace Hotel, 17th and Tremont Pl.

Buchtel Bungalow, 2100 S. Columbine St.

Buckhorn Exchange/Zeitz, 1000 Osage St.

This statue, "The Old Prospector" by Alphonse Pelzer, on 15th Street, between Curtis and Arapahoe, in Denver salutes the thousands of gold seekers who rushed to Colorado beginning in 1859. The model for the statue was Col. John W. Straughn.

Alfred Butters House, 1129 Pennsylvania.
Carter-Rice Building, 1623-1631 Black St.
Cathedral of the Immaculate Conception, Colfax and Logan.
Central Presbyterian Church, 1660 Sherman St.
Chamberlin Observatory, 2930 E. Warren Ave.
Chapel No. 1/Eisenhower Memorial, Lowry AFB.
Allen Delos Chappel House, 1555 Race St.
Cheesman-Boettcher Mansion/Governor's Mansion, 400 E. 8th St.
Cheesman Park Duplex, 1372 S. Pennsylvania St.
Christ Methodist Episcopal Church/Greater Temple of Jerusalem, 2201 Ogden.

Civic Center, between Grant and Delaware Sts.
Clements Rowhouse, 2201-2217 Glenarm Pl.
Cornwall Apartments, 921 E. 12th Ave.
Creswell Mansion, 1244 Grant St.
F. W. Crocker & Co., 1860 Blake St.
Croke-Patterson-Campbell Mansion, 428-430 E. 11th Ave.
Curry-Chucovich House, 1439 Court Pl.
Daniels and Fisher Tower, 1101 16th St.
Denver Athletic Club, 1325 Glenarm Pl.
Denver City Cable Railway Building/Spaghetti Factory, 1801 Lawrence St.
Denver City Railway Building, 1635 17th St.
Denver Dry Goods Co. Building, 16th and California Sts.
Denver Mint, W. Colfax Ave. and Delaware St.
Dow-Rosenzweig House, 1129 E. 17th Ave.
Dunning-Benedict House, 1200 Pennsylvania St.
William J. Dunwoody House/LaLoma Restaurant, 2637 W. 26th Ave.
Elitch Theater, W. 38th and Tennyson.
John Elsner House, 2810 Arapahoe St.
Emmanuel Shearith Israel Chapel, 1201 10th St.
Eppich Apartments, 1266 Emerson St.
Equitable Building, 730 17th St.
Evans Memorial Chapel, University of Denver campus.
Evans School, 1115 Acoma St.
Eugene Field House, 715 S. Franklin St.
Thomas M. Field House, Colorado State Home for Dependent Children, 2305
S. Washington St.
William G. Fisher House/International House, 1600 Logan.
First Congregational Church, 980 Clarkson St.
Fitzroy Place/Warren/Iliff Mansion, 2160 S. Cook St.
Fleming-Hannington House, 1133 Pennsylvania.
Flower-Vaile House, 1610 Emerson St.
John S. Flower House, 1618 Ogden St.
Barney L. Ford Building, 1514 Blake.
Justina Ford House, 3091 California St.
A. C. Forest Building/University Building, 912 16th St.
Ernest LeNeve Foster House, 2105 Lafayette St.
Four Mile House, 715 S. Forest.
General Electric Building, 1441 18th St.
The Grafton/The Aldine, 1001-1020 E. 17th Ave.
Guerrieri-De Cunto House, 1650 Pennsylvania.
Hanigan-Canino Terrace, 1421-1435 W. 35th Ave.
Haskell House, 1651 Emerson St.
Hendri and Bolthoff Warehouse Building, 1743 Wazee.
Ideal Building, 821 17th St.
Jeffery and Mary Keating House, 1207 Pennsylvania.
Kistler-Rodriguez House, 700 E. 9th St.
Kittredge Building, 511 16th St.
William Lang Townhouse, 1626 Washington St.
Owen E. LeFevre House, 1311 York St.
Littleton Creamery-Beatrice Foods Cold Storage Warehouse, 1801 Wynkoop.
Loretto Heights Academy, 3001 S. Federal Blvd.
The Marne, Wilbur S. Raymond House, 1572 Race.
Masonic Temple Building, 1614 Welton St.
Peter McCourt House, 1471 High St.

McPhee and McGinnity Building, 2301 Black St.
Midwest Steel & Iron Works Co. Complex, 25 Larimer St.
Moffat Station, 2101 15th St. Montgomery Court, 215 E. 11th Ave.
Dora Moore School, E. 9th Ave. at Corona St.
Frederick W. Neef House, 2143 Grove St.
Neusteter Building, 720 16th St.
New Terrace, 900-914 E. 20th Ave.
Norman Apartments, 99 S. Downing St.
Orlando Flats, 2330 Washington St.
Oxford Hotel, 1612 17th St.
Pacific Express Stable, 2363 Blake St.
Judge Peter L. Palmer House, 1250 Ogden St.
Paramount Theatre, 519 16th St.
Peters Paper Co. Warehouse, 1625-31 31 Wazee.
Pierce-Haley House, 857 Grant St.
Public Service Building/Insurance Exchange Building, 910 15th St.
Richthofen Castle, 7020 E. 12th Ave.
Rocky Mountain Hotel, 2301 7th St.
Amos H. Root Building, 1501 Platte St.
George Schleier Mansion, 1665 Grant St.
Schlessinger House, 1544 Race St.
George Schmidt House/Zang Brewery, 2345 7th St.
Shorthorn Building/Goodwill Building, 2257 Larimer St.
Smith House, 1801 York St.
Pierce T. Smith House, 1751 Gilpin St.
Smith's Irrigation Ditch/City Ditch/Big Ditch, Washington Park.
Spratlen-Anderson Wholesale Grocery Co., 1450 Wynkoop St.
St. Andrews Episcopal Church, 2015 Glenarm Pl.
St. Elizabeth's Church, 1062 11th St.
St. Elizabeth's Retreat Chapel, 2825 W. 32nd Ave.
St. John's Cathedral, 1313 Clarkson St.
St. Joseph's Polish Roman Catholic Church, 517 E. 46th St.
St. Joseph's Roman Catholic Church, 600 Galapago.
St. Mark's Parish Church, 1160 Lincoln.
St. Patrick Mission Church, 3325 Pecos.
Stearns House, 1030 Logan.
Stuart St. Historic Structures/West Colfax, 1389, 1390, 1435, 1444, 1471
Stuart St.
Sugar Building, 1530 16th St.
Tallmadge & Boyer Block, 1926-2942 Zuni.
Tears-McFarland House, 1290 Williams St.
Temple Emanuel, 2400 Curtis.
Temple Emanuel (1st Southern Baptist), 1595 Pearl St.
H. H. Thomas House, 2104 Glenarm Pl.
Tivoli Brewery Co., 1320-1348 10th St.
Tramway Building, 1100 14th St. (University of Colorado).
Treat Hall, E. 18th Ave. and Pontiac St.
Trinity United Methodist Church, E. 18th Ave. and Broadway.
U.S. Custom House, 721 19th St.
U.S. Post Office/Federal Building, 18th and Stout Sts.
Union Station, 17th at Wynkoop.
Vine Street Houses, 1415, 1429, 1435, 1441, 1453 Vine St.
Weckbaugh House, 1701 E. Cedar Ave.
Wood-Morris-Bonfils House, 707 Washington St.

This is a detail from "Colorado Chronicle," 150 year time line at the Colorado History Museum.

Zang House/Gargoyle House, 1532 Emerson St.
Adolph Zang Mansion, 709 Clarkson.
(Please remember that many of these sites are private residences or private property. Please do not disturb the occupants.)

Chapter 3
A Side Trip to Estes Park

This chapter covers Boulder, Lyons and Estes Park. Provided is a list of museums and historical places and sites.

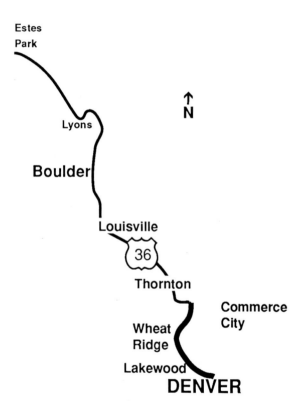

Estes
Park

Lyons

↑
N

Boulder

Louisville

36

Thornton

Commerce
City

Wheat
Ridge

Lakewood

DENVER

Chapter 3
A Side Trip to Estes Park

Boulder (pop. 76,685), county seat of Boulder County, is 30 miles northwest of Denver via US 36. It is home of the **University of Colorado**, founded in 1861. Construction on the university did not begin until 1874. Today the campus occupies 600 acres. Many of the 160 buildings are built in the Italian Renaissance style.

A. A. Brookfield helped to organize the **Boulder City Town Company** on February 10, 1859. At the time, the new town was part of Nebraska Territory. The town was organized in 1871. The first schoolhouse in Colorado was erected at the southwest corner of Walnut and 15th Streets in 1860.

M. Scott Carpenter, one of the first U.S. astronauts and the second American to circle the earth in a spacecraft, was born in Boulder on May 1, 1925. He joined the Navy after graduating from high school and returned to Boulder after World War II to study aeronautical engineering at the University. Carpenter rejoined the Navy in 1949 and became a pilot, serving in the Korean War. He became a test pilot and was selected to be an astronaut and assigned to the Mercury program in 1959. He made a three-orbit flight in the **Aurora 7** spacecraft on May 24, 1962. In 1965, Carpenter took a leave of absence from NASA to become an aquanaut in the **Navy's Man-in-the-Sea** program. He participated in the **Sealab II** experiment by spending 30-days at a depth of 205 feet on the floor of the Pacific Ocean in 1965. Carpenter was awarded the Legion of Merit for his part in this experiment. He retired from the Navy in 1969.

The historic attractions in Boulder include:

UNIVERSITY OF COLORADO MUSEUM is located in the Henderson building between 15th and 16th Streets on Broadway on the University of Colorado campus. The museum maintains collections in anthropology, archaeology, enthnology, botany, entomology and zoology. It is open 9 a.m. to 5 p.m. weekdays, 9 a.m. to 4 p.m. Saturday and 10 a.m. to 4 p.m. Sunday. It is closed on all University holidays. Admission is free.

UNIVERSITY OF COLORADO HERITAGE CENTER is located on the third floor of Old Main, the oldest building on

Astronaut Scott Carpenter gets set . . .   Takes a last look around . . .   Gets ready to go . . .

ELGIN DAILY COURIER-NEWS

A Good Neighbor and Friendly Servant Since 1874

Eighty Eighth Year — 123   ELGIN, ILLINOIS, THURSDAY, MAY 24, 1962   Twenty-Six Pages   7 Cents Per Copy

GREAT SCOTT! CARPENTER'S
- WHEW - OKAY!

Farm Bill Passes Big Test

WASHINGTON (UPI) — President Kennedy's program to trim the government's $4 billion a year farm surplus storage bill passed a major test today. The Senate adopted an amendment writing the administration's wheat surplus reduction plan into a catch-all farm bill.

The Senate moved immediately on other business to head an early vote on a second key feature of the administration bill. This was an amendment which would restore to the bill Kennedy's proposal for mandatory acreage control to reduce feed grain surpluses.

The wheat program would require farmers to choose between strict acreage controls with high support prices and relaxation in the crop or reduction of supports to no more than 50 per cent of the last running power parity level.

The program is designed to allow production cuts to about 25 million bushels below present domestic and export needs. Administration experts figure this would allow the present 1.3 billion bushel surplus to be cut in half in about four years.

Inside Courier-News

It'll Remain Fairly Mild

Fair tonight. Low in 5th. Friday fair with little temperature change. High in 70s. West to northwest winds diminishing tonight and becoming mostly northerly 10-15 mph Friday. Saturday showers likely with little temperature change.

Elgin Gets New Contract

WASHINGTON — The Army Signal Corps has awarded Elgin National Watch Co. a contract to produce a telephone equipment.

Sen. Paul Douglas (D-Ill.) today announced the award in a $40,157 and prepared to bring two panels onto the water at Cape Canaveral if necessary.

Meanwhile two panels were dispatched from the aircraft carrier Intrepid, which was stationed in the intended drop zone 200 miles away.

The Virgin Islands Coast Guard

Navy Searchers Sight Raft, Happy Astronaut

CAPE CANAVERAL, Fla. (AP) — Astronaut Malcolm Scott Carpenter successfully orbited the earth three times today and then—after a harrowing 35 minutes when it was not known whether he had survived the re-entry—he was sighted sitting on a raft in the Atlantic Ocean.

A Navy P2V Neptune bomber flashed the word that Carpenter apparently was all right after spotting him in the raft some 135 miles northeast of Puerto Rico.

Floating nearby was the Aurora 7 spacecraft which had carried him three times around the globe in 4 hours and 56 minutes at 17,532 miles an hour.

The capsule overshot its intended landing area by 200 miles and Carpenter apparently decided to leave it and wait out recovery in the one-man inflatable life raft which he carried aboard the capsule.

The Neptune reported it was circling the raft and said that Carpenter was "sitting upward." There...

(CAPE CANAVERAL, Fla.)

MORE ORBIT NEWS ON PAGE TWO

After Two Orbits

Lt. Cmdr. Malcolm Scott Carpenter, USN

Salan Escapes Death In Surprise Verdict

PARIS (UPI) — A high rate at which the army court-martial...

Fine Acquitted

LUXEMBURG, Ky. (AP)—Jim...

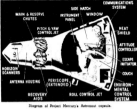

Diagram of Project Mercury's Astronaut capsule.

COMMUNICATIONS SYSTEM
SIDE HATCH
INSTRUMENT PANEL
WINDOW
MAIN & RESERVE CHUTES
PITCH & YAW CONTROL JET
HEAT SHIELD
ATTITUDE CONTROLLER
HORIZON SCANNERS
ESCAPE INITIATOR
COUCH
ANTENNA HOUSING
PERISCOPE (EXTENDED)
RECOVERY AIDS
ROLL CONTROL JET
ENVIRONMENTAL CONTROL SYSTEM

New Guinea Exclusive

Indonesian Force Poised For Attack

Copley News Service
JAKARTA, Indonesia — An account force of several thousand Indonesian troops is poised in the Moluccas Islands ready to invade Dutch-held West New Guinea, according to a top government of Israel here.

In an exclusive interview Wednesday, the official said the troops, armed with U.S. and Russian weapons, are based within 130 miles of New Guinea. He said the men are "exceedingly well armed"...

Astronaut Scott Carpenter, a Boulder native, turned up missing for 35 minutes when his space craft Aurora 7 splashed down 200 miles from its intended landing area in the Atlantic Ocean on May 24, 1962. He was one of the first U.S. astronauts and was the second American to circle the earth in a spacecraft.

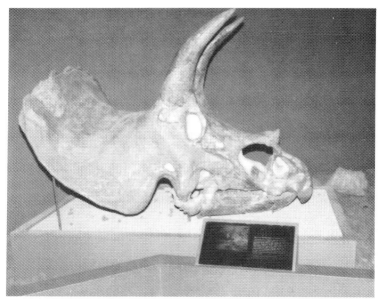

This skull of a Triceratops Calicorns, a common dinosaur of Western North America, found in the Henderson Museum on the CU campus dates back some 70 million years ago. Its teeth and beak indicate the triceratops was a herbivore, feeding on tough, woody plants.

The footprint of a giant duckbill dinosaur, some 70 million years old, is exhibited in CU's Henderson Museum in Boulder. This footprint filling was found on the roof of a coal mine in Western Colorado.

The Giffen-Klingler House, 1040 Mapleton Avenue in Boulder, was built in 1890 and is an excellent example of the noted American architect Henry Hobson Richardson's Shingle Style.

The Harbeck House, 1200 Euclid, houses the Boulder Historical Society Museum. The museum is open Tuesday through Friday and on Saturday afternoons.

"The Wedding Cake House" is the nickname given to the historic McInnes House, 1020 Mapleton Avenue in Boulder. The stately home was built in 1905 and the style of architecture is Greek Revival.

The McKenzie House, 809 Pine Street in Boulder, is listed on the National Register of Historic Places. This Queen Anne style home was built in 1877 for a local bank vice president.

the CU campus. It contains memorabilia documenting the history of the university in its seven rooms. It is open 10 a.m. to 3 p.m. Tuesday through Friday and 9 a.m. until kickoff before every home football game. Special tours are available. Admission is free.

HARBECK HOUSE, 1200 Euclid, houses the Boulder Historical Society museum. It includes over 35,000 interesting objects from Boulder's past. It is open 10 a.m. to 4 p.m. Tuesday through Friday and 12 noon to 4 p.m. Saturday. An admission is charged.

There are several buildings in Boulder listed on the National Register of Historic Places. These include the Carnegie Library, 1125 Pine St.; Chautauqua Auditorium and Colorado Chautauqua, both in Chautauqua Park; Highland School, 885 Arapahoe Ave.; Northern Colorado Park Company Substation/U.S. Express Building, 1590 Broadway; Squires-Tourtellot House/Malick House, 1019 Spruce St.; Swedish Evangelical Lutheran Church of Ryssby, N. 63rd St.; Woodward-Baird House/Little Gray House, 1733 Canyon Rd.; and Boulder Post Office, 1905 15th St.

There are three historic districts in Boulder and the area. The Boulder Downtown Historic District; the Nolin Quadrangle Historic District, on the CU campus; and the Walker Ranch Historic District, west of Boulder.

The **Bolder Boulder**, one of the top 10 10K races in the world, is held in Boulder every Memorial Day and draws more than 20,000 runners each year.

Lyons

About half way to **Estes Park** is **Lyons** (pop. 1,332), designated a historic district by the Colorado Historical Society and the U.S. Department of Interior. Lyons was founded in 1881 and incorporated in 1891.

E. S. Lyon came to the area northwest of Boulder in the 1880s to be a farmer. What he found instead was a wealth of sandstone cliffs, which he turned into a booming quarry business. The sandstone structures reflect a unique era of prosperity in Lyons. During the peak years, Lyons sandstone was shipped as far as Boston and New York. Lyons sandstone was used in the construction of several buildings on the University of Colorado campus in Boulder. The industry thrived until cement replaced it as a more convenient building material in

The Lyons Redstone Museum is housed in this school building that dates back to 1881.

1916, although the stone is in demand today for its aesthetic appeal.

There are several buildings listed on the National Register of Historic Places in Lyons. These include the First Congregational /Old Stone Church, 717 4th Ave.; Longmont Power Plant, Old Apple Valley Rd.; Lyons Railroad Depot Library (now the town library), 400 block of Broadway; The Lyons Redstone Museum, 338 High St.; and several other Lyons Sandstone Buildings, on US 36 and CO 7.

LYONS REDSTONE MUSEUM, is located in the 1881 school building, 338 High St. It houses the Photographic Display on **Lyons** by Manual Weiss; a video, "Lyons History—Past and Present" by Joel Goldfain; and a number of exhibits and displays depicting the community's and area history. Of special interest is a collection of 570 telephone insulators on display. The museum is open 9:30 a.m. to 4:30 p.m. Monday through Saturday and 12:30 to 4:30 p.m. Sunday from June through October. Admission is free. Pick up a brochure at the museum for a "drive-by" tour.

The Old Stone Church at 4th and High Streets in Lyons is listed on the National Register of Historic Places.

The famed Stanley Hotel in Estes Park is listed on the National Register of Historic Places.

Estes Park

Estes Park is north of Boulder via US 36, only an hour from Denver. The scenic Village of Estes Park was platted in 1905 and incorporated in 1917.

Freelan O. Stanley is credited with much of what has happened in **Estes Park** and this area since the turn of the century.

Freelan Stanley (1849-1940), who with his twin brother, Francis, built the first **Stanley steamer automobile** (simply called the Stanley). Suffering from tuberculosis, Freelan Stanley came to Estes Park for relief and built the historic Stanley Hotel that helped build Estes Park into a popular tourist destination. The hotel has hosted such famous personages as the **"Unsinkable Molly Brown," John Phillip Sousa,** and **Theodore Roosevelt. Author Stephen King** stayed for some time at the hotel, drawing on its turn-of the-century ambience for his popular thriller, "The Shining." The hotel is home to the U.S. Chess Championship every autumn.

The Stanley brothers organized businesses and invented products together. They invented dry plate film and organized the Stanley Dry Plate Company in 1883. In 1905 they sold out

The McGregor Ranch Museum in Estes Park is a 1,200 acre working homestead ranch.

to Eastman Kodak Company. They built their first Stanley in 1897 and sold their car company to the Locomobile Company in 1899. In 1902 they bought back their patents and organized the Stanley Motor Carriage Company. They retired in 1917. Ironically and tragically, Francis was killed a year later in an auto accident. Freelan died in Estes Park in 1940. The **Stanley Hotel** is listed on the National Register of Historic Places.

   William Byers, founder and editor of the *Rocky Mountain News* named the Park in 1864 in honor of **Joel Estes**, his host at the time, who had settled here with his family to raise cattle. Estes first visited the Park in 1859 but left after the harsh winter of 1866. Estes sold out his interests to Michael Hollenback for either a yoke of oxen or $50. After two other owners the land was acquired by **Griffith J. Evans** who became the first dude ranch operator in Estes Park. Among his many guests was the **Earl of Dunraven.** The English lord enjoyed the experience so much that he wanted to acquire Estes Park for a private hunting preserve for the exclusive use and pleasure of his English friends and himself. Under the Homestead Act he was unable as a foreigner to purchase the land so he hired **Theodore Whyte** to acquire it for him. Whyte proceeded then to pull off

Estes Park Area Historical Museum on US 36 provides exhibits and displays relating to area history dating back to 1859.

the Knowlton & McLeary co.

This old advertisement displayed in the Estes Park Area Historical Museum shows the Stanley Brothers in their 1897 Steamer. They were instrumental in the development of the Park.

95

Baldpate Inn, south of Estes Park, was the setting for the novel and 1920s comedy mystery, "The Seven Keys to Baldpate." On display is one of the largest key collections in the world.

one of the biggest land swindles in the history of Colorado. He hired loafers and drifters from Denver's Larimer Street to file on 160 acres under the Homestead Act. It is said that some claims were even filed by fictitious persons. The earl formed the **Estes Park Co., Ltd.**, a corporation organized under the laws of Great Britain doing business in Colorado. The company was known simply as the **English Company**. Lord Dunraven sold his property in Estes Park in 1907.

ESTES PARK AREA HISTORICAL MUSEUM, located at 4th St. and US 36, Estes Park, provides memorabilia depicting history of the town and valley since its 1859 discovery. It is

The Enos A. Mills Cabin and Museum, located eight miles south of Estes Park on CO 7, was built in 1885. It is listed on the National Register of Historic Places.

open 10 a.m. to 5 p.m. Monday through Saturday and 1 to 5 p.m. Sunday, May through September, and the same hours, except Monday when it is closed, March and December. Other months it is open by appointment. Admission is free.

MACGREGOR RANCH, on Devil's Gulch Rd., is a 1,200 acre educational working homestead ranch and ranch house museum. It is open 11 a.m. to 5 p.m. Tuesday through Sunday, Memorial Day through Labor Day. Admission is free.

BALDPATE INN'S KEY ROOM, located seven miles south of Estes Park on CO 7, boasts the largest key collection in the world. The novel, "Seven Keys to Baldpate," gave the Inn its name, as well as inspiring a Broadway play, radio play and movie. The story plot, seven people who each believe they hold the only key to an isolated mountain hotel, was the basis for the

The Key Room in the Baldpate Inn features the largest collection of keys in the world. The historic inn is located seven miles south of Estes Park.

famous key collection. The inn is open from Memorial Day to Labor Day. Admission to the key display is free.

ENOS MILLS CABIN & NATURE TRAIL, located eight miles south of Estes Park on CO 7, is an informal museum in the cabin of naturalist **Enos Mills**, "Father of Rocky Mountain National Park." It is listed on the National Register of Historic Places. It is open 8 a.m. to 7 p.m. daily. Admission is free.

There are several buildings and a trail in Rocky Mountain National Park listed on the National Register of Historic Places. These include Thunder Lake Patrol Cabin, Wild Basin House, Wild Basin Ranger Station and House, Milner Pass Road Camp Mess Hall and House, Timber Creek Campground Comfort Stations (No. 245, 246, 247), Timber Creek Road Camp Barn, Timber Creek Road Camp Storage Buildings, Timberline Cabin, and Trail Ridge Road.

Chapter 4
The Colorado Springs Area

Home of the U.S. Air Force Academy, Colorado Springs became home to many of the early-day millionaires, who struck it rich in the Victor and Cripple Creek goldfields near the turn of the century. Also included is Manitou Springs and Cascade. The museums and historical sites in this area are included.

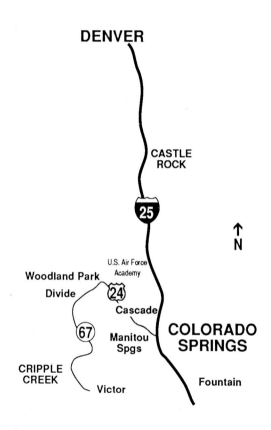

DENVER

CASTLE
ROCK

25

↑
N

U.S. Air Force
Academy

Woodland Park

Divide **24**

Cascade

67 Manitou
Spgs

CRIPPLE
CREEK

Victor

**COLORADO
SPRINGS**

Fountain

Chapter 4
The Colorado Springs Area

Colorado Springs (pop. 375,000), county seat of El Paso County, is 65 miles south of Denver, via I-25.

Several military bases are located in this area including **Fort Carson**, established by the Army in the early 1940s; the **U.S. Air Force Academy**, opened here in 1958, the **North American Air Defense Command (NORAD)**, constructed in Cheyenne Mountain in 1966; **Peterson Air Force Base**; and **Falcon Air Force Base**. The **U.S. Space Foundation** was established here in 1983. The USAF and the Space Commands at Peterson AFB have paved the way for future space related industry and visitor attractions to the area.

The **North American Air Defense Command (NORAD)** is located deep inside Cheyenne Mountain, south of Colorado Springs. NORAD is manned by U.S. and Canadian airmen who work in 11 windowless steel buildings mounted on heavy springs, under granite a quarter-mile thick. The buildings are protected by 30-ton blast doors.

Fort Carson, named in honor of the famous frontiersman, **Kit Carson**, was established in 1942 as an Army infantry training center. **Lt. Clark Gable** (1901-1960), one of the world's best-known motion picture personalities, was stationed at Fort Carson during World War II. His most famous film roles were in "It Happened One Night" (1934), "Mutiny on the Bounty" (1935), and "Gone With The Wind" (1939). During World War II, a section of Fort Carson, headquarters for the 4th Infantry Division (Mechanized) today, served as a German POW camp. Fort Carson is south of Colorado Springs, off CO 115.

Peterson Air Force Base was selected as the Space Command September 1, 1982. The base began as Colorado Spring's municipal airport in 1925. The government took control of the field in 1941 for an Army Air Corps training base. In December, 1942, the Army named it Peterson Field in honor of **Lt. Edward J. Peterson**, a native of **Inglewood**, Colorado, who was killed in a crash of his F-4 airplane here on August 8, 1942. Peterson, serving as the operations officer for the 14th Photographic Reconnaissance Squadron, was one of his squadron's top pilots. The airfield was returned to Colorado Springs in 1948 but was reactivated as a military base in 1951. It was designated an Air Force base in 1976. Peterson AFB is east of Colorado Springs, off US 24.

The **U.S. Olympic Complex**, on 36 acres, was established in 1978 and is the home of 20 of the 38 national governing bodies. Thousands of athletes annually train at the Olympic Training Center, on the site of former Ent AFB. Admission to the Complex is free. (**Ent Air Force Base** was established in 1943 as an Army Air Corp airbase and was named for **Major Gen. Uzal G. Ent**, who commanded the 2nd Air Force during World War II.)

Pikes Peak, six miles west of Colorado Springs, is probably the best known of the Rocky Mountain Peaks. **Lt. Zebulon Pike**, leading a 23-man expedition, made his historical discovery of the now famous mountain that bears his name on November 13, 1806. The first white man to reach the summit of Pikes Peak was **Dr. Edwin James**, a member of **Major Stephen Long's expedition**, in July, 1820. The famous explorer, **Charles Fremont**, built the first trail to the summit, in 1846. The famous **Pikes Peak Auto Race** is held here every summer. The National Weather Service once maintained a meteorological station on Pikes Peak. It was here that **Dr. Robert Andrews Millikan** (1868-1953), a Nobel prize winner in 1923, did much of the work that culminated in his discovery of the cosmic ray.

On August 12, 1901 a **Locomobile** made history by reaching the top of Pikes Peak. A carriage road, called the U.S. Grant Road, had been built to the summit in the early 1880s. The carriage road right-of-way was purchased by the Pikes Peak Automobile Club in 1915. In July, 1916, the company completed a road to the summit for automobiles. The cog-railroad from Manitou Springs to the summit was completed in 1891.

It was from atop Pikes Pike that **Katharine Lee Bates**, a young teacher at Wellesly College in Massachusetts, was inspired to write four stanzas of a poem that almost remained unforgotten. She had gone to the top of Pikes Peak with several other teachers who had chartered a prairie wagon to take them to the summit. It was from this point that the young school teacher from New England glimpsed the magnificent panorama that made her feel as if she were seeing in those brief moments, all the natural beauty of the world. Two years later, Katharine Lee Bates came across her poem and sent it to a church publication which published it on July 4, 1895. The poem was an instant success, but it was not until 1904 that the revised version of the verse was set to the familiar music of Samuel A. Ward—"America The Beautiful."

Thousands of persons visit **Pikes Peak** annually.

Colorado City, a narrow strip extending two miles along **Fountain Creek**, was founded in 1859 as **El Dorado City** which was soon renamed Colorado City. When the Colorado Territory came into existence in 1861, Colorado City was named as its capital. The 2nd Territorial Legislature met here for four days in 1862, before the capital was moved to **Golden**. The governor never transferred his office to Colorado City.

Colorado Springs came into existence in 1871 when Gen. William J. Palmer's **Denver & Rio Grande Railroad** tracks reached today's Pikes Peak and Cascade Avenue. Originally Palmer's town was called **Fountain Colony** for its position on **Fountain Creek**. Later it was renamed Colorado Springs for the mineral springs at the nearby village of Manitou. It was incorporated in 1886.

Colorado College was founded here in 1874.

Interestingly, written into all land deeds in Colorado Springs was a clause prohibiting the manufacture or sale of intoxicating liquors on the premises, a restriction enforced until the repeal of prohibition in 1933.

The **Colorado Midland Railroad** pushed westward to the silver camps from the city in 1885. Colorado Springs was selected as the western terminal of the **Chicago, Rock Island & Pacific Railway** in 1889.

In the meantime, Colorado City continued to be a rowdy, bawdy town. It had its share of labor problems, the most important in 1903 when the members of the **Mill and Smeltermen's Union** called a strike. For a time the town was an armed camp with loud charges and countercharges. After 1912, the old mills were closed or torn down, replaced with the Golden Cycle Mill which used a new and better reduction process. Population soon dwindled and for a period it appeared the town might slip into oblivion. In 1917, Colorado City became **West Colorado Springs**, and, while retaining marks of its identity, gradually conformed to the Palmer way of life.

Many of the "new" rich, the "bonanza kings," invested heavily in Colorado Springs, building lavish homes and expensive

103

The Indians once believed that their great god, Manitou, became angry with lesser gods and turned them into stone to create the Garden of the Gods. It is said the name originated in 1859 in a conversation between M. S. Beach, a founder of Colorado City, and R. E. Cable, a visitor from Kansas City. According to the legend, Beach said, "This would be a fine place for a beer garden." Cable responded, "Beer garden! Why, this is a fit place for the gods to assemble." Helen Hunt Jackson described it as a wonderland of "red rocks of every conceivable and inconceivable size and shape. . ." This park is owned by the City of Colorado Springs.

offices. Between 1900 and 1910, Colorado Springs laid claim to being the wealthiest city per capita in the United States.

Several artists and writers made their homes in Colorado Springs. Among them was **Helen Hunt Jackson**, author of "Ramona."

Among Colorado Springs' great assets is the GARDEN OF THE GODS, presented to the city by the children of **Charles Elliott Perkins** in 1909. Perkins had acquired the land in 1879 for a homesite. It is a registered Natural Landmark.

Centuries ago the Indians met in the **Garden of the Gods** here to hold religious ceremonies. They called it **Old Red Land**. The grotesque, massive and fantastically shaped rocks, now known as **Cathedral Spires**, were, according to Indian legend, huge invaders turned to stone by the great god, Manitou, as punishment for desecrating the hallowed soil.

The original claimant of the area was **Bill Garvin**, who operated the first store in Colorado City. Colorado Springs acquired the Balanced Rock property from the **Curt Goerke estate**. At one time, Goerke fenced the famous rock and charged a fee to those who wanted a close up look and photograph. Today, the park includes 770 acres and admission is free.

The **Easter Sunrise Services** at the Garden of the Gods attracts upward of 20,000 persons annually and millions through the radio broadcast. The service was inaugurated in 1921 through the efforts of **Rev. W. A. Luce** of Colorado Springs.

The Trading Post, constructed in the style of the traditional Pueblo Indian homes, was established in the Garden of the Gods in 1900. It offers fine Indian jewelry, arts, and crafts. The **Southwestern Art Gallery** at the Trading Post offers the best contemporary Indian jewelry, Santa Clara pottery, Hopi kachinas, Navajo rugs and sandpaintings. It is open daily throughout the year.

High Point and Camera Obscura offer an excellent view of the Garden of the Gods and the Pikes Peak region. Camera Obscura, one of three in the nation, projects the entire panorama through a set of lenses onto a disc shaped viewing table. It is open 7:30 a.m. to 9 p.m. daily during the summer. An admission to Camera Obscura is charged.

Another natural attraction is CAVE OF THE WINDS, six miles west of Colorado Springs on US 24 (Exit 141, off I-25). The 40 minute guided walking tour begins every 15 minutes. This tour is through 20 rooms of subterranean beauty. A two-hour guided tour is rugged and involves climbing and crawling through tunnels and underground rooms. This tour is conducted three times a day, Memorial Day through Labor Day and at other times by reservation. It is open 9 a.m. to 9 p.m. during the summer; 10 a.m. to 5 p.m. the balance of the year. An admission is charged.

SEVEN FALLS AND SOUTH CHEYENNE CANYON, referred to as "The Grandest Mile of Scenery in Colorado," is only 10 minutes from downtown Colorado Springs. It is west on West Cheyenne Boulevard. The canyon and waterfall are completely illuminated at night. Helen Hunt Jackson's grave is at the summit of the falls, a mile east of the top of the falls. The canyon is open 8 a.m. to 11 p.m. during the summer months; 9 a.m. to 5 p.m. during the winter months. Admission is free. Just a few miles north of Colorado Springs, off I-25, is the U.S. AIR FORCE ACADEMY, authorized by Congress, April 1, 1954. The permanent campus was opened here in 1958. The first class of 306 cadets trained at the temporary academy site at Lowry AFB at Denver. The Academy Cadet Chapel, a national landmark, is also a major attraction. It has 17 gleaming aluminum spires soaring 150 feet skyward. Protestant and Catholic chapel services are open to visitors at 9 and 11 a.m. on Sunday and Jewish services at 8 p.m. Friday. It is just one of several buildings open daily to the public. The Visitor Center provides information and schedules for all Academy activities. It offers free movies and presents several displays relating to the Academy's past. It is open 9 a.m. to 5 p.m. every day of the week. Cadet training takes place year-round. Visitors enjoy watching cadets march to lunch on weekdays during the academic year. Occasional Saturday morning parades are also open to the public.

Some of the buildings are open to the public. The Planetarium offers free shows periodically. Public restrooms are available. Call 472-2778 for the show schedule. Cadet Social Center, in Arnold Hall, houses historical exhibits and a theatre and is open daily from 9 a.m. to 5 p.m. Public restrooms and a cafeteria are available. The Theater Variety Series and Allied Art Series are presented here also. For information, call 472-4499. The Cadet Chapel is described above. Cadet Field House is the setting for two of the Academy's most popular spectator sports, ice hockey and basketball. Call 472-1895 for ticket information. In the cadet area is an F-105 fighter that commemorates academy graduates killed in Viet Nam.

Sijan Hall, a dormitory on campus, is named in honor of **Capt. Lance P. Sijan**, class of 1965, the first Academy graduate to receive the Congressional Medal of Honor. Just past the front gate, at the entrance, a B-52 bomber is displayed.

NATIONAL CARVERS MUSEUM, Exit 158, off I-25, one exit north of the Air Force Academy, was incorporated in November, 1969, to foster, cultivate, promote, sponsor, and develop the understanding of the art, craft, and skill of woodcarving. To reach the museum, after leaving I-25, turn west toward the mountains, then drive to the first road on the left. On dis-

This B-52 bomber is displayed at the entrance to the U.S. Air Force Academy near Colorado Springs. The USAFA Visitors Center (below) provides visitors with complete information about the Academy and its offerings.

This statue at the Air Force Academy salutes "The Tuskegee Airmen of World War II," the black aviators who served in the U.S. Army Air Corps during the war. The blacks served in segregated units until 1948 when the armed forces were desegregated by an executive order issued by President Truman. The Department of the Air Force was created in 1947. Before then, the Department of War controlled military aviation.

Lt. General Hubert R. Harmon was the first superintendent of the U. S. Air Force Academy, authorized by Congress in the spring of 1954. Temporary quarters were established at Lowry Air Force Base in Denver in 1955 and the permanent campus was opened in 1958. This statue was erected in June, 1984, in General Harmon's honor by the first graduating class at the Academy.

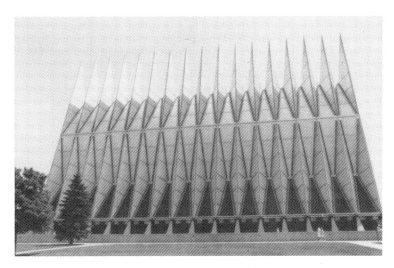

The Cadet Chapel at the U. S. Air Force Academy near Colorado Springs is a national landmark and attracts thousands of visitors annually. Most visitors to the Academy enjoy watching the cadets drill or march to their various exercises also.

play are carvings by over 4,000 American artists with daily changing of displays. It is open 9 a.m. to 5 p.m. daily. An admission is charged.

WESTERN MUSEUM OF MINING AND INDUSTRY, Exit 156-A off I-25 (125 Gleneagle Dr.) just east of the North Gate of the U.S. Air Force Academy. Relive Colorado's rich and colorful mining past and find out what's happening in mining today. Unique to this "hands on" museum is the actual operation of its multi-ton steam engines, drills, hoists, mine locomotives, and other carefully restored mining machines. Visitors learn to pan for gold and see how miners timbered, drilled, blasted, mucked, and moved ore from the mine to the stamp mill, where ore was crushed and processed at the turn of the century. An 18-minute multi-media show traces the history of western mining. It is open 9 a.m. to 4 p.m. Monday through Saturday, noon to 4 p.m. Sunday. It is closed Thanksgiving, Christmas, New Year's Day, and Easter. An admission is charged.

PRORODEO HALL OF CHAMPIONS & MUSEUM OF THE AMERICAN COWBOY, 101 ProRodeo Dr. (Exit 147, off I-25), Colorado Springs, was created to preserve the legacy of the cowboy and his competitions, and to honor the champions of the American legend in action. The guided tour begins with a multi-media presentation that traces the history of the early West. Heritage Hall features displays that trace the development of cowboy gear over the past 100 years. Atop a brahma bull, through special photographic techniques, a visitor will get the feel of a bull ride. The rodeo greats are honored in the **Hall of Champions**. The **Hall of Fame** and museum are open 9 a.m. to 5 p.m. daily from Memorial Day to Labor Day and 9 a.m. to 4:30 p.m. Tuesday through Saturday, noon to 4:30 p.m. Sunday the rest of the year. It is closed on New Year's Day, Easter, Thanksgiving and Christmas. An admission is charged.

PETERSON AFB MUSEUM, located at Peterson AF Base off US 24, displays military uniforms and memorabilia, military aircraft models and photographs, and other displays depicting the history of Peterson AFB and its present missions, which includes support to Cheyenne Mountain AFB and Falcon AFB. Located at Peterson AFB are headquarters for the North American Aerospace Defense Command, U.S. Space Command, Air Force Space Command, 1st Space Wing and 3rd Space Support

Wing. The museum is open 8:30 a.m. to 4:30 p.m. Tuesday through Saturday (closed between 12 noon and 1 p.m. for lunch). Admission is free.

CHEYENNE MOUNTAIN ZOO AND WILL ROGERS SHRINE OF THE SUN are both located on Cheyenne Mountain Hwy. The zoo houses a collection of animals from around the world. The shrine was built as a monument to the late Will Rogers (1879-1935), the American humorist and social critic, by **Spencer Penrose**, who struck it rich in the gold fields in **Cripple Creek**. A spectacular view of the Pikes Peak region is offered from the shrine which is also lighted at night. The zoo and shrine are open 9 a.m. to 5 p.m. daily during the summer, and 9 a.m. to 4 p.m. daily, Labor Day through Memorial Day. An admission is charged.

JOHN MAY CENTER, nine miles southwest of the center (the Court House) of Colorado Springs on CO 115 (Nevada Ave.) includes the MAY NATURAL MUSEUM OF THE TROPICS exhibiting over 7,000 of the world's most beautiful and unusual giant insects and related vertebrates from all the

The ProRodeo Hall of Fame also features the Museum of the American Cowboy. Rodeo greats are featured in the Hall of Champions. It is located just off I-25 in north Colorado Springs.

The Will Rogers Shrine of the Sun Memorial on Cheyenne Mountain.

This bust of Will Rogers, the famous American humorist, stands at the Will Rogers Shrine of the Sun on Cheyenne Mountain near Colorado Springs. Rogers died in an air crash with Wiley Post in Alaska in 1935. The shrine is lighted at night and has become a well-known landmark in the region.

Spencer Penrose struck it rich in the Cripple Creek District goldfields. An admirer of Will Rogers, he built this shrine to the humorist on Cheyenne Mountain just outside Colorado Springs. This bust of Penrose is setup at the Will Rogers Shrine. He also built the historic Broadmoor Hotel in Colorado Springs in 1918.

tropical areas on the globe. **James F. May** (1884-1956) spent over a half century of collecting and mounting over 100,000 of these specimens while exploring many of the world's jungles. The newest addition to the Museum Center is the Museum of Space Exploration with hundreds of actual photographs taken by our planetary spacecraft and many models of the space machines. The Museum Center is located on Golden Eagle Ranch which has a large RV Park and Campgrounds. The museum is open daily from April 15 through September 30. An admission is charged.

McALLISTER HOUSE MUSEUM, 423 N. Cascade Ave., Colorado Springs, was built by **Major Henry McAllister** in 1873 for his family and is filled with furnishings, clothing, books and family items. As the first brick house in Colorado Springs, it is listed on the National Register of Historic Places. It is open 10 a.m. to 4 p.m. Wednesday through Saturday and

Giant insects and other creatures are displayed in the May Natural History Museum located in Golden Eagle Ranch RV Park south of Colorado Springs.

noon to 4 p.m. Sunday, May through August, and 10 a.m. to 4 p.m. Thursday through Saturday, September through April. An admission is charged.

AMERICAN NUMISMATIC ASSOCIATION MUSEUM, 818 N. Cascade Ave., Colorado Springs, features exhibits and displays of a wide selection of coins, medals, tokens, and currencies of the world. The Association, founded in 1891 as a non-profit educational association, is the largest and most active numismatic body in the world. Of particular importance in the museum are the **Kenneth Keith** collection of Mexican coins, the **Norman H. Liebman** collection of paper money relating to Abraham Lincoln, and the **Robert T. Herdegen and Richard W. Lloyd Memorial Collections** of worldwide coins. It is open from 8:30 a.m. to 4 p.m. Monday through Saturday. An admission is charged.

PIONEER MUSEUM, 215 S. Tejon St., Colorado Springs, is located in the 1903 El Paso County Courthouse. It features exhibits and programs on the history of the Pikes Peak Region. It is open 10 a.m. to 5 p.m. Monday through Saturday and 1 to 5 p.m. Sunday. Docent guided tours are offered at 1 and 2 p.m. Tuesdays and 10 a.m. and 11 a.m. Thursdays throughout the

The McAllister House, built in 1873, is the oldest house in Colorado Springs. It houses a museum.

115

The American Numismatic Association Museum is located in this Colorado Springs building that also serves as the national headquarters for the Association.

Colorado Springs' Pioneer Museum is housed in the 1903 El Paso County courthouse.

The front entrance to Fort Carson, named for frontiersman Kit Carson. The fort is located just south of Colorado Springs.

summer. Reservations are suggested for groups of 12 or more. Call 578-6650 for additional information. Admission is free.

HALL OF PRESIDENTS WAX MUSEUM, 1050 S. 21st St. (Exit 141 west off I-25), Colorado Springs, presents over 100 lifelike wax representations of U. S. presidents and other famous persons. It is open 10 a.m. to 5 p.m. daily. An admission is charged.

WORLD FIGURE SKATING HALL OF FAME AND MUSEUM is located at the National Headquarters of the United States Figure Skating Association, 20 1st St., Colorado Springs. The museum contains permanent displays of costumes of figure skating champions, along with antique skates, pins and medals from around the world. It is open 10 a.m. to 4 p.m. Tuesday through Saturday, June through August; Monday through Friday, September through May. Admission is free.

The Colorado Springs sites listed on the National Register of Historic Places include the Alamo Hotel, 128 S. Tejon St.; Amarillo Hotel/Stockbridge House, 2301 W. Colorado Ave.; Atchison, Topeka & Santa Fe depot, 555 E. Pikes Peak Ave.; Bemis House/Hearthstone Inn, 506 N. Cascade; Chambers Ranch/White House, 3202 Chambers Way; the City Hall of Colorado City, 2902 W. Colorado Ave.; Claremont, 21 Broadmoor Ave.; Colorado Springs Fine Arts Center, 30 W. Dale St.; Colorado Springs Post Office and Federal Courthouse, 210 Pikes Peak Ave.; Cutler Hall, Colorado College campus, 912 N.

Cascade Ave.; the De Graff building, 116-118 N. Tejon St.; El Paso County Courthouse, 215 S. Tejon St.; Emmanuel Presbyterian Church, 419 Mesa Rd.; Giddings building, 101 N. Tejon St.; Glen Eyrie, 3820 N. 30th St.; Gwynne-Love House, 730 N. Cascade Ave.; the Hagerman Mansion, 610 N. Cascade Ave.; the McAllister House, 423 N. Cascade Ave.; the Midland Terminal Railroad Roundhouse/Van Briggle Art Pottery, 600 S. 21st St.; Palmer Hall, Colorado College campus, 116 E. San Rafael St.; the Pioneer Cabin, U.S. Air Force Academy campus; the Plaza Hotel, 830 N. Tejon St.; Rio Grande Engine No. 168, 9 S. Madre; the Second Midland School/Old Midland School, 815 S. 25th St.; St. Mary's Catholic Church, 26 W. Kiowa St.; and YWCA Building/Colorado Springs Company, 120 E. Kiowa St.

The historic districts include the Boulder Crescent Place Historic District, 9 and 11 W. Boulder, 312, 318, 320 N. Cascade Ave.; the North Weber St.-Wasatch Ave. Historical Residential District, on N. Weber St. between Boulder and Del Norte; North End Historic District, bounded by Monument Valley, Wood, Nevada, Madison and Unitah Sts.; and the Old Colorado City Historic Commercial District, on the north side of Colo-

World Figure Skating Museum and Hall of Fame is located in the U.S. Figure Skating Association's national headquarters in Colorado Springs.

rado Ave. from 24th St., west to 2611 Colorado Ave., and also includes 115 S. 26th St. and 2418 W. Pikes Peak Ave. Pikes Peak has been designated a National Historic Landmark.

Manitou Springs

West on US 24 is **Manitou Springs** (pop. 4,475), founded in 1872 and incorporated in 1888 as a resort with mineral springs. The Ute Indians believed the region was sacred and the word manitou means "Great Spirit." **President and Mrs. Ulysses S. Grant** visited Manitou Springs and its famous natural mineral water. The community is listed as a National Historic District. Among the attractions here:

PIKES PEAK COG RAILWAY climbs 46,158 feet to the top of Pikes Peak and the view is spectacular enroute and at the summit. Modern Swiss trains operate daily from Manitou Springs from May through October. The depot is at 515 Ruxton Ave., off Manitou Ave. For reservations and information, call 685-5401. An admission is charged.

PIKES PEAK HIGHWAY is a toll road to the summit of Pikes Peak. The 19-mile road is paved for the first seven miles and gravel the other 12 miles. A spectacular view awaits the travelers on this trip to the 14,110-foot peak.

MIRAMONT CASTLE, 9 Capitol Hill Ave., off Ruxton Ave.,

Miramont Castle, a National Historic Landmark in Manitou Springs, was built in 1895.

119

Manitou Springs, is a National Historic Landmark. It was built in 1895 by **Father Jean Baptiste Francolon**. Miramont is a museum dedicated to preserving the Victorian heritage of Manitou Springs and the Pikes Peak Region. It is open 10 a.m. to 5 p.m. daily Memorial Day through Labor Day. An admission is charged. Between Labor Day and Memorial Day it is only available for tours and special functions for groups of 20 or more. For information, call 685-1011.

Other sites in Manitou Springs listed on the National Register of Historic Places include the Barker House/Navajo Apartments, 819 Manitou Ave.; Briarhurst/William A. Bell House, 404 Manitou Ave.; the bridge over Fountain Creek, on US 24; Cliff House, 306 Canon Ave.; Crystal Valley Cemetery, on Plainview Ave.; First Congregational Church, 101 Pawnee Ave.; the Manitou Bath House, 934 Manitou Ave.; the Manitou Springs Post Office, 307 Canon Ave.; the Wheeler Bank, 717-719 Manitou Ave.; and two bridges, one on Park Ave. and the other on Canon Ave. both over Fountain Creek.

The two historic districts in Manitou Springs are the Keithly Log Cabin Development District, Santa Fe Pl., Crystal Rd. and Spur Rd., and the Manitou Springs Historic District, bounded by El Paso Blvd., Ruxton Ave., US 24, and Iron Mt. Ave.

The Stage Coach Inn (Restaurant) building, 702 Manitou Ave., began as a stage stop in the late 1880s. It was later turned into a power plant but wasn't able to produce enough power. It served as a summer cottage for **Helen Hunt Jackson**, author of "Ramona."

There are a number of mineral springs in Manitou, including: Cheyenne Soda Spring, 934 Manitou Ave.; Iron Springs, 431 Ruxton Ave.; Navajo Spring, Arcade, 900 block of Manitou Ave.; Seven Minute Spring, 514 El Paso Blvd.; Shoshone Soda Spring, 816 Manitou Ave.; Stratton Spring (restored), 953 Manitou Ave.; Twin Spring, 121 Ruxton Ave.; Ute Chief (restored), 1311 Manitou Ave.; and Wheeler Spring (restored), 60 Park Ave. The Jerome B. Wheeler Clock Tower, Y of Manitou and Canon Aves., was contributed to the town by the multi-millionaire. Atop the clock is the Goddess Hygeia, goddess of health. Wheeler was the first banker in Manitou and served as president of the once world famous Manitou Water Bottling Co.

MANITOU CLIFF DWELLINGS MUSEUM, west on US 24, was established in 1904 and opened to the public in 1907. The

The Manitou Cliff Dwellings Museum presents the Anasazi tribal culture.

preserve offers visitors a collection of some of the finest architecture of the cliff dwelling Indians and artifacts of the Anasazi culture acquired throughout the Southwest. It demonstrates the fine stone work of the early Indians, 1100 to 1200 A.D. and makes their architectural achievements easily accessible to visitors. It is open 10 a.m. to 5 p.m. every day May, September and October and 9 a.m. to 6 p.m. daily June, July and August. Indian dancing is performed daily June through August. An admission is charged.

BUFFALO BILL WAX MUSEUM, 404 W. Manitou Ave., Manitou Springs, includes over 100 life-sized wax figures of the famous and infamous of yesterday. Prominently displayed is the famous **Buffalo Bill (Col. William F. Cody)** who typifies a glorious and romantic period in American history. His life and exploits captured the imagination and enthusiasm of the entire world and dramatized the adventures of settling the West. Among some of the other displays are The Dalton gang, Black Bart's Stage Holdup, The Texas Rangers, Judge Roy Bean, The Fight at the OK Corral, Belle Starr, the Pony Express, the James and Younger gangs, The Plummer gang, Western Indian chiefs and many others. It is open daily April 15 through September 30. An admission is charged.

Cascade

Cascade is an unincorporated community west of Manitou Springs on US 24.

UTE PASS MUSEUM, at Pikes Peak Exit off US 24 in Cascade, provides a view of the early-day Ute Indians and other area historical events through its various exhibits. A special display is the miniature Colorado Midland Railway, the first railroad into the Rocky Mountains. It is open 10 a.m. to 5 p.m. daily Memorial Day weekend through Labor Day weekend and 10 a.m. to 5 p.m. weekends May and September through December. An admission is charged.

There are three other sites in El Paso County listed on the National Register of Historic Places. These are the Old Livery Stable, 217 W. Missouri, in Fountain, south of Colorado Springs; the Inez Johnson Lewis School, 146 Jeffeson St., in Monument, north of the USAF Academy; and the First Presbyterian Church of Ramah, 113 S. Commercial St., in Ramah, in the northwestern corner of the county.

The Ute Pass Museum just off US 24 in Cascade.

Cripple Creek and Victor

Cripple Creek (pop. 655) and **Victor** (pop. 265), about 40 miles southwest of Colorado Springs, via CO 67 off US 24 at Divide, became the district for the last of the great gold rushes. Cripple Creek is the county seat of Teller County, established in 1899. Gold at Cripple Creek was discovered by Bob Womack, a "hard drinking cowboy," in 1890. He struck it rich in a place called Poverty Gulch on the ranch homesteaded by his father in 1876. Later, on a drinking spree in Colorado City, Womack sold his claim for only $500. He died penniless in Colorado Springs in 1909.

Originally, Cripple Creek was known as **Fremont**. It was renamed for the stream, Cripple Creek, that ran through the ranch and was incorporated in 1892. Victor, six miles southeast of Cripple Creek, became the district's second city when it was established in 1893. Called the "City of Mines," after **Battle Mountain** where the largest and richest mines were located, Victor was destroyed by a fire, started in a dance hall, on August 21, 1899. Within a few days, 100 merchants were back in business in makeshift shacks. Cripple Creek suffered two major fires in 1896. The first fire broke out on April 25, 1896 in a dance hall in the red-light district and destroyed much of the mining town. Four days later, another fire wiped out the remaining buildings, except for a few houses on the west side of town. It also rebuilt quickly.

The Cripple Creek District grew rapidly and by 1900 more than 55,000 persons lived here. The town's population was 25,000, making it the fourth largest city in the state. Victor, with more than 18,000 residents, was the state's fifth largest city. There were 11 other towns in the gold camp, long gone, with such names as Goldfield, Cameron, Altman, Independence, Elkton, Anaconda, Midway, and Gillett. The Portland Mine, on Battle Mountain, just above Victor, was the largest and richest mine and over a 50 year period produced $60 million in gold. The Cresson, midway between Cripple Creek and Victor, was the second largest producer in the district. The field's richest discovery was made here in 1914. Some of the gold coming out this mine was worth $50 per pound.

Victor, named for **Victor Adams**, a local, was founded in 1893. It is one of the best preserved of the Old West mining towns documented on the National Register of Historic Places. The Gold Coin Mine was discovered while excavating for the foundation of a hotel in the middle of town. The remains of this rich mine are still visible off Diamond Ave.

Thirty millionaires came out of the Cripple Creek District gold fields. The first was **Winfield Scott Stratton**, of Colorado Springs, who hit it big in 1891 with his discovery of the Independence. **Spencer Penrose**, who built the **Broadmoor Hotel** in Colorado Springs in 1918, gained his wealth from the Cash-on Delivery Mine in Poverty Gulch at Cripple Creek.

At Cripple Creek's zenith it supported eight newspapers, five of them dailies. It also supported 72 lawyers, 60 doctors, 40 brokers, and 39 real estate agents as well as 73 of the district's 150 saloons. Myers Avenue was the city's red light district where one could gamble away his money, drink it up or spend it on one of many prostitutes on the street. Victor supported two daily newspapers. There were some 35 gambling houses and saloons on Victor's First Street. Several of these operated 24-hours a day.

Both Cripple Creek and Victor had large, modern hospitals. Each had two undertakers. Bennett Street was Cripple Creek's business center. Only five blocks long it had four department

The "Old Homestead" is the last of Cripple Creek's notorious parlour houses on Myers Avenue, once the town's red light district. Seventy three saloons and numerous parlour houses served Cripple Creek during it heyday as a gold camp.

stores, two dance schools, a business college, four book stores, nine photographers, and many other shops. Several banks were also located on Bennett Street. The town supported 49 grocery stores, 14 bakeries, 11 laundries, and 11 blacksmith shops. While the several towns in the district had reputations as raw, rowdy communities, they also supported 34 churches and 19 schools.

News commentator, author and world traveler, **Lowell Thomas**, grew up in Victor. Although his boyhood home is marked, it is a private residence and is not open to the public.

Jack Dempsey, one of the most popular heavyweight boxing champions of all times, began fighting in mining camps in 1912. He worked in the mines in the Cripple Creek district and appeared on several local fight bills, drawing as many as 2,000 fight fans. He won the heavyweight crown in 1919 when he knocked out **Jess Willard**. **Jack Johnson**, the first black to win the heavyweight boxing crown, also appeared in the ring in Cripple Creek. Johnson won the championship from **Tommy Burns** in 1908.

A drive through this historic district is a must.

Among the attractions:

THE LOWELL THOMAS MUSEUM, in Victor, features a **Lowell Thomas** family collection and mining memorabilia. An admission is charged.

The Midland Terminal Railroad Depot, 230 N. 4th St., and Victor Hotel, 4th and Victor, both in Victor, are listed on the National Register of Historic Places.

THE CRIPPLE CREEK DISTRICT MUSEUM, Cripple Creek, is located in the Midland Terminal Railroad depot and two other adjacent buildings. Its 12 rooms are filled with displays relating to the mining, transportation and social history of the district. The Colorado Trading & Transfer Building houses a natural history exhibit, a collection of historic photos, and a gallery of locally produced art. The third building, the Assay Office, houses a large collection of mining and geological exhibits. Also demonstrated is the testing of ores mined here. The museum is open 10 a.m. to 5 p.m. daily from Memorial Day through September. The main building is open during the months of May and October and from noon to 4 p.m. on weekends the balance of the year. An admission is charged at the main building. The other two buildings are open without charge.

MOLLIE KATHLEEN GOLD MINE, Cripple Creek, descends 1,000 feet underground. The gold mine, open for tours, began operating in 1892 and ceased gold production in 1961 because of the low price of the precious metal. Visitors to the mine are accompanied throughout their tours by a trained guide. It is open 9 a.m. to 5 p.m. daily and Sunday, May through October. An admission is charged.

THE OLD HOMESTEAD, on Myers Ave., Cripple Creek, is one of the last of the notorious parlour houses that once flour-

The Midland Terminal Railroad depot serves as the main building in the Cripple Creek District Museum complex.

News commentator and author Lowell Thomas grew up in this house in Victor. Today it is a private residence.

ished in the gold camp. The town's red light district was fairly well concentrated on Myers Avenue but there were a number of saloons and gambling halls found on Bennett Street, the town's main thoroughfare. The Homestead is open 10 a.m. to 5 p.m. daily. An admission is charged.

THE IMPERIAL HOTEL, a half block north of Bennett Ave. at 3rd St., is the only one of Cripple Creek's original hotels that still stands. It was built in 1896, shortly after the disasterous fire that destroyed much of the original town. With the exception of two years during World War II it has been in continuous operation. A feature of the hotel during the summer months is the Melodramas presented in the Gold Bar Room Theatre. For information call (719) 471-8878.

CRIPPLE CREEK NARROW GAUGE RAILROAD AND GHOST TOWN JOURNEY departs every 45 minutes from the Cripple Creek Museum, formerly the old Midland Railroad Terminal. The train passes through many historic mines and ghost towns. The train is pulled by a 15-ton locomotive of the 0-4-0 type, typical of the early steam engines so important to the winning of the West. The four-mile, round-trip includes a fascinating narration on the rich history of the area with special stops at points of interest and impressive photo locations. It is in operation from the end of May to the first weekend in October. For information, telephone (719) 689-2640.

The Cripple Creek Historic District, on CO 67, is listed on the National Register of Historic Places.

Chapter 5
The Pueblo Area and I-25 South

Pueblo began as a trading post in 1842 and later became a steel city; once claiming to be the smelting capital of the world. This southern area, covering Walsenburg and Trinidad, is rich in history and has many offerings to those interested in the past.

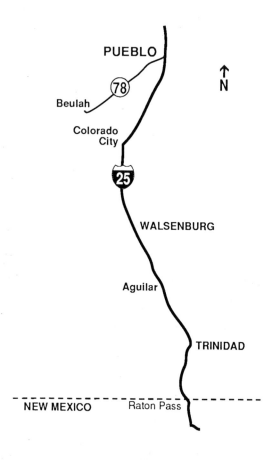

Chapter 5
The Pueblo Area and I-25 South

Forty-two miles south of Colorado Springs via I-25, is **Pueblo** (pop. 101,686), county seat of Pueblo County. Pueblo was organized in 1859 and incorporated in 1885. A trading post, called **Fort Pueblo**, was established in 1842. Soon after, in the winter of 1846-47 a party of Mormons enroute to Utah established temporary quarters here. Fort Pueblo, the trading post, was abandoned after the Ute Indians massacred the inhabitants while they were celebrating Christmas in 1854. Pueblo was originally called **Independence**.

Uncle Dick Wootton, an early-day trapper and trader, was ranching less than 20 miles from Pueblo during the Fort Pueblo massacre of 1854. His ranch was spared by the Utes during this rampage. Wootton began his ranching operation in the area in 1840 in anticipation of a settlement here. He worked his ranch off and on for more than two decades.

Gen. William Jackson Palmer, founder of the Denver & Rio Grande Railroad, arrived with his line in 1872. He began the town of **South Pueblo** that was incorporated in 1873. Another town, **Central Pueblo**, was incorporated in 1882. The three towns merged in 1886.

Early-day Spanish conquistadors once searched in this general area for Cibola, the legendary city of gold. The United States acquired all of Pueblo south of the Arkansas River in the Louisiana Purchase of 1803. The Indians—the Arapahoes, Cheyennes, Comanches, Kiowas, and the Utes—dominated until the white man came searching for gold. The U.S. gained control of the territory in the **Treaty of Guadalupe Hidalgo** in 1848 at the conclusion of the Mexican War. During the Civil War, Confederate sympathizers failed in an attempt to take Pueblo and the rest of Colorado for the South. A band of 600 rebels trained in **Beulah Valley** during the early days of the war but broke up before they became fully organized.

Bat Masterson, the sheriff of Ford County, Kansas, was one of the many gunmen hired by the Santa Fe Railroad in their fight with the Denver & Rio Grande Railroad over the route to **Leadville**. Masterson led a gang of gunfighters who captured

131

the Denver & Rio Grande roundhouse in Pueblo. General Palmer and his Denver & Rio Grande workers were able to regain possession of the several stations and the roundhouse but not until they killed two Santa Fe men and wounded two others.

Pueblo became a steel city early on and by the turn of the century, the city not only had the largest steel plant west of the Mississippi but had become the smelting capital of the world. Four mills specialized in the refining of gold, silver, zinc, and lead.

Meyer Guggenheim (1828-1905), a native of Langnau in Emmental, Switzerland, built a copper smelter in Pueblo in 1888 and eventually invested his fortune in mining ventures. In 1901, he won control of the American Smelting and Refining Company, the leading company in the industry. A son, Daniel (1856-1930), followed his father as head of the family copper interests. Another son, Murry (1858-1939), was in charge of the Pueblo smelter. Still another son, Simon (1867-1941), served as a U. S. Senator from Colorado from 1907-1913. Senator and Mrs. Guggenheim established the **John Simon Guggenheim Memorial Foundation** in 1925, in memory of their son, John Simon.

Over 100 persons in Pueblo died in the January 3, 1921 Arkansas River flood. Hundreds downstream were saved by the actions of **Josephine Pryor** and 13 other Pueblo telephone operators who remained at their stations to warn the residents of the area. The telephone operators were trapped on the second floor of the telephone building for several hours before the waters began to recede. Later, when awards were given, the men who saved the business records were presented gold medals while the women were presented with only silver and bronze medals for saving lives.

Pueblo boasted as having the largest industrial YMCA in the world from World War I to 1963 when it was torn down. The "Y" was located on Jones, between Abriendo and Evans, and served steelworkers and their families.

The Army established an Ordnance Depot 16 miles east of Pueblo during World War II. Today the depot is called the **Pueblo Army Facility**.

Pueblo Army Air Base was established during World War II to train B-17, B-24 and B-29 air crews. The air base was transferred to the City of Pueblo and today serves as Pueblo

Memorial Airport.

The **University of Southern Colorado** was established in Pueblo in 1963.

Three Congressional Medal of Honor recipients came from the Pueblo area. They are **Pvt. William J. Crawford**, 36th Infantry Division, for his daring actions near Altavilla, Italy, September 13, 1943; **2nd Lt. Raymond G. Murphy USMC**, 5th Marines, 1st Marine Division, for bravery in battle in Korea, February 3, 1953; and **Capt. Carl L. Sitler USMC**, 1st Marines, 1st Marine Division, for service above the call of duty at Hagaru-ri, Korea, November 29-30, 1950.

There are many monuments and historical markers as well as historical attractions in the Pueblo area.

President Woodrow Wilson made his last public address in Pueblo's Memorial Hall, September 25, 1919. He fell ill on the train upon leaving Pueblo and died on February 3, 1924. Memorial Hall, honoring Puebloans who had served in the military during World War I, is part of Pueblo's City Hall at Grand and Union. When it was completed in 1919, Wilson appeared for the dedication. A plaque, commemorating President Wilson's visit, has been placed in the main corridor of City Hall.

A life-sized bronze figure of a World War I doughboy is set in a small park just south of City Hall and Memorial Hall. It honors the soldiers and sailors of World War I.

A memorial, set in a native boulder, serves as a tribute to the World War I soldiers and sailors. It is in Elizabeth Memorial Parkway, near 28th Street.

A stone shaft topped with a circle enclosing the letter "W" has been erected to honor the 27 Puebloans who served in the 89th Infantry Division during World War I. It is in Elizabeth Memorial Parkway, north of 25th Street.

A tablet set in a concrete pillar commemorates the sinking of the *U.S.S. Maine*, the battleship sunk in Havana Harbor in 1898. It is in Elizabeth Memorial Parkway, near 29th Street. A second memorial plaque in rememberance of the sinking of the *Maine* is in the lobby of the Post Office, Main and 5th Streets. Among the volunteers from Pueblo in the Spanish-American War, that resulted from the sinking of the *Maine*, was **Ben Lear**. He served in the Army for 56 years and retired in 1954 as a full general.

There are two major memorials to railroads in Pueblo. One is

The Pueblo monument to Christopher Columbus.

a large steam locomotive given to the City of Pueblo by the Santa Fe Railroad, and the other is the old redstone Union Station which today does not offer any rail service. At one time, 55 passenger trains arrived and departed from this station daily. The steam locomotive is set diagonally across Union Avenue from City Hall.

Christopher Columbus is honored in Pueblo with a monument at Mesa Junction, south of the Pueblo Regional Library. The monument, sponsored by the Columbian Federation, was erected on October 12, 1905. This was the second statue of Columbus erected in the United States.

Two Civil War memorials are located in Pueblo. One, just inside the entrance to Roselawn Cemetery, includes three cannons and balls with a marker dedicated to the memory of the soldiers and sailors of the Civil War. The other, including four cannon balls mounted on a stone pedestal, is located just south of the Federal Building, 5th and Main Streets. It includes the words: "15-Inch Shells Used by the Army and Navy from 1861 to 1865."

A large boulder with a bronze plaque, at Joplin and Damson in East Pueblo, identifies **Jacob Fowler's Lookout**. Fowler and other trappers lived in a log house near this point in January, 1822.

A simple white shaft in Mineral Palace Park honors the veterans of all American Wars.

A granite monument with an inscription marks the site of old

This monument marks the site of the historic Jacob Fowler's Lookout in Pueblo.

135

The Zebulon Pike historical marker in Pueblo.

Fort Pueblo on the Arkansas River and the site of the Indian massacre there in 1854. This is located at 1st and Court Streets, next to the Pueblo Ice Palace.

Along US 50, near the Salt Creek Overpass, one and a half miles east of Santa Fe Ave., is a monument to **Lt. Zebulon Montgomery Pike**, who arrived at the Pueblo site on November 23, 1806. The plaque is almost a mile from the Pike encampment site.

136

The Mormons established the first Anglo-Saxon settlement in Colorado during the winter of 1846-47. A party of 43 Mormons, with 19 wagons, established the camp. In the meantime, several Mormon soldiers with **Brig. Gen. Stephen Kearny's Army of the West** fell ill and were sent to the Pueblo settlement to recuperate. In time the settlement grew to 275 persons. The first white children born in Colorado came into the world in this settlement. Seven births and nine deaths were recorded that winter. The Mormon Battalion was demobilized the next spring and they joined the group at Pueblo for the trip to Utah where they arrived July 27, 1847. About a half mile from where the settlement was located stands a monument, which is a varicolored stone shaft near the junction of US 50 and Santa Fe Ave.

A miniature replica of the Statue of Liberty was erected by the Boy Scouts in front of the County Court House in 1950. This was part of the community's U.S. loyalty crusade.

Among the unmarked historical sites are:

HISTORIC GOVERNORS' MANSION, Orman and Colorado, was built by Gov. James B. Orman, who served from 1901 to 1903. Gov. Alva Adams, who served in 1905, and his son, Sena-

The historic Orman-Adams House in Pueblo is listed on the National Register of Historic Places.

tor Alva B. Adams, also made their home here. Until 1978, it served as the administrative building for Pueblo School District 60. It is listed on the National Register of Historic Places.

DR. HUBERT WORK RESIDENCE, on the northwest corner of Court and 19th Sts., was the home of Dr. Hubert Work, who served as Postmaster General under President Calvin Coolidge and Secretary of Interior under President Warren G. Harding. It is privately owned.

PUEBLO'S OLDEST BUILDING, 126 Oneida St., was built in 1869 and has been used as a flour mill, brewery, mattress factory and distributing plant. A section of it is currently the home of the Impossible Players. It is a private museum and is listed on the National Register of Historic Places.

CHARLES GOODNIGHT BARN, about a mile west of Pueblo on CO 96, still stands but is in poor condition. The original stone barn was part of the headquarters of the Goodnight Ranch. **Charles Goodnight** was one of the early cattle drovers from Texas who settled here. When observed in 1988, the historic old barn was being used as a storage shed by a gravel company.

DAMON RUNYON'S HOME was near 6th and present I-25. Pueblo's athletic field and baseball park are named in his honor. Runyon, who became one of America's famous writers, started his career on Pueblo newspapers.

The historical attractions include:

EL PUEBLO MUSEUM, 905 S. Prairie Ave., Pueblo, directly behind the Colorado Fairgrounds, is a full-sized reproduction of the trading post established in 1842 by a company of independent fur traders. The occupants of the post lived by hunting and farming as well as trading goods for Indian buffalo hides. Although the Indians were usually friendly, an attack by a Ute band in December, 1854, and continued unrest along the Arkansas River in early 1855 left Pueblo abandoned. The walls of the fort were neither high nor portholed and surrounded a corral, several storage bins, and a dozen or more adobe huts for the families that lived here. One of the exhibits on display is a cross section of **Old Monarch**, a 388-year old cottonwood tree cut down in 1883. Legend has it that 14 men were hanged from its branches and the first white woman to die in Colorado died beneath it. Old Monarch, claimed to be one of the largest trees in the West, stood in the middle of the 300 block of South Union Street. The museum is open 10 a.m. to 5 p.m. Tuesday through

An exhibit in El Pueblo Museum.

Friday and 10 a.m. to 4 p.m. Saturday from Memorial Day weekend through Labor Day weekend. It is open the rest of the year from 10 a.m. to 3 p.m. Wednesday through Saturday. An admission is charged.

ROSEMOUNT VICTORIAN HOUSE MUSEUM, 14th and Grand, Pueblo, is a three-story mansion built in 1891 for **Mr. and Mrs. John Albert Thatcher**. Thatcher was a successful merchant and banker. The Victorian-styled residence, known as "Rosemount," is a 37-room pink lava stone building. The lower two floors remain as originally decorated. The third floor, which served as guest and servant's quarters, features changing exhibits and displays focusing on Pueblo and Colorado history. It is open 10 a.m. to 4 p.m. Monday through Saturday and 2 to 4 p.m. Sunday, June 1 to September 1 and 1 to 4 p.m. Tuesday through Saturday and 2 to 4 p.m. Sunday, September 1 to June 1. It is closed on Mondays and during the month of January. An admission is charged.

FRED E. WEISBROD AIRCRAFT MUSEUM, Pueblo Memorial Airport, six miles east of Pueblo, is a tribute to American military airmanship. The museum, named for City Manager **Fred Weisbrod**, became a reality in 1972 with the arrival

139

A museum is housed in Pueblo's Rosemount Victorian House on West 14th Street.

of a Douglas Invader. The first acquisitions were donations from the Naval Air Systems Command in Washington, D. C. Some of the aircraft on display are on loan from various military services. One plane, the Voodoo, is the only F-101 recorded as having a civilian owner. Among some of the aircraft on display—B-29 Superfortress, F-6A Skyray, C-119 Boxcar, F9F-8 Cougar, F-80 Shooting Star, F-4 Phantom, F-100-D Super Sabre, F-84 Thunderjet, SH-34J Seahorse, and CH-21B Shawnee. Missiles on display include the Boeing Bomarc CMQ-10A and Martin Marietta Pershing 1. Among the research vehicles displayed are the Garret Linear Induction Motor Research Vehicle, the Grumman Tracked Levitated Research Vehicle, and the Rohr Prototype Tracked Air Cushion Vehicle. The museum is open daily. Admission is free.

There are a number of sites in Pueblo and the area listed on the National Register of Historic Places. These include the Barndollar-Gann House, 1906 Court St.; Baxter House/Bishop House, 325 W. 15th St.; the Allen J. Beaumont House, 425 W. 15th St.; the Dr. John A. Black House Complex, 102 W. Pitkin Ave.; the Bowen Mansion, 229 W. 12th St.; the James N. Carlile

House, 44 Carlile Pl.; Central High School, 431 Pitkin Ave.; City Park Carousel, in City Park; Colorado State Hospital Superintendent's House, 13th and Francisco; Doyle Settlement/White House/Casa Blanca, on Doyle Rd. 18 miles southeast of US 50; Nathaniel W. Duke House, 1409 Craig St.; Edison School, 900 W. Mesa St.; Farris Hotel, 315 N. Union; First Congregational Church, 225 W. Evans; First Methodist Episcopal Church/Trinity Methodist, 400 Broadway; Fitch Terrace, 401, 403, 405, 407, 409 and 411 W. 11th St.; R. T. Frazier House, 2121 Elizabeth St.; the Galligan House, 501 Colorado Ave.; the Gast Mansion, 1801 Greenwood St.; J. S. Glass Clothing Store, 308 S. Union Ave.; the Goodnight Barn, west of Pueblo at CO 96; Hazelhurst/Berkely House, 905 Berkely; Henkel Duke Mercantile Co. Warehouse, 212-222 W. 3rd Ave.; Dr. Alexander T. King House and Carriage House, 229 Quincy St.; T. G. McCarthy House, 817 N. Grand Ave.; Mechanics Building/Masonic Building, 207-211 N. Main St.; Orman-Adams House, 102 W. Orman Ave.; Frank Pryor House, 1325 Greenwood St.; Pueblo County Courthouse, 10th and Main St.; Pueblo Federal Building/U.S. Post Office, 421 N. Main St.; Quaker Flour Mill, 102 S. Oneida St.; Ward Rice House, 1825

The Fred E. Weisbrod Aircraft Museum is located on the former site of the Pueblo Army Airbase, established during World War II.

141

"Peachy" was the name given to this B-29 Superfortress, commanded by Capt. Robert T. Haver of Pueblo. It is displayed in Pueblo's air museum. The B-26 (below) was used as a light bomber and reconnaissance plane by the Army Air Corps and later, the U.S. Air Force.

One of the aircraft displayed in the Weisbrod Aircraft Museum is the C-47, workhorse of the Army Air Corps during World War II. The passenger/cargo plane was built by Douglas Aircraft. The F-80 "Shooting Star" (below) was the first true jet powered fighter. Introduced January 9, 1944, the F-80 was the first American fighter to exceed 500 mph.

143

The Department of Transportation ordered research on high-speed trains and among some of the vehicles on display at the Pueblo air museum are these research vehicles.

Grand Ave.; Rood Candy Co. Building, 408-416 W. 7th St.; Sacred Heart Cathedral, 1025 N. Grand Ave.; Sacred Heart Orphanage, 2316 Sprague St.; Star Journal Model House, 2920 High St.; Charles H. Stickney House, 101 E. Orman Ave.; J. L. Streit House, 2201 Grand Ave.; Tooke-Nuckolls House, 38 Carlile Pl.; Tutt Building, 421 Central Plaza; Union Depot, Victoria and B Sts.; Vail Hotel, 217 S. Grand; Martin Walter House, 300 W. Abriendo Ave.; Asbury White House, 415 W. 11th St.; Woodcroft Sanatorium, 1300 W. Abriendo Ave.; and YWCA-Pueblo, 801 N. Santa Fe Ave.

There are two historic districts, the Pitkin Place Historic District and the Union Avenue Historic Commercial District, Main St., Grand, and Victoria Aves.

St. Charles Bridge, on RD 65, is also listed on the National Register of Historic Places.

Nine miles east of Pueblo, on US 50 on the west side of the highway, near the south end of the Vineland-Devine bridge across the Arkansas River, is a marker commemorating the first Indian reservation established by the government in 1860. The idea proved to be premature and the plan did not work out even though several buildings were constructed and hundreds of acres were plowed and irrigation ditches laid out. The Indians were not ready to become farmers and soon left for the open country.

About 20 miles east of Pueblo, on US 50 between Avondale and the Huerfano River, is a marker commemorating **Fort Reynolds**, established by the Army, July 3, 1867, on the right bank of the Arkansas River. The fort was named in honor of **Gen. John F. Reynolds**, killed at Gettysburg in 1863. Troops assigned to Fort Reynolds were never involved in any battles or skirmishes with the Indians. The fort was abandoned July 15, 1872.

At **Avondale** the Butler House, 6916 Broadacre Rd., and Avondale Bridge, on RD 327, are listed on the National Register of Historic Places.

The Indian Petroglyphs and Pictographs, in Turkey Creek Canyon near **Penrose**, are listed on the National Register of Historic Places.

About 20 miles southeast of Pueblo, on Doyle Road just before it crosses the Huerfano River, is a large marker describing Joseph Doyle's ranch, established in 1859. Doyle was one of the

The monument to Chief Cuerno Verde in Greenhorn Meadows Park at Colorado City.

men who built Fort Pueblo in 1842. He purchased two miles of the Huerfano Valley and began farming here with his family. He called his large ranchhouse Casa Blanca, and the settlement included a school, a post office, and a flour mill. Doyle and his wife are buried on the hill above the marker.

Twenty miles southwest of Pueblo, via CO 78, is **Beulah**, hot bed of activity on behalf of the Confederate cause during the Civil War. A regiment met secretly at Mace's Hole, near Beulah, to drill. They were aided and abetted by **Zan Hicklin**, also known as "Old Seceh," a prominent early-day settler. The regiment finally was disbanded in late 1861. Historical markers regarding Colorado's part in the Civil War may be found in rest areas on I-25, 16 miles south of Pueblo.

Colorado City

Twenty-five miles south of Pueblo, via I-25, is the new **Colorado City**, established in Greenhorn Valley in 1963.

A historical marker in Greenhorn Meadows Park briefly tells the story of the **Comanche Chief Cuerno Verde** (Greenhorn), killed in a battle, September 2, 1779, by a large force led by **Juan Bautista de Anza**, governor of New Mexico. Cuerno Verde, leading 50 Comanche warriors, attacked de Anza's force of nearly 800 and was killed along with four sub-chiefs, his son, his high priest, and 32 of his braves. He had killed de Anza's father and had raided the ranches and villages in the Taos, New Mexico, area.

Walsenburg

Forty-eight miles south of Pueblo is **Walsenburg** (pop. 4,329), county seat of Huerfano (Orphan) County. Walsenburg was laid out on the site of a Spanish village in 1873.

Originally a New Mexican settlement called **Plaza de los Leones** (Plaza of the Lions), the town was renamed Walsenburg for a German storekeeper, **Fred Walsen**. Huerfano and Las Animas counties produced 60 percent of Colorado's coal shortly after the turn of the century. At one time Colorado had the distinction of possessing the nation's largest bituminous coal reserve. Coal mining in this region dates back to the 1860s.

WALSENBURG MINING MUSEUM, 101 E. 5th St., Walsenburg, represents an era when Coal was King. It provides insights into how miners lived and worked and how times have changed. It is open 11 a.m. to 6 p.m. weekdays. (It is closed from 2 to 3 p.m. for lunch). An admission is charged.

The Huerfano County Courthouse and Jail, 400 Main St., are

147

The Coal Miner's statue in Walsenburg.

The monument commemorating the Ludlow Massacre.

The Walsenburg Mining Museum.

listed on the National Register of Historic Places.

Ludlow

Twenty-two miles south on I-25 is **Ludlow**, once a tiny mining camp that became famous in a labor dispute between the United Mine Workers and the southern coal operators. In September 1913, the union called a strike in the Trinidad mines calling for a 10 percent wage increase, recognition of the Union, and enforcement of Colorado mining laws. The Union also demanded that miners be given the choice of where they lived and the right to trade somewhere other than the Company store. The strike continued and thousands of miners, with their families, moved into makeshift tent cities set up by the Union.

Coal production was crippled, tempers flared, and the tent cities remained throughout the winter. The Colorado militia was called in to maintain order as tensions mounted. On April 20, 1914 the tensions that had welled up for months broke and the militia lost control. Troops opened fire and set fire to the tent city at Ludlow. Five miners and a trooper were killed as were two women and 11 children who had taken refuge in a hole to avoid the conflict. The United Mine Workers reported the **"Ludlow Massacre,"** and national attention focused on Colorado and this tragedy.

Ludlow did not resolve the labor problems immediately but

The Bloom House in Trinidad.

the industry rebounded quickly after the strikes and violence came to an end. The next several years, an all time record high of 12,483,000 tons of coal were mined. Colorado's coal fields in Adams, El Paso, Boulder and Weld counties (Northern) and in Huerfano and Las Animas counties (Southern) made her the largest coal producing state west of the Mississippi.

The **Ludlow Tent Colony Site**, on Del Aqua Rd., Ludlow, is listed on the National Register of Historic Places.

Trinidad

Fifteen miles south of Ludlow is **Trinidad** (pop. 9,901), settled on the old Santa Fe Trail in 1859 and incorporated in 1879. It is the county seat of Las Animas County.

Don Felipe Baca, a former New Mexican, donated land for the establishment of Trinidad in the 1870s. He had become wealthy raising sheep and cattle along the Purgatoire River. He also donated land for the town's Catholic church and a convent. He served as a representative to the territorial legislature.

The region has been developed as a rich farm area. After the Civil War, Trinidad became the headquarters for some of the largest cattle firms in the West—the **Bloom Cattle Company, Thatcher Brothers & Company**, and the **Matador Land & Cattle Company, Ltd.**

Coal mining became an important industry in the Trinidad area. The Denver & Rio Grande and the Santa Fe railroads both arrived in Trinidad to take advantage of the lucrative coal business. The need for the legendary Santa Fe Trail came to an end shortly after the arrival of the railroads in 1878.

Bat Masterson, the colorful Kansas sheriff, turned up in Trinidad in 1882 to accept an invitation to become city marshal. During his year in this post his most notable achievement was to block the extradition of **John "Doc" Holliday**, the dentist gunfighter who had been involved in the shootout at the O.K. Corral in Tombstone, Arizona, on October 26, 1881, with Wyatt Earp and two of his brothers.

Three major buildings, all owned and operated by the Colorado Historical Society, are located together in the Corazon de Trinidad's National Historic District. These are:

BACA HOUSE, in the 300 block of East Main St., Trinidad, was built by merchant **John S. Hough** in 1870 and purchased by **Maria Baca** in 1873. It is a two-story territorial-style adobe reflecting an eclectic mixture of Spanish and Anglo furnishings typical of a prosperous Spanish-American family of the region.

PIONEER MUSEUM, located behind the Baca House, was once used to house the families of Baca's farmhands and sheepherders. It now features exhibits interpreting the history of the large ranches and the people who played prominent roles in the development of Trinidad. Wagons and buggies used to transport goods and people along the Mountain Branch of the Santa Fe Trail are displayed in the courtyard.

BLOOM HOUSE, near the Baca House, is a three-story Second Empire-style mansion built for **Frank G. Bloom** and his family in 1882. He arrived in Trinidad in 1867 to work as a store manager for Thatcher Brothers & Company and eventually became one of the town's bankers and a director of the Bloom Cattle Company. The mansion has been restored and furnished in the fashion of the 1880s.

The three historic buildings are open 10 a.m. to 5 p.m. Monday through Saturday and 1 to 5 p.m. on Sunday, Memorial Day through Labor Day. The last tour begins at 4 p.m. In September they are open 10 a.m. to 4 p.m. Saturday and 1 to 4 p.m. Sunday. An admission is charged.

The other sites listed on the National Register of Historic

The Baca House in Trinidad.

Places include the Jaffa Opera House/Hausman Drug, 100-116 W. Main St.; the Trinidad Post Office, 301 E. Main St.; and the Commercial Street Bridge.

The LOUDEN-HENRITZE ARCHAEOLOGY MUSEUM, Freudenthal Memorial Library, Trinidad State Junior College, presents a series of dioramas of the local landscape through various geologic eras. Also shown are dioramas of both inside and outside views of the famed **Trinchera Cave**, a nearby archaeological site occupied thousands of years ago by prehistoric man. Fossils and geologic samples are displayed as well. It is open 10 a.m. to 4 p.m. Monday through Saturday, May 28 through September 1. Admission is free.

CHILDREN'S MUSEUM/OLD FIREHOUSE NO. 1, 314 N. Commercial, is housed in the historic firehouse which also once served as Trinidad's first city hall and jail. On display are an original firecart and fire engine as well as other hands-on displays for children. Summer tours are offered June 15 to August 15. Hours are posted at the museum.

There are several other sites in Las Animas County listed on the National Register of Historic Places. These include the Cokedale Historic District, Church, Maple, Pine, Elm and Spruce Sts., in **Cokedale**; the Colorado Millennial Site/Hackberry Spring/Bloody Springs, at **Ruxton**; the Elson Bridge on RD 36, El Moro; **Raton Pass**, five miles north of Raton, N.M.; the Bridge over Burro Canyon, CO 12, **Madrid**; the Avery Bridges at **Hoehne** and **Aguilar**; and in the eastern part of the county, the Torres Cave Archaeological Site at **Villegreen.**

Richens Lacy Wootton "Uncle Dick" built a 27 mile toll road over Raton Pass in 1865 and operated it until 1878 when the Santa Fe Railroad paid him a $50 per month pension for his right-of-way. Wootton, who was born in Virginia in 1816 died in 1893. Many stories surrounded this unusual frontier character.

It is 13 miles south, via I-25, to the New Mexico state line.

Chapter 6
Northeast Area—I-76 and I-25

The Indians ravaged the Overland Trail from Julesburg to Denver in the mid-1860s. This story and others are described in this chapter. There were many heroes in the development of this area and many of their stories are told here. A complete listing of museums and historical sites is included.

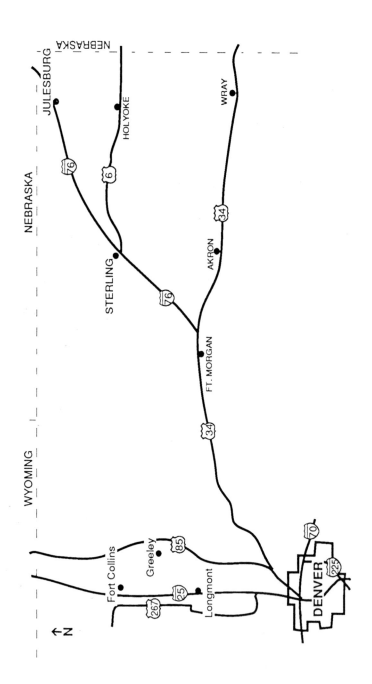

Chapter 6
Northeast Area—I-76 and I-25

This chapter will cover three basic routes in northeastern Colorado. These include the 185-mile I-76 route from Julesburg to Denver, the 95-mile I-25 route from the Wyoming state line to Denver, and the 54-mile US 85 route from Greeley to Denver.

Julesburg

The chapter begins with the I-76 route from **Julesburg** (pop. 1,578), county seat of Sedgwick County. There were actually four Julesburgs. Julesburg was named for **Jules Beni** who established a trading post on the south side of the river, near the junction where the Lodgepole entered the South Platte River, in the 1850s. This trading post was established south of the site of today's Ovid, Colorado.

In 1859, the Overland Stage inaugurated its service and Beni became the station agent. Jules Station was the only Colorado station on the line initially. When Beni was replaced as the agent by **Jack Slade** bad blood developed between the two men. Beni ambushed Slade and severely wounded him. When Slade recovered he killed Beni.

When the **Pony Express** was inaugurated in April 1860, Julesburg was the only Colorado station. It is claimed that teen-age **William F. Cody**, later to become famous as "Buffalo Bill," was hired here as a Pony Express rider. Later he served as a scout at **Fort Sedgwick** and the last performance of his Wild West Show was in Julesburg, going on to **Denver** where it was attached for debts. The Pony Express came to an end in 1861 when the transcontinental telegraph was completed. Until the telegraph was continued to Denver in 1863, messages were relayed from Julesburg by stage.

In the summer of 1864, the Sioux, Cheyenne and Arapahoe Indians went on a rampage from Big Sandy in southeastern Nebraska to Denver. The road was closed for several weeks as the Indians burned and pillaged ranches and stations along the trail. The Indian outbreak was reported in the *New York Times*, September 8, 1864 thusly:

"Upon the overland trail, devastation, terror, murder has held a perfect carnival. From Denver to Fort Larimee (sic) to the Lit-

157

tle Blue in Kansas, and to the Big Sandy in Nebraska, both within 150 miles of the Missouri, the Rebel Indians have swept like a hurricane. In a distance of 400 miles along this great route they have captured at least 50 trains of merchandise or Government freight, driving stock, plundering and destroying to the value of at least a quarter of a million dollars. They have murdered 200 white persons, among them many women and children. The stark bodies lie stripped and mutilated in the glaring sunlight, festering and rotting for the want of burial, or half charred, (and) are seen smouldering amid the ruins of ranches, cabins and stage-stations."

Company F, **7th Iowa Cavalry**, under the command of **Capt. Nicholas O'Brien**, was sent from Fort Cottonwood, Nebraska, to Julesburg to establish a post to protect the area from Indians. The soldiers built a post about a mile from the Julesburg settlement and named it **Camp Rankin**. Within weeks, on November 29, 1864, the **Sand Creek Massacre** in southeastern Colorado sparked the flames of rage in the Indians.

On January 7, 1865, over 1,000 Indians were in the hills surrounding **Fort Rankin** (the post had been designated a fort). That morning a small band of Indians approached the fort as decoys to draw out the troops. The ruse worked and Captain O'-Brien and 37 troopers from Company F rushed out to attack. Once they were in the open, the larger band swooped down from their hiding places and attacked with full fury. The soldiers were driven back to the fort, but not before 14 were killed. It was reported that the Indians suffered 50-60 casualties. The Indians kept the fort under siege for several hours before breaking off their attack.

Brig. Gen. Robert Mitchell, commanding general of the Nebraska District with headquarters at Fort McPherson, Nebraska, ordered the prairies to be burned to keep the Indians from foraging during the next few months. The prairies were burned from Fort McPherson west to Denver.

On January 15, 1865, Indians attacked every ranch between **Fort Sedgwick** (the new name given to Fort Rankin later in 1865) and **Fort Morgan**, a distance of nearly 100 miles. **Lt. Judson J. Kennedy** commanded a company of cavalry sent to this area to guard some of the ranches and stage stations. Kennedy and his troops reached **Valley Station**, 3.8 miles north of the Overland Trail Museum in Sterling, as the Indians were attacking. The station was so badly damaged, Kennedy ordered his men to fortify it with "government corn and adobes that were nearby." **Wisconsin Ranch** was also abandoned after this raid. **William Morris** and three hired men were killed by the Indians in their raid on the **American Ranch** on January 15th. **Godfrey's Ranch** (later known as **"Fort Wicked"**) also came under attack on that day as the Indians rampaged up and down the trail.

The Indians were still fighting in late January when the **Washington Ranch**, just south of Sterling, came under attack January 30th.

On February 2, 1865, the Indians returned to burn and sack the Julesburg settlement while the townspeople watched from the safety of the fort, later in 1865 to be designated Fort Sedgwick, named for **Maj. Gen. John Sedgwick**, who commanded the Army of the Potomac's Sixth Corps during the Civil War. He had distinguished himself in battle and as a brigadier general was wounded at the Battle of Antietam, Maryland, on September 17, 1862. He was killed in the Battle of Spotsylvania Court House, May 8-12, 1864.

The second Julesburg was laid out and platted in March, 1866 and remained a stagecoach station until June, 1867 when the railroad arrived. The third Julesburg was moved to the north side of the river to the new railroad. For a period of time Julesburg carried the title as the "Wickedest City in the West." During this time it became a shipping point for cattle and a hangout for hunters, trappers, and adventurers.

In 1865, the stations on the Overland Trail from Julesburg to Fort Morgan included **Upper Crossing, Spring Hill Station, Lillian Springs Station, Dennison's Station, Valley Station, Washington Ranch, Wisconsin Ranch, American Ranch, Fairview Station, Godfrey's Station ("Fort Wicked"),** and **Beaver Creek Station.** Some of these are marked with trail markers. (For those who wish to locate the stations that have been found, please contact the Logan County Chamber of Commerce in Sterling.)

In May, 1871 Fort Sedgwick was abandoned by the Army.

In the spring of 1880, the Union Pacific decided to lay out a new town six miles east; the town was called **Denver Junction.** Most of the residents of the third Julesburg moved to Denver Junction which was incorporated in 1886 and the name was formally changed to Julesburg.

The FORT SEDGWICK HISTORICAL MUSEUM is located in the old railroad depot, 202 W. 1st St., in Julesburg. Among the many displays and exhibits are Indian tools, pottery, skeletons, and other relics; fossil bones of pre-historic animals found in Sedgwick County; memorabilia of World Champion Rider Thad Sowder, featured in Buffalo Bill's Wild West Show; an unusual exhibit of 250 pieces of barbed wire; displays and relics from the three older Julesburg sites; and many others. It is open 9 a.m. to 5 p.m. weekdays and 11 a.m. to 5 p.m. Sunday, Memorial Day to Labor Day. An admission is charged.

Ovid—Sedgwick

Two other communities on US 138 in Sedgwick County are noted. **Ovid**, southeast of Julesburg, was platted in 1908 and incorporated in 1925. **Thad Sowder**, Cowboy Hall of Famer, is buried in the Ovid Cemetery.

Further west is **Sedgwick**, laid out in 1887 and incorporated in 1906. The first school in the county was established here in 1884.

Crook—Iliff

Southwest of Sedgwick, on US 138, in **Crook** (pop. 177) is the CROOK HISTORICAL SOCIETY MUSEUM, on the corner of 4th Ave. and 4th St. It is open 2 to 4 p.m. Sunday, June 1 to Labor Day weekend. An admission is charged. The town of Crook is named in honor of **Brig. Gen. George Crook**, noted for his campaigns against the Apache Indians.

Further west is the small town of **Iliff**, named in honor of **John W. Iliff**, the Cattle King of the Plains. In the 1870s, the **Iliff Cattle Company** is said to have had 50,000 head of cattle and claimed about 3,000 square miles for their cattle ranges.

Iliff arrived in Denver in 1859 and became a merchant. He started buying Texas cattle on their way to market or to Wyoming ranges. He found the beef market lucrative with the Army's buildup during the problems with the Indians, the building of railroads, and even more naturally the hordes of gold seekers. Iliff left a part of his estate to the founding of the **Iliff School of Theology** in Denver.

Sterling

Further west, the next major town is **Sterling** (pop. 10,636), county seat of Logan County. Logan county was named in honor of **Gen. John A. Logan** (1826-1886), who gained fame as a Union general and political leader. He helped to organize the

Grand Army of the Republic (GAR), a veterans organization, after the Civil War. He is also credited with selecting May 30, 1868 as the first Memorial Day.

There have been two Sterlings. Old Sterling, established in the 1870s, was about three miles northeast of the present day community. In 1881, as the Union Pacific rails came closer from the east, it was decided a new town should be platted and built along the railroad. By 1883, the residents of Old Sterling had moved to the new town.

Two presidents—**Theodore Roosevelt** and **Herbert Hoover** — made brief stops in Sterling as did **Thomas Dewey**, the 1944 and 1948 Republican presidential candidate.

Seven buildings in Sterling are listed on the National Register of Historic Places. These include: the Logan County Courthouse, dedicated in 1910; the I and M Building, 223 Main, dating back to 1920 and still in use by the Henderson Company; the Union Pacific Depot, Main and Front Sts., dating back to 1903; the First United Presbyterian Church, 4th and Ash Sts., dating back to 1918; St. Anthony's Roman Catholic Church, S. 3rd and Cedar, dating back to 1911; the W. C. Harris House, 102 Taylor, dating back to 1910; and the J. Conrad Luft House, 1429 Hwy 14, dating back to 1902. Other than the courthouse, these are private businesses or residences. The Sterling Post Office/Federal Building/Courthouse, 3rd and Popular Sts., is listed on the National Register (Theme Resource).

OVERLAND TRAIL MUSEUM, on US 6, east of Sterling, only a few minutes off I-76, records the greatest migration of people our country has experienced on the Overland Trail, the famous road that led to the goldfields and the Far West. Indians and later fur trappers, explorers and early government expeditions, had long followed this well-trodden pathway. The museum building, built of native stone, is a replica of an old fort. Inside is a large fireplace of petrified wood. Trees, native grasses and wildflowers beautify the grounds. A shaded, well-equipped picnic area offers an ideal resting place. On display is a Concord stage, and scattered throughout the grounds are pieces of pioneer farm machinery. Indoor exhibits present artifacts that belonged both to the pioneers who crossed the prairie and to Indians who had inhabited the vast open spaces for generations. There is a one room school, where prairie school sessions are held each summer; a small country church, where small family weddings may be held; a blacksmith shop and a shed housing machinery on the grounds also. One of the largest branding iron collections found anywhere is also on display. The museum is handicapped accessible and is open 9 a.m. to 5 p.m. Monday through Saturday and 10 a.m. to 5 p.m. Sunday and holidays, May 1 through September 30. Admission is free.

Battle of Summit Springs

Summit Springs, site of the last Plains Indian conflict in Colorado, is located 16 miles south of Sterling. From the Atwood interchange, off I-76, drive south on CO 63, then turn east and follow the road signs to the site of the **Battle of Summit Springs**.

In the summer of 1869, **Chief Tall Bull** led a large force of Cheyenne Dog Soldiers on a rampage among settlements on the plains. Tall Bull's band swooped down on a Swedish colony in Kansas and captured two white women. **Major (Bvt. Maj. Gen.) Eugene A. Carr**, commanding the **5th U.S. Cavalry** at Fort McPherson, just east of North Platte, Nebraska, was ordered to pursue and corral Tall Bull and his men. Also riding with the cavalry were 150 **Pawnee Scouts** commanded by

The Overland Trail Museum in Sterling records the early days of cattle ranching and pioneer life.

162

The monument marking the site of the 1869 Battle of Summit Springs.

A second monument at the Battle of Summit Springs site commemorates the heroism an unknown 15-year old Cheyenne herd boy killed during the Battle of Summit Springs.

Major Frank North and his brother, Luther, a captain, and **"Buffalo Bill" Cody** serving as a scout.

The expedition started in the Republican Valley and headed west as the Cheyennes fled toward the Colorado plains. Tall Bull, realizing soldiers were in hot pursuit, split his band into three groups and each went in a separate direction. Carr did the same with his troops and their support forces. Early Sunday afternoon, July 11, 1869, a scouting party located the Indian camp. The Pawnee Scouts rejoined the main force to lead the attack on the unsuspecting Cheyennes. Some of the warriors were forced to flee on foot and hid in the nearby sand hill coulees.

As the soldiers were regrouping, a women, **Mrs. G. Weichel** who had been kidnapped from the Swedish colony, appeared. The body of **Mrs. Susannah Alderdice**, another white female captive, was found nearby with her skull crushed by the blow of a tomahawk. Her infant had been killed a few days earlier when his crying threatened to betray the Indians' location.

In the meantime, Frank North and his brother found Tall Bull, his wife and daughter hiding in a ravine. Major North killed the chief in an exchange of shots. Later Ned Buntline, the western novelist, wrote and published a fictionalized version of the battle and credited Cody, who was still miles away, with the killing of Tall Bull. A monument has been established at the site but may be difficult to locate. It is at the edge of a pasture some distance from the oil road.

Traveling Bear, one of Frank North's Pawnee Scouts, single handedly killed four Cheyenne Indians. For his daring he was awarded the Medal of Honor.

There are two historical markers in a pasture on this site. One marks the Summit Springs Battlefield and reads: "Fleeing after a series of bloody raids on the Kansas frontier, a band of 450 marauding Cheyenne Dog Soldiers led by Tall Bull camped here. On the afternoon of July 11, 1869, 300 men of the 5th Cavalry and the Pawnee Scouts under Maj. Gen. (his brevet rank) E. A. Carr made a successful surprise attack on the camp. Chief Tall Bull was among the 52 Indians killed in the battle. 418 horses and mules were captured and 84 lodges were put to the torch. 5th Cavalry Scout Buffalo Bill Cody later made this Plains battle in Colorado a regular feature of his "Wild West Show." The other marker commemorates the memory of an unknown 15-year Cheyenne herd boy killed in the conflict at Summit Springs.

Fleming—Holyoke

East of Sterling, via US 6, is **Fleming** (pop. 388) and the FLEMING HISTORICAL SOCIETY MUSEUM, at Tower Park on US 6. The museum is open 1 to 4 p.m. Sunday during the summer months. An admission is charged. AL'S COUNTRY AND WESTERN MUSEUM, two miles west of Fleming on US 6, is open the year-round. Admission is free.

It is 47 miles east on US 6 from Sterling to **Holyoke** (pop. 2,092), county seat of Phillips County. Holyoke was incorporated in 1888.

The W. E. Heginbotham House, 539 S. Baxter in Holyoke, is listed on the National Register of Historical Places. Elsewhere in Phillips County, the First National Bank of Haxtun, 145 S. Colorado Ave., is also listed on the NRHP.

THE PHILLIPS COUNTY HISTORICAL SOCIETY MUSEUM, located one block east of the lights on US 6 in the middle of town, is open from 1 to 5 p.m. weekends and holidays from Memorial Day to Labor Day. An admission is charged.

This monument on the Arikaree River in Yuma County marks the site of the 1868 Battle of Beecher Island.

A historical marker a mile west of the Colorado-Nebraska state line on US 6 commemorates the 1860 trail used by stage lines and wagon trains.

Battle of Beecher Island

Another famous Indian battle, the **Battle of Beecher Island**, occurred in Yuma County in 1868. The site, covered only by a monument, can be reached by taking CO 63 south to Akron, east on US 34 from **Akron** to **Wray** then south on US 385 to the Beecher Island site. It may also be reached off US 36. From Wray, take US 385 six miles south to County Rd. 30 and then 11 miles south on this road. From US 36, take County Rd. KK nine miles north to the site.

Col. George A. Forsyth had organized and commanded 50 scouts and was tracking renegade Indians led by Cheyenne **Chief Roman Nose**. In early September, 1868 Forsyth and his men had reached a point on the Arikaree River when they were attacked by Roman Nose and his Northern Cheyenne, Ogallalah and Brule Sioux Dog Soldiers. As the Indians appeared Forsyth and his men took refuge on a small island in the river and took their positions for the fight that followed. The battle was fought September 17-19 but the Indians held Forsyth and his men on the island for over a week. **Lt. Fred Beecher** and five other scouts were killed and half of the defenders wounded. Forsyth was wounded four times. The beleaguered scouts subsisted on horse and mule meat and wild plums they found on the little island. Roman Nose's death during the second day of the battle took some of the heart out of the attackers. Seventy-five Indians were killed and many were wounded. Indian women and children watched the battle from a small hill that became known as Squaw Hill.

The first night of the battle two pairs of scouts were able to escape and go for help. The nearest Army post was Fort Wallace in northwest Kansas, 110 miles away. Forsyth and his men were rescued by the 10th U.S. Cavalry (the Buffalo Soldiers) 10 a.m. the ninth day of the battle. The survivors and their rescuers began their trip back to Fort Wallace, September 27th.

Forsyth had joined the dragoons in 1861 at the outbreak of the Civil War. He rose to the rank of brevet major general and served as an aide to Union cavalry hero, Gen. Philip Sheridan.

The Beecher Island Battleground is listed on the National Register of Historic Places.

167

This signboard west of Yuma tells the story of the railroad worker, who was only known as Yuma, who died and was buried here in the early 1880s. The body was later discovered by railroad workers.

Wray—Eckley—Yuma—Akron

Wray (pop. 2,131), on US 34, is the county seat of Yuma County. Wray was incorporated in 1906.

The WRAY MUSEUM, 140 W. 4th St., is open 2 to 4 p.m. every Friday the year-round. An admission is charged.

At **Eckley** (pop. 262), between Wray and Yuma, the Boggs Lumber and Hardware Building, 125 N. Main, is listed on the National Register of Historic Places.

It is 26 miles west to **Yuma** (pop. 2,824) from Wray. It was incorporated in 1887.

Three miles east of Yuma on US 34 is the burial site of "Yuma," an Indian laborer. The town was named for this Indian railroad worker who died and was buried at this site in the late 1800s. Thirty miles southeast of Yuma was a hideout used by rustlers for stolen livestock in the 1870s and 80s.

YUMA MUSEUM, located on CO 59, features a collection of Yuma memorabilia and Indian artifacts. It is open 1 to 6 p.m. Sunday, June through August. Admission is free.

It is 28 miles west to **Akron** (pop. 1,716), county seat of Washington County. Akron was founded in 1882 and incorporated in 1887.

This monument pinpoints the site of "Fort Wicked," a famous Overland Stage Station. The official name of this station was Godfrey's Ranch. The agent here and his family were able to drive off marauding Indians in 1864. It was one of a handful of stage stations the Indians were unable to capture or destroy.

It is home of the WASHINGTON COUNTY MUSEUM, 225 E. 1st St. There are three buildings included in the museum complex. The Rock Building and School House were acquired in 1958 and 1975 respectively. The Burlington Northern Dormitory was acquired in 1987 and is located at 301 W. Railroad. The museum is open from 2 to 4 p.m. Sunday during the summer months. Admission is free.

Fort Wicked

Back to Sterling and driving south on US 6, two-and-a-half miles south of **Merino**, is a historical marker on the west side of the highway commemorating **Godfrey's Station** on the Overland Stage route. It became known as **"Fort Wicked"** by the Indians during their 1864-65 rampages because of the fighting spirit of the agent, 52-year old **Holdon Godfrey**, his wife and two daughters. It was the only station between the forks of the Platte River and Denver that the Indians were unable to destroy. During one major attack on the station, the Godfreys were able to hold off the Indians two full days, enough time for troops to arrive from Fort Morgan.

Brush

Thirty-five miles south of Sterling, via I-76, is **Brush** (pop. 4,082), incorporated in 1884. It is named for **Jared L. Brush**, a well-known cattle rancher and one-time Lieutenant Governor.

Eben Ezer All Saints Church, 122 Hospital Rd., Brush, dates back to 1903 when it was founded as a tuberculosis sanitarium and deaconess motherhouse. All Saints Church is located in Eben Ezer and was dedicated in 1918. It is listed on the National Register of Historic Places. A Danish Pioneer Museum is also on the site.

Fort Morgan

Ten-miles south is **Fort Morgan** (pop. 8,768), county seat of Morgan County. Fort Morgan, founded in 1884 and incorporated in 1887, was settled on the site of an early Army post, also called Fort Morgan, established July 1, 1865. This post, established to protect travelers on the Overland Trail, began as **Camp Tyler** and a short time later was renamed **Camp Wardwell**. It was initially manned by regular Army officers and 150 "galvanized Yankees" (Confederate POWS who gave their allegiance to the Union to fight Indians.) The Army elevated its status to a fort, June 23, 1866 and it was named Fort Morgan for **Col. Christopher A. Morgan**, a deceased friend of the commanding officer, Major General Pope, commanding general of the Department of Missouri. The fort protected the stage route between Julesburg and **Fort Sedgwick** and **Camp Weld** in Denver until it was abandoned, May 18, 1868. The site of the fort is marked by a monument on Riverview Avenue in Fort Morgan.

This part of the state was hard-hit by the dust storms and grasshopper plagues during the Depression years of the 1930s. In 1938, a plague of grasshoppers was so overwhelming, the National Guard distributed truckloads of poisoned bran to kill them off. The area became over populated by jack rabbits and county-wide rabbit drives were held to rid farms of the unwanted pests. Morgan County was inundated by two major floods, one in 1935, the other in 1965, that created massive destruction. Several persons and large numbers of livestock were lost.

During World War II, German POWs were housed in the Fort Morgan Armory and worked on farms in the surrounding area. One prisoner was killed while attempting an escape.

Glenn Miller (1904-44), the popular orchestra leader in the

The Fort Morgan Museum is located in the local library located in City Park.

1930s and early '40s, lived in Fort Morgan as a boy and was a graduate of Fort Morgan High School.

President Theodore Roosevelt spoke here during a brief stop at Union Station in 1918. The Danish Crown Prince and Princess also stopped here briefly while enroute to nearby Brush.

The Sherman Street Historic Residential District, including the 400 and 500 blocks of Sherman St., is listed on the National Register. The Fort Morgan Main Post Office, 300 State St., and the Rainbow Arch Bridge, on CO 52, are listed on the National Register (Theme Resource).

FORT MORGAN LIBRARY AND MUSEUM, in the City Park, was dedicated in 1975. It is open 10 a.m. to 5 p.m. weekdays and 1:30 to 4:30 p.m. Saturday the year-round. Admission is free.

In 1910, several black families filed on land about 30 miles east of Greeley, on US 34, (or about 60 miles west of Brush) to establish a black colony they called **Dearfield**. Within seven years, the colony had grown to 700 people as they developed farms here. The Depression of 1919-23 wiped out the colony as it did many farmers across the nation. Dearfield has since disappeared.

From Fort Morgan it is an 80-mile drive to Denver.

Along I-25 and US 85 from Wyoming

These routes, criss-crossing to the historical places from the Interstate to US 85, cover a little more than 100 miles. The **Lindenmeier Site** is located just south of the Colorado-Wyoming state line, and several miles west of I-25. It was first discovered in 1924 by several local inhabitants, who found examples of projectile points known as Folsom points. Their subsequent research on the distinctive points led to the scientific excavations by the Smithsonian Institution in the 1930s. The significance of the site lies in the fact that it was a Paleo-Indian camp site, dating to approximately 10,000 years ago, while most Folsom man sites are either kill sites or butcher sites. The Lindenmeier Site is a National Historic Landmark.

In the spring of 1862, Sioux depredations on the Overland Stage line in central Wyoming caused so many interruptions of service, that the stage company decided to change the route. The new main line was established in July 1862, and it followed the South Platte River from Julesburg southwest to the mouth of the Cache la Poudre River where **Latham Station** was established (just south of **Greeley**). It then turned northwest and followed the Poudre River to **Laporte**. At Laporte it again went northwest to follow a portion of the Cherokee Trail (roughly following US 287) into south central Wyoming. This new route was much safer, shorter, and easier to travel. A branch line went from Latham Station to Denver, and a branch line ran from Denver to Laporte, following another portion of the **Cherokee Trail** (paralleling I-25).

Fort Collins

During the changeover to the new line, the stage company requested and received U.S. Army escorts to guard their personnel, stock and equipment. Troops from Fort Laramie were assigned to the task, and during this time established two new posts to help guard the line. One of these posts was **Camp Collins**, established near Laporte, and named for **Lt. Col. William O. Collins**, who was the commanding officer at Fort Laramie. The camp remained at Laporte until August 1864, when it was moved further downstream to avoid the annual spring flooding and conflicts with settler claims to land in Laporte. Permanent structures were erected, and the post began to be called **"Fort Collins"** to denote its more permanent status, although the name was never made official. It continued its mission to guard the stage line and local settlers from Indians until September, 1866, when the last troops were evacuated.

After the demise of the fort, squatters quickly pre-empted claims on the military reservation, although the land was not legally available for settlement until 1872. On May 15 of that year the land was released for claims, and in October the **Larimer County Land Improvement Co.** was incorporated to buy land upon which to establish the **Fort Collins Agricultural Colony**. The advertisements circulated by the Agricultural Colony soon brought in new settlers, who joined with those that had established themselves near the fort, and began to build a small agricultural community. The town struggled for survival its first few years, but its existence was firmly rooted when in 1870 the **"Agricultural College of Colorado"** (now **Colorado State University**) was established, and then in 1877 when the first railroad through Fort Collins began its service.

Fort Collins (pop. 85,000), was founded in 1864. It was incorporated in 1873 and is the county seat of Larimer County.

Colorado State University was opened in Fort Collins in 1870. There are 17 buildings in Fort Collins listed on the National

Coloradoan Serves on Supreme Court

Byron R. "Whizzer" White, born in Fort Collins June 8, 1917, became the 93rd justice on the U.S. Supreme Court on April 16, 1962 and the first native of Colorado to serve on it. He grew up in Wellington, 10 miles north of Fort Collins. He graduated from the University of Colorado in 1938 Phi Beta Kappa. At the same time he probably was one of the best known collegiate football players in the country. A halfback, he was a star punter, passer and runner. In his senior year he led the Colorado Buffalos through an unbeaten season and to the Cotton Bowl game. That season he was named to the All America team.

The Pittsburgh Steelers offered him $15,800 to play one season, more money at the time than any player in the NFL was getting. During the 1938 season with Pittsburgh, White led the league in ground gaining and made the Associated Press All Pro team. He was also awarded a Rhodes scholarship.

Late in 1939, White entered the Yale Law School. While at Yale he played pro football with the Detroit Lions during the 1940 and 1941 seasons. Years later he was named to the National Football Hall of Fame.

Upon the United States entry into World War II, White entered the U.S. Navy. He came out of the Navy in 1946 with two Bronze Stars and a Presidential unit citation. He returned to Yale law school and was graduated magna cum laude in 1946.

After a year as one of Chief Justice Fred M. Vinson's law clerks, he moved to Denver and joined a law firm, later becoming a partner.

During John F. Kennedy's campaign for the presidency White headed the National Citizens for Kennedy organization. He also headed the Colorado Kennedy committee and was credited with delivering 27 of the state's 42 convention votes for Kennedy.

After Kennedy's election and Robert Kennedy's appointment as Attorney General, White was appointed deputy Attorney General, second in command of the Justice Department.

He was appointed to fill the vacancy on the Supreme Court created with the resignation of Associate Justice Charles Evans Whittaker because of poor health.

Associate Justice of the Supreme Court
Byron R. White

Register of Historic Places. These are: the Avery House, 328 W. Mountain Ave.; the Old Federal Building, College Ave. at Oak St.; Spruce Hall, Old Domestic Economy Building, Ammons Hall, the Botanical and Horticultural Lab, all on the campus of Colorado State University; Peter Anderson House, 300 S. Howe St.; the Andrews House, 324 E. Oak; the Baker House, 304 W. Mulberry; the Bouton House, 113 N. Sherwood St.; the Fort Collins Municipal Railway Birney Safety Street Car No. 21, 1801 W. Mountain Ave.; Fort Collins Post Office, 102 S. College St.; Kissock Block Building, 115-121 E. Mountain Ave.; the R. G. Maxwell House, 2340 Mulberry; the McHugh-Andrews House/Mayor's House, 202 Remington St.; Montezuma Fuller House, 226 W. Magnolia; and Opera House Block/Central Block Building, 131 N. College Ave.

There are two National Historic Districts in Fort Collins and these include the Laurel School Historic District, off US 287, and the Old Town Historic District.

A historical marker has been placed near **Bellvue** east of Fort Collins to mark the naming of the Cache la Poudre River. The Cache la Poudre River received its name in February, 1825, when a group of trappers in the employ of William H. Ashley camped along the river while on their way westward to the Green River area. They remained in the area for three weeks, and made a temporary cache of gunpowder and other supplies on the bank of the river, while they traveled in different directions for the purpose of trade. Thereafter the river was called the Cache la Poudre, which roughly translated from French means "hide the powder."

FORT COLLINS MUSEUM, 200 Mathews St., is a general museum that emphasizes the local history of people and the natural environment. Its collections range from mammoth molar fossils, Folsom points, and mineral samples to Indian and early settler artifacts. The museum's collection of Folsom points, found at the Lindenmeier Site, is the largest outside of the Smithsonian Institution, in Washington, D.C. Three historic buildings in the Pioneer Courtyard, just outside the museum, represent three eras in the history of Fort Collins. These include: the Janis Cabin, representing the early settlement era, the home of Antoine Janis, dating to 1858-59; the "Auntie" Stone Cabin, representing the Army fort era, built in 1864 as

The Fort Collins Museum at 200 Matthews Street. Several historic buildings are found in the courtyard (below) at the Fort Collins Museum.

the fort's officers' mess and the fort's only remaining structure; and the Boxelder Schoolhouse, representing the agricultural and settlement era, built in 1884. The museum is open 10 a.m. to 5 p.m. Tuesday through Saturday and 12 noon to 5 p.m. Sunday. It is closed on Monday and all major holidays. Admission is free.

Loveland

Thirteen miles south of Fort Collins is **Loveland** (pop. 38,200), founded in 1877 as a railroad town and incorporated in 1881. Known as "The Sweetheart City," it was named in honor of **W.A.H. Loveland**, president of the Colorado Central Railroad.

There had been other settlements in the area before this. **Mariano Medina**, a trader from Taos, New Mexico, established a trading post, called **Namaqua**. Namaqua became a station for the Overland Stage Line in 1862. The town of **St. Louis** developed about three miles downstream from present-day Loveland after the Civil War. When the railroad was built in 1877 a better grade was found west of St. Louis and a new town, which became Loveland, was laid out on a 64-acre field contributed by **David Barnes**, who became known as the "Father of Loveland." Fifty historical homes have been identified by a Loveland committee. A folder describing these homes is available at the Loveland Chamber of Commerce.

Listed on the National Register of Historic Places are the Rialto Theatre, 228-230 E. 4th Ave.; Colorado & Southern Railroad Depot, 405 Railroad Ave.; and Chasteen's Grove Living History Farm, 3142 N. County Rd. No. 29.

LOVELAND MUSEUM AND GALLERY, 5th and Lincoln, provides a look at Loveland's past and future through a variety of art exhibits. Turn-of-the-century period rooms depict Loveland homes and the commercial district in the early 1900s. Loveland's burgeoning art community is featured in the art gallery which changes monthly. Walking tours, films and lectures, outreach trunks, concerts and special summer events are also offered. It is open 9 a.m. to 5 p.m. Tuesday through Friday, except Thursday, when it is open until 9 p.m. and 10 a.m. to 4 p.m. Saturday. Admission is free.

The VALENTINE MUSEUM, at the Loveland Visitor's Center on East US 34, pays tribute to the internationally-known

The museum and art gallery in Loveland.

Loveland's Valentine Museum.

This exhibit in the Loveland Museum features Mariano Medina, a Colorado mountainman.

Sculptor George Ludeen called this bronze sculpture "Prairie Flowers." It is one of several sculptures found in Benson Park in Loveland.

"Girl with Ribbons" is the title of this bronze sculpture by Glenna Goodacre in Loveland's Benson Park.

Benson Park is home of this bronze work by Dennis Anderson entitled, "Common Ground." Dan Ostermiller's "A Friend Indeed" (below) is another sculpture displayed in the Loveland park.

The Little Thompson Valley Pioneer Valley Museum is located in the original blacksmith shop owned by A.G. Bimson in Berthoud. The 1893 structure is a National Historic Site.

Valentine Remailing System. It is open 12 noon to 4 p.m. Thursday through Sunday.

LOVELAND'S OUTDOOR SCULPTURE GARDEN is located in Benson Park. Major works by nationally noted sculptors are displayed here.

Berthoud

South of Loveland seven miles on US 287 is **Berthoud** (pop. 2,362), named for **Capt. Edward L. Berthoud**, a surveyor for the Colorado Central Railroad.

LITTLE THOMPSON VALLEY PIONEER MUSEUM is housed in the stone blacksmith shop built by A. G. Bimson in 1893. Upon the arrival of the automobile the City Star Barn livery on Mountain Avenue became the Jefferes' garage. The building is listed on the National Register of Historic Places. The museum contains exhibits and memorabilia reflecting the area's history. It is open 1 to 5 p.m. weekends from Memorial Day through Labor Day. Admission is free.

Greeley

East of Loveland, via US 34, is **Greeley** (pop. 53,006), county seat of Weld County. It was founded in 1870 by **Nathan C. Meeker**, as the cooperative **Union Colony**. **Horace Greeley** was the founder of the *New York Tribune* and Meeker was his agriculture editor. Greeley had visited the region a decade earlier. Meeker and his colonists purchased 72,000 acres of land in April, 1870, and established an irrigation system. In late 1876, Meeker received an appointment as agent for the Ute White River Indian Agency in northwest Colorado. Here he was killed in what became known as the Meeker Massacre, September 29, 1879.

The **Monfort Feed Lots** near Greeley have a capacity of 200,000 head of cattle, making this one of the largest cattle-feeding operations in the world.

The **University of Northern Colorado** was established in 1889 in Greeley.

The museums in Greeley include:

MEEKER HOME MUSEUM, 1324 9th Ave., is housed in the two-story adobe house built in 1870 for Nathan Meeker. Through the display of personal belongings, artifacts, and home furnishings of the period, the history of Greeley and the founding of the Union Colony is illustrated. It is listed on the National Register of Historic Places. It is open from April 15 to October 15. Call (303) 350-9220 for the hours. An admission is charged.

CENTENNIAL VILLAGE, on 1475 A St., is a six-acre complex including 21 historical structures. In addition to historic homes, the museum includes reproductions of a blacksmith's shop, firehouse, and newspaper building. It is the site of the Union Pacific depot from Burns, Wyoming, built in 1910; a replica of a Cheyenne Indian tepee; the homestead shed from the Joe Filer Ranch near Buckingham, Colorado, dating back to 1908; and the Bolin homestead from Osgood, Colorado, dating back to 1909, as well as other memorabilia. In the summer, the Village becomes the site of a dramatized history, known as the "History Alive" program. All of this is in a landscaped setting with gardens. It is open from April 15 to October 15. Call (303) 350-9220 for the hours. An admission is charged.

The MUNICIPAL MUSEUM, located in the City Library at 919 7th St., features a gallery which changes interpretive exhib-

The Meeker Home Museum in Greeley once served as the home of Nathan C. Meeker, founder of the Union Colony and Greeley.

This bust of Nathan Cook Meeker, in front of the Meeker Home Museum, commemorates the founder of Greeley.

The train depot in Greeley's Centennial Village.

its on local history topics. The museum archives contain the original Union Colony records, minute books, correspondence, and an extensive photographic collection pertaining to Greeley and Weld County. It is open 9 a.m. to 5 p.m. Tuesday through Saturday, the year-round. Admission is free.

Up in the northeastern corner of this very large county is Wild Horse Creek. Southwest of the creek is the Keota Stone Circles Archaeological District/Shull Tipi Rings listed on the National Register of Historic Places.

Platteville

South of Greeley, via US 85, is **Platteville** (pop. 1,662). The **"Battle of Rattlesnake Hill"** is an interesting story in connection with this area. **Kate Slaughterback** owned a farm east of Ione. On October 28, 1925, Kate and her three-year old son, Ernie, heard duck hunters shooting a short distance from their farmstead and went out to see if they could find a duck that may have been killed but not found by the hunters. Kate took along her shotgun in case she should run across a wounded mallard. When she and Ernie opened a farm gate a rattlesnake appeared which Kate quickly dispatched with a shot. Three more appeared and she killed them. Soon it appeared a nest of

A view of one of the walls of Fort Vasquez in Platteville. The Fort Vasquez Visitors Center (below) features a small museum.

rattlers had been aroused and before Kate and Ernie could flee snakes seemed to be everywhere. Kate clubbed them after she ran out of ammunition and after two hours of fighting off snakes killed 140 of them. She gathered up the dead reptiles, skinned them and made an evening dress and purse from the skins. On several occasions she appeared at local dances and other affairs dressed in her rattlesnake dress. She soon became known as "**Rattlesnake Kate.**"

Kate Slaughterback died October 6, 1969 and is buried in Mizpah Cemetery in Platteville. The inscription on her tomb simply reads "Rattlesnake Kate."

FORT VASQUEZ, 13412 US 85, is a reconstruction of an adobe fur trading post built about 1835 by **Louis Vasquez** and **Andrew Sublette**. The fort, as described in early accounts, was about 100 feet square with 12 foot walls. Inside the fort were living quarters, a barn, storage rooms, and trade rooms. The operators traded such items as black silk handkerchiefs, ivory combs, blankets, brass kettles, and liquor for buffalo robes. Vasquez and Sublette sold the fort in 1841 and it was abandoned about a year later. The walls have been rebuilt and signs provide some idea of the layout of the fort's interior. It is listed on the National Register of Historic Places. The Colorado Historical Society owns the property and has established a visitors center here. It is open 10 a.m. to 5 p.m. Monday through Saturday and from 1 to 5 p.m. Sunday from Memorial Day weekend to Labor Day weekend. An admission is charged.

A historical marker on the west side of the highway, just south of Fort Vasquez, describes the site of **Fort Lupton. Lt. Lancaster P. Lupton** established the trading post, which became known as Fort Lupton, a quarter of a mile west of this marker in 1836.

The United Church of Christ of Highland Lake, in the vicinity of Mead, is listed on the National Register of Historic Places.

Brighton

South on US 85 is **Brighton** (pop. 12,773), county seat of Adams County. It was incorporated in 1887.

Brighton is home of the ADAMS COUNTY MUSEUM, located at 9601 Henderson Rd. Displays include Indian and mountain men articles, minerals and fossils from the area. It is open 10 a.m. to 4:30 p.m. Tuesday through Saturday the year-round. Admission is free.

Longmont

West of **Platteville**, via CO 66 to US 287, is **Longmont** (pop. 42,942), founded in 1871 by the **Chicago Colorado Colony**. The colony was organized in Chicago in 1870 by a group of investors in the Kansas Pacific & Denver Pacific Railroads. By the fall of 1871, 600 persons had settled here.

The buildings listed on the National Register of Historic Places in Longmont include the T.M. Callahan House, 312 Terry St.; Dickens Opera House, 300 Main St.; St. Stephen's Episcopal Church, 470 Main St.; Empson Cannery, 15 - 3rd Ave.; Longmont Fire Department, 667 4th St.; and Longmont College (The Landmark), 546 Atwood St. The East Side Historic District is bounded by Long's Peak Ave., Collyer St., 4th Ave. and Emery St. The West Side Historic District is bounded by 5th, Terry, 3rd and Grant. The Sandstone Ranch, east of Longmont off CO 119, is also listed on the National Register.

OLD MILL PARK, 237 Pratt St., Longmont, contains original buildings, plantings and artifacts preserved by pioneers who settled in the St. Vrain Valley from 1859 to 1890. Among the old

The Longmont Museum is operated by the Department of Human Services, City of Longmont.

The Lafayette Miners' Museum is housed in this old home on East Simpson in Lafayette. The building is listed on the National Register of Historic Places.

residences in the park—Townley House, dating back to 1871; Affolter Cabin, built in 1860 on Left Hand Creek near Haystack Mountain; and Billings Cabin, built in 1890 as a hunting and fishing resort west of Lyons. Also included here is the Mill Pond and Secor Centennial Garden. The east wall of the pond is the only remaining portion of the Longmont Flour Mill built in 1873. The Secor Garden contains wild plum, cherry, peach, pear, apple, and mulberry, Chinese elm, green ash, locust, catalpa, black walnut, hawthorn, and American elm trees which attract a variety of birds. The park is open 8 a.m. to 5 p.m. daily.

LONGMONT MUSEUM, 375 Kimbark St., interprets the history of the people of Longmont and the St. Vrain Valley from the time of the Plains Indians to the present day. It is open 9 a.m. to 5 p.m. weekdays and 10 a.m. to 4 p.m. Saturdays. It is closed on Sundays and holidays. Admission is free.

Lafayette

South of Longmont on US 287 is **Lafayette** (pop. 8,985), incorporated in 1890.

Union organizer and martyr **Joe Hill** is memorialized with

191

five other union miners buried in a Lafayette cemetery. Six miners had been slain at the Columbine Mine on November 21, 1927. The memorial to the six killed by state militiamen and mine guards was dedicated in 1989 when Hill's ashes were scattered over the slain miners graves. Hill, an organizer for the Industrial Workers of the World, known as the Wobblies, was executed in 1915 by a Utah firing squad for the murder of a grocer in Salt Lake City. Hill's supporters claimed he had been framed. The sixth miner killed in the Columbine Mine disaster is listed on the memorial in Lafayette. He is buried in a family plot in nearby Louisville.

An interesting side note to this story about Hill and the six miners: Hill's body was cremated in 1916. His last request was that his ashes be scattered in several states—except Utah, where he said he wouldn't be caught dead. The five miners in Lafayette had lain in unmarked graves until 1989. The envelope containing Hill's ashes wound up at the National Archives in Washington, D.C., through a postal error and were undiscovered for seven decades.

The MINER'S MUSEUM is located at 108 E. Simpson in Lafayette. It is housed in the Lewis House, one of the Lafayette Coal Mining Era Buildings. It is listed on the National Register of Historic Places. For information, telephone (303) 666-9555.

There are five other buildings depicting the Lafayette Coal Mining Era. These include the Congregational Church, 300 E. Simpson St.; the Lafayette House, 600 E. Simpson St.; The Terrace, 207 E. Cleveland St.; the Kullgren House, 209 E. Cleveland St.; and the Miller House, 409 E. Cleveland St. Also listed on the NRHP is the Boulder Valley Grange No. 131, 3400 N. 95th St.

Louisville

Nearby is **Louisville** (pop. 5,593), incorporated in 1892.

The first coal field in the area of what is now Louisville was opened in 1877 by **C. C. Welch** on land belonging to **Dave Kerr**. The man in charge of boring the mine was **Louis Nawatny**. Kerr gave Nawatny 40 acres of land and Nawatny platted it into the Original Town. He named the new town for himself, thus calling the town Louisville which was registered in the fall of 1878.

The two LOUISVILLE HISTORICAL MUSEUMS are lo-

This statue on the grounds at the Louisville library is dedicated to the coal miners in this area.

The Louisville Historical Society is housed in two buildings on Main Street. This is the latest addition to the museum complex.

cated at 1001 and 1013 Main St. They are open from 1 to 3 p.m. on Thursday and Saturday and by appointment. Admission is free.

There are several buildings listed on the National Historic Register in Louisville. These include Tego Bros. Drugstore (State National Bank), 700 Main St.; National Fuel Company Store, 801 Main St.; Jacoe Store, 1001 Main St.; Petrelli-Del Pizzo House, 1016 Main St.; LaSalle House/Wilson House, 1124 Main St.; the Robinson House, 301 Spruce St.; Lackner's Tavern, 1006 Pine St.; the Ginacci House, 1116 LaFarge St.; the Rhoades House, 1024 Grant St.; the Stolmes House, 616 Front St.; the Thomas House, 700 Lincoln St.; and the Denver Grain Elevator, Tract 712 near CO 42.

From Louisville it is a short drive to either Boulder or Denver.

Chapter 7
Through the State on I-70

This route through Colorado begins and ends on the plains. From the west it comes out of the arid region of Utah and from the east it covers the plains leading to the mountains. There are many historical towns and places along this route. The story of the men who first discovered gold is told as well as many other famous and infamous characters. The museums and historical sites are listed for every community.

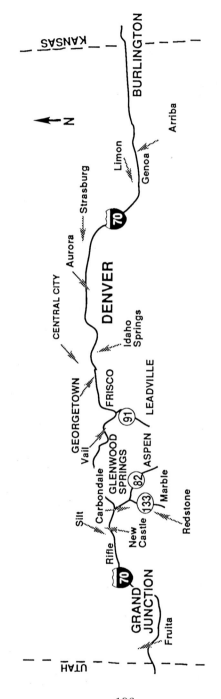

Chapter 7
Across Colorado on I-70

It is 450 miles across Colorado on I-70. This chapter will cover the historic points and attractions along this Interstate Highway from Kansas to Utah.

Burlington

Driving west from Kansas the first community is **Burlington** (pop. 3,107), county seat of Kit Carson County. Burlington was founded in 1888.

There are two main attractions in Burlington:

OLD TOWN, on south 14th St., just off Rose Ave., can be accessed from either exit off I-70. The Old Town Museum consists of 19 buildings and the Heritage Hall, a 250 foot museum with living exhibits, antiques, clothing, machinery and a vintage wagon collection. The museum tells the history of the early 1900s eastern plains town and the lives of its citizens. The Old Town Emporium has approximately 5,000 handcrafted items for sale. The museum is open 8 a.m. to 9 p.m. daily from Memorial Day to Labor Day and from 9 a.m. to 6 p.m. the rest of the year. The summer months include a variety of entertainment such as can can shows, melodramas, gunfights, and madam shows along with special events every weekend. Fred and Doc provide transportation on the Old Town Express to the Kit Carson County Carousel. An admission is charged.

KIT CARSON COUNTY CAROUSEL, located in the Kit Carson County Fairgrounds, is a beautifully restored and fully operating carousel manufactured by the Philadelphia Toboggan Company in 1905. PTC No. 6 has been designated a National Historic Site and has been awarded National Landmark status, making it one of only 13 National Landmarks in Colorado. The carousel features 45 hand carved wooden animals, including a hippocampus (seahorse). The carousel was originally built for Elitch Gardens, an amusement park in Denver. It was sold to Kit Carson County in 1928 for $1,250. It is open from 1 to 4 p.m. and 7 to 8:30 p.m. daily from late May through Labor Day. Private tours are available the rest of the year. A minimum of two weeks notice is required. An admission is charged.

The Burlington State Armory, 191 14th St., and the Winegar

The museum in Burlington's Old Town, a popular historical attraction in eastern Colorado. Another attraction in Burlington is the Kit Carson County Carousel, a restored and operating 1905 wooden merry-go-round.

Building, 494-498 14th St., are listed on the National Register of Historic Places.

Arriba

Fifty-three miles west is **Arriba** (pop. 236), home of the TARADO MANSION. This museum is just south of Arriba, via Exit 383 from I-70. Built in 1917 as the Adams Hotel, the building was purchased in 1973 and moved to its present location and rebuilt as Tarado Mansion (Tara of Colorado). Today it houses an eclectic collection of historical and art treasures. Among some of the items housed here is a harp which belonged to Gen. George Custer's wife, a tea coat worn by the "Unsinkable Molly Brown," and several porcelains including a large Italian grouping by Capo di Monte hand-sculptured in the late 1700s. Furnishings in the Greek Revival mansion range from period styles to the elaborate Victorian. Other rare pieces include hand-carved rosewood, walnut and oak furniture and a gold leaf curio cabinet containing a miniature carved ivory piano and chess table. It is open for tours from 10 a.m. to 5 p.m. daily. It is closed New Year's Day, Easter Sunday, Thanksgiving Day, and Christmas Day. An admission is charged.

The elegant Tarado Mansion just south of Arriba was built in 1917 as the Adams Hotel.

The Genoa Tower is the only pictograph museum in the country.

The Pioneer Schoolhouse Museum in Limon.

Genoa
Continuing west it is 12 miles to **Genoa** (pop. 165) and GENOA TOWER, the only pictograph museum in the United States. Not only can visitors see six states from the tower, they may also see a large collection of fossil skulls, guns, bottles and other items as well as 20,000 Indian artifacts. The 20-room museum can be reached by taking Exit 371 off I-70. It is open 8 a.m. to 8 p.m. daily from Memorial Day through Labor Day. An admission is charged.

Limon
It is another nine miles to **Limon** (pop. 1,805) and the SCHOOL HOUSE MUSEUM, 517 D Ave. The museum is housed in one of the early day school houses in Lincoln County, dating back to 1895. Although it is open only by appointment, admission is free.

Strasburg Significant in Transportation History
Back on I-70, the interstate continues toward Denver. It is 48 miles northwest from Limon to Byers and eight miles from Byers to unincorporated **Strasburg** on US 36.

Strasburg is a significant site in transportation history. Kansas Pacific Railroad crews from Kansas City east and Denver west met to drive the last rails in a system that provided rail

This historical marker in the Rest Area off I-70 three miles west of Strasburg describes the linking of the transcontinental railroads. This last link, the 640 miles connecting Denver and Kansas City, came together in August 1870. On the final day, August 15, the crews laid a record-breaking 10 and a quarter miles of track in nine hours to win a barrel of whiskey which canny foremen had placed midway in the final gap.

service from coast-to-coast at 3 p.m. on August 15, 1870, to form the first continuous chain of railroads from the Atlantic Coast to the Pacific Coast. The last 10 and a quarter miles of track were laid by two crews, one working from the east and one from the west, in a recordbreaking nine hours. With the connection of the rails at Strasburg it was possible to board a train in New York and travel to San Francisco. The 640 mile trip from Kansas City to Denver that took two months by prairie schooner and a week by stagecoach now only took a day and a half by rail. Fifteen months earlier, the Union Pacific and Central Pacific joined at Promontory Summit in Utah to join the east and the west, however, this joint venture only provided continuous rail service between Omaha and Sacramento. A historical marker in

The historical marker (above) commemorates the rail linkage of the Pacific and Atlantic coasts with the completion of the Kansas Pacific Railroad line between Kansas City and Denver. Displays in the Comanche Crossing Historical Society Museum (below) in Strasburg.

Lions Park provides a brief explanation of this historic event. A second historical marker commemorating this achievement is located in the rest area just off I-70 three miles west of Strasburg.

COMANCHE CROSSING MUSEUM, at the west end of town on US 36, features a 1917 U.P.R.R. Depot, caboose, 1891 one-room school, 1910 homestead, and over 3,000 artifacts on display. It is open 2 to 5 p.m. daily, June 1 through August 31. Admission is free.

Comanche Crossing, east of the depot in Strasburg near Mile Post 602 is listed on the National Register of Historic Places.

It is 36 miles from Strasburg to Denver. (See Chapter 2—the Greater Denver Area.)

Central City/Blackhawk

West of Denver is **Central City** (pop. 329), county seat of Gilpin County. From Golden take US 6 west through Clear Creek Canyon. Once a railroad bed, this route offers spectacular scenery with rushing streams and sheer black rock canyon walls.

Proceeding west on US 6 12 miles to the CO 119 turnoff it is another nine miles to the **Central City/Blackhawk National Historic District**. This area is known as "the Richest Square Mile on Earth." Over a half-billion dollars in mineral wealth has been mined from here. The district appears today much as it did a century ago, and was listed as a National Historic Landmark in 1966.

In Blackhawk, the Lace House, built in the 1860s, is a National Historic Landmark. It is open to the public. An admission is charged.

LITTLE COLONEL MINE, 301 Gregory St. in Blackhawk, is also open to the public for tours. It is open 10 a.m. to 5:30 p.m. daily from Memorial Day to Labor Day. An admission is charged.

Central City was first known as **Gregory's Diggings**. This was the beginning of the mining interests of **John H. Gregory**, a penniless Georgian who had come to Colorado in search of gold.

John Gregory's and his companions' gold discovery May 6, 1859, launched the great Colorado gold rush. After their discovery of gold, Gregory and **D. Joseph Casto** drew up rules and regulations for the Gregory Mining District. Their plan, the first recorded, became the basis for all mining law in the Terri-

203

The historic Lace House in Blackhawk is leased by the Gilpin County Historical Society. It is listed on the National Register of Historic Places.

The Lost Gold Mine in Central City is open for tours.

The Thomas-Billings House Museum in Central City.

tory and later in the state. The plan provided that each man was entitled to 100 feet on the "lead" or vein. As the discoverer of the vein, Gregory was entitled to two plots. A monument just west of Blackhawk commemorates the spot where the Gregory Mining District plan was laid out.

Quickly Gregory's Diggings became **Mountain City**. A few weeks later it became Central City.

The town flourished. The first Masonic temple between the Missouri River and the Pacific Ocean, was built here in June 1859. The site, just east of Central City, is marked with a monument.

At the outbreak of the Civil War the Army established **Camp Gilpin**, a temporary post, in Central City in 1861.

Many famous persons visited early-day Central City. Among those who visited here on western sightseeing trips in 1865 were **Schuyler Colfax**, speaker of the House of Representatives, and **Samuel Bowles**, editor of the *Springfield (Mass) Republican* and author of a number of travel books. In 1867, **Henry M. Stanley**, the journalist, visited here before making his trip to search for Dr. Livingston in Africa.

Gen. U.S. Grant, along with other generals, arrived on a stagecoach in 1868. President Grant, accompanied by his wife and daughter, visited in 1873. In a show of wealth, silver ingots were laid out in front of the **Teller House** for the president to walk from the stagecoach to the hotel steps. Teller House, financed principally by **Henry M. Teller**, was the largest and finest hotel in Colorado at the time. The Teller family owned the hotel until 1935.

City Hall and the Henry M. Teller law office are the oldest buildings in town. City Hall began as a log cabin in 1862 and later was sided. It served as a courthouse, jail and sheriff's office in the 1860-70s. Teller's law office dates back to the 1860s. Teller, a prominent attorney and railroad executive, represented Colorado in the U.S. Senate for nearly 30 years. Later, President Chester A. Arthur appointed him Secretary of Interior (1882-1885).

Early-day Central City suffered disasterous fires as did other mining camps and towns. In 1873 a major fire destroyed most of downtown. The 1874 fire, that destroyed most of the central part of town, was believed to have been set off by celebrating Chinese.

Two women, **Anne Evans** and **Ida McFarlane**, are credited with much of the restoration that occurred in the 1930s to develop Central City into a national historic attraction. Anne Evans was the daughter of John Evans, the second territorial governor of Colorado. Ida McFarlane, whose husband and his father and family had lived in Central City most of their lives, was head of the English department at the University of Denver. The two women not only saved and restored the Opera House but went on to launch productions in it. They are also credited with the restoration of the Teller House. Both buildings have since been listed on the National Register of Historic Places. Through their Central City Opera House Association they acquired several other historic holdings.

There are several historical attractions in Central City. Among them is a 30-minute historic tour of the community which may be taken on the Black Hawk & Central City Narrow Gauge Railroad pulled by an 1898 coal burning engine. It is open 10:30 a.m. to 5:30 p.m. daily except Tuesday, May through September. An admission is charged.

TELLER HOUSE AND THE FACE ON THE BARROOM FLOOR, 120 Eureka St., was built in 1872 as a hotel. "The Face on the Barroom Floor" was painted on the Teller bar floor by

The legendary "Face on the Barroom Floor" is located in Central City's Teller House bar.

Herndon Davis in the summer of 1936. It was inspired by a ballad written by Hugh Antoine d'Arcy in August, 1877. The ballad, originally called "The Face Upon the Floor," was not published until 1912. Davis drew his "face" in the Teller Hotel bar as a lark. The bar is open 11 a.m. to 5 p.m. daily Memorial Day through Labor Day. Admission is free.

The CENTRAL CITY OPERA HOUSE, on Eureka St., was built by Cornish and Welsh miners in 1878 at the height of Central City's heyday as a booming mining town. After the turn of the century, it suffered a decline, but was revived by a group of Denver business leaders and re-opened in 1932 with Lillian Gish in "Camille." In the 1980s, the historic Opera House has been beautifully restored to its original splendor with exquisite ceiling murals by John Massman.

Today, the Central City Opera Festival is one of the oldest in the United States, and presents some of the finest voices in America. All Central City Opera productions are performed in English. The Opera Festival runs each summer from early July through mid-August. Each summer two operas and one operetta are presented. For information call (303) 292-6700.

The THOMAS-BILLINGS HOME, 209 Eureka St., is a historic home furnished with everything from the original household. It is open 9:30 a.m. to 5 p.m. daily, year-round. An admission is charged.

LOST GOLD MINE, 229 Eureka St., gives the visitor an opportunity to gain an understanding of the main shaft, tunnels, drifts and other nomenclature of a typical mine. It is open 8 a.m. to 8 p.m. daily during the summer and 10 a.m. to 6 p.m. during the winter months. An admission is charged.

*This monument in Central City marks the site of the
first Masonic Temple built in Colorado.*

CENTRAL CITY GOLD MINING MUSEUM, Main and Spring Sts., provides a good illustration of mining. The mine was opened in 1888 and the present building was constructed in 1906. The museum is open 11 a.m. to 5 p.m. daily from Memorial Day to Labor Day. An admission is charged.

GILPIN COUNTY HISTORICAL SOCIETY MUSEUM, 228 E. High St., is housed in the old high school building. It features exhibits and displays concerning mining as well as a toy and doll collection and 19th century clothing dating back as far as 1869. It is open 11 a.m. to 5 p.m. daily from Memorial Day to Labor Day and by appointment at other times. An admission is charged.

Also recommended is a trip to **Anne Evans Point** and the **Glory Hole** for spectacular views. The Glory Hole, created by dynamiting for low grade ore, is 500 feet across and 900 feet deep.

Some other interesting designated historic places in Gilpin County are the Winks Panorama/Winks Lodge in the Pinecliffe area and the Denver NW & Pacific Railway Historic District at Rollinsville and Winter Park.

A visitor can return to I-70 by backtracking on CO 119 or by driving over the **"Oh My God Road,"** a drive through country dotted with old abandoned mines that is only nine miles to Idaho Springs. This back road is not suitable for all vehicles at all times and before taking it, it might be prudent to talk to some of the natives about its condition. A self guided tour of the "Oh My God Road" is available at the Chamber of Commerce Visitor's Center in Idaho Springs.

Idaho Springs

Back on I-70 or via "Oh My God Road" it is a short drive to **Idaho Springs** (pop. 2,077). It is 32 miles west of Denver on I-70.

While on a hunting trip, January 7, 1859, **George A. Jackson** discovered gold in Chicago Creek where it runs into Clear Creek. He was able to keep his find a secret until May. Once the news was out, a mining camp, called **Jackson's Diggings**, instantly sprang up. Eight years later it was permanently named Idaho Springs for its mineral springs which the Indians considered sacred.

Two monuments have been erected to George Jackson in

This monument in Idaho Springs marks the site where George A. Jackson first discovered gold in the Rocky Mountains. This historic event occurred January 7, 1859.

The historic Argo Gold Mine in Idaho Springs.

Idaho Springs. One is on the campus of Clear Creek School one-quarter mile south on CO 103 (Clear Creek Rd.). A boulder here marks the site where Jackson made his gold discovery. A quarter mile south is a 12-foot statue of Jackson provided by Gene and Carolyn Kidd, local business owners.

Twenty eight miles south on this same highway is Mount Evans (14,260 feet high) with the highest paved highway in North America.

Other historical attractions include:

ARGO GOLD MILL, off Riverside Dr., began with the discovery of placer gold in 1859 by George Jackson just a short distance from the present Argo Mill site. As mines opened the need for a mill became apparent and Argo was planned and built. It became one of the largest and most modern mills in the world, designed to process 120 tons per day. On January 19, 1943, the Argo tunnel was flooded killing four men. The flooding was caused when miners blasted a lateral loose. The tunnel was closed and today stands as a monument to the mining adventures of the area. The mill is listed on the National Register of Historic Places. The Argo Gold Mill and Clear Creek Mining and Milling Museum is open daily May through October.

STEVE CANYON STATUE, located in front of the Chamber

This statue of Milt Caniff's comic strip character Steve Canyon is located outside the Visitor's Center in Idaho Springs. It honors Colorado airmen who have and who defend our country.

of Commerce Visitor's Center, salutes the airmen of Colorado. The statue of Milt Caniff's comic strip hero Steve Canyon was commissioned by the cartoonist and owners of the strip after the Colorado legislature renamed Squirrel Gulch for the cartoon character. The Visitor's Center is located at the junction of Miner St. and Colorado Blvd.

UNDERHILL MUSEUM, in the 1400 block of Miner St., contains mining artifacts and photographs. The museum is located in the former office of a local assayer, **James Underhill**, and features a collection of assay equipment.

"Old Number 60" was the designation of the locomotive that operated between Denver and Graymont (now Bakerville) for 64 years without an accident, a remarkable record in early railroad days. In 1941, the Chicago and Southern Railroad donated the engine and a coach to Idaho Springs. "Old Number 60" with the coach today is located on a site behind City Hall on Miner St.

EDGAR EXPERIMENTAL MINE, opened in 1921 by the Colorado School of Mines as a working mine and underground laboratory for students, is open for tours and demonstrations Wednesday through Saturday, June to September. It is at the west end of town off Virginia St.

BRIDAL VEIL FALLS, off Soda Creek Rd. south of I-70, offers a spectacular sight to visitors. In the winter, the falls freeze on the rock cliffs facing Idaho Springs from the south, forming a natural, free form ice sculpture. In the summer, the falls flow off the rock wall into Clear Creek. The Taylor Water Wheel at the base of the falls is being restored.

The Idaho Springs Downtown Commercial District, bounded by Center Alley, Riverside Dr., and Idaho St., was designated a National Historic District in 1984. The Miner Street Bridge is listed as a National Register Theme Resource. The Evans-Elbert Ranch/Elbert-Austin Ranch, on Upper Bear Creek Rd., is listed on the National Register of Historic Places.

Georgetown/Silver Plume

Georgetown (pop. 830), county seat of Clear Creek County, is 13 miles west of Idaho Springs. Georgetown, the "Silver Queen" of the Rockies, was incorporated in 1868.

George and David Griffith, brothers, discovered gold near the corner of 11th and Rose Streets in June 1859. They staked out a claim and within a year established the Griffith Mining District. Georgetown got its name from George Griffith, who became District Recorder. Although the gold discovery was not

213

spectacular, silver turned out to be the boon. For more than two decades Georgetown and neighboring Silver Plume rode the crest of the silver boom.

By the time Colorado reached statehood in 1876, Georgetown's population was nearly 5,000. By then the town boasted a telegraph office, two newspapers, several hotels and a bank along with five churches, four fire companies and a waterworks. Silver mining was hard hit in 1893 with the repeal of the Sherman Silver Purchase Act, which placed the country on a gold standard. Mining operations soon closed and it was not until the 1960s that the area was revived as the Georgetown-Silver Plume National Historic Landmark District.

Among some of the historic sites in the District include:

HOTEL DE PARIS, 409 6th St., Georgetown, was opened in 1875 by **Louis Dupuy**, a Frenchman, who arrived here in 1870. Dupuy rented the building formerly occupied by the Delmonico Bakery, and proposed to keep a first-class hotel and restaurant. The museum is owned by the National Society of the Colonial Dames of America in the State of Colorado. Today it is listed on the National Register of Historic Places. It is open 9 a.m. to 5 p.m. daily from Memorial Day through September. The rest of the year it is open from noon to 4 p.m. except Mondays and the traditional holidays. An admission is charged.

A brief explanation concerning Dupuy's background is of interest. He actually was **Adolphe Francois Gerard** who was educated at a Roman Catholic seminary in France. Being a free spirit, the rigid life did not suit him, and at age 20 he left for other pursuits in Paris, London and New York. He had become skilled in both the English language and French cuisine which would help him more than he possibly realized. In 1868 he joined the Army and was assigned to the 2nd U.S. Cavalry stationed at Fort D.A. Russell near Cheyenne, Wyoming. He served briefly in the Army and in mid-1869 turned up in Denver with a new identity, Louis Dupuy. He was hired by the *Rocky Mountain News* to travel the mining camp circuit and send back stories. Louis was lured by prospects of an easy fortune, and became a miner himself. In 1873 he was maimed while saving his partner during a mine explosion. Louis was very popular, and the people of Georgetown took up a collection to help him get started in business. Louis purchased the building which he continued to remodel and expand into a fine hotel and restaurant reminiscent of the Normandy inns of Alencon. He

Georgetown's Old Stone Jail was built c. 1868 and contains only two small cells and a watchman's room.

The Hotel de Paris in Georgetown was established by Louis Dupuy, an alias for Adolphe Francois Gerard, an Army deserter. It is listed on the National Register of Historic Places.

The Hamill House in Georgetown is listed on the National Register of Historic Places. William Hamill acquired the home, built in 1867, in 1874. He was a successful silver mining speculator.

considered the Hotel de Paris his souvenir of France in America. Louis Dupuy's true identity was finally revealed when he died in 1900 of pneumonia.

HAMILL HOUSE MUSEUM, 301 Argentine St., was the home of **William A. Hamill** who arrived in Georgetown in 1867. The house was begun in 1867 by Joseph Watson, Hamill's brother-in-law. When Hamill became successful as a silver mining speculator in 1874, he acquired the home. His other business interests included two wagon roads, three ranches and various small enterprises. He also served as a State Senator in the first Colorado Legislature. Between 1879 and 1885, Hamill expanded his residential property to its present dimensions and maintained his silver mining company offices here. Hamill died in 1904 and his wife, Priscilla, died in 1910. The last of the Hamills left Georgetown in 1914. The Hamill House is listed on the National Register of Historic Places. There are five buildings on the grounds. The home is an excellent example of early Georgetown architecture. The museum is open 9 a.m. to 5 p.m. daily Memorial Day through September 30 and 12 noon to 4 p.m. Tuesday through Sunday during the winter months. An admission is charged.

THE STONE JAIL, on the Clear Creek Courthouse grounds on Argentine St., was built c. 1868 for the Town of Georgetown. The building contains two cells and a watchman's room. It was used primarily to keep drunks off the street overnight or to hold stray animals. Most lawbreakers in early-day mining towns and camps were banished rather than given jail sentences. It is not open to the public.

There are several other historic structures in Georgetown. Among these are the Georgetown Depot, on Rose St.; the covered portal of the Griffith Mine, on 11th St.; the Old Missouri Firehouse, on Taos St.; the Church-Hamilton House, off Rose St.; Bowman-White House, on Rose St.; the Log Cabin built sometime before 1870, off 9th St. facing Clear Creek; and the Tucker Rutherford House, on 9th St. at Clear Creek. The Georgetown Society, Inc., owns the Hamill House, Bowman/White House, Tucker Rutherford House and Old Log Cabin.

Other structures listed on the National Register of Historic Places are the Georgetown Loop Railroad, the Grace Episcopal Church, on Taos St. between 4th and 5th Sts.; and the Julius G. Pohle House/Mine Manager's House/Toll House, on the west side of town adjacent to I-70. The Alpine Hose Company No. 2, 507 5th St.; the McClellan House, 919 Taos St.; and the Ore Processing Mill and Dam/Lebanon Dam, one mile southwest of Georgetown off I-70, are listed as (Individual) National Historic Districts.

GEORGETOWN LOOP HISTORIC MINING DISTRICT AND RAILROAD PARK are owned by the Colorado Historical Society. The railroad played a vital role in the development of the various mining camps and towns in Colorado. The Colorado Central Railroad reached Georgetown in the summer of 1877. At that time the narrow-gauge locomotives could only pull a four percent grade and the grade rose six percent between Georgetown and Silver Plume. **Robert Blickensderfer**, a Union Pacific engineer, solved the problem by designing a series of curves and a grand loop whereby the railroad crossed over itself on a 300-foot trestle nearly 100 feet above Clear Creek. In the meantime other railroads were developed in the region and the great Georgetown Loop became a tourist attraction. The line was given a boost in 1884 when **William Henry Jackson**, the noted photographer, took promotional photos for the line. Today, the

Georgetown Loop Railroad covers six miles and includes an optional guided tour of the Lebanon Silver Mine. The train can be boarded in either Georgetown or Silver Plume. It is open 10 a.m. to 4 p.m. daily from Memorial Day through Labor Day. An admission is charged.

In **Silver Plume** the Lebanon and Everett Mine Tunnels, northeast of Silver Plume adjacent to I-70, are listed on the National Register of Historic Places. The Silver Plume Depot, off I-70, is listed as a National Historic District (Individual).

From Georgetown and Silver Plume I-70 continues west to the Utah state line. There are several museums and historical attractions in the Grand River region.

Dillon

West of Silver Plume is **Dillon** (pop. 182).

THE SUMMIT HISTORICAL SOCIETY MUSEUM, on LaBonte St., features a number of buildings moved from the Old Dillon site and **Keystone** as well as the Dillon School House. Tours are available for a fee.

The Porcupine Peak Site, east of Dillon, is listed on the National Register (Archaeology).

Frisco

Five miles west of Dillon is **Frisco** (pop. 1,221).

FRISCO HISTORICAL PARK is located at 2nd and Main Sts. The Park offers a look into Frisco's past. It houses seven historic buildings including Frisco's original one-room school house. This building remains on its original site and is on the National Register of Historic Places. The school house is now an exhibit museum of artifacts and pictorial displays. Also available for public viewing is the Staley House exhibit which is a turn of the century home complete with an interpretive exhibit of domestic life during the early 1900s. Other buildings in the Park include Frisco's original jail, log chapel, and several homes dating back to the late 1800s. Local merchants and craftspeople are located in some of these buildings. Admission through the Park is free.

Wildhack's Grocery Store-Post Office, 510 Main St., Frisco, is also listed on the National Register of Historic Places.

Breckenridge

Breckenridge (pop. 818), county seat of Summit County, is nine miles south of I-70 on CO 9 (Exit 203). **Gen. George E.**

Spencer is credited with the founding of **Breckinridge**, as it was first spelled, in 1860. He named his new town for **Vice President John Cabell Breckinridge**. Unfortunately, Breckinridge's sympathies were with the South when the Civil War broke out and he was commissioned a Confederate brigadier general. The little Colorado town quickly and quietly changed the spelling of its name to "Breckenridge," replacing the "i" with an "e." The discovery of gold drew many to this area from late 1859. Eventually the gold was mined out and the little town stood still for a number of years. In 1961, the Breckenridge Ski Area was opened and thus the town became one of the more popular ski resorts in Colorado.

Over 40 buildings have been included in the Breckenridge National Historic District. Victorian-era architecture has been preserved in this over 130-year old mining town. Guided group tours (six or more) of this district are available for a fee. Reservations are required by calling (303) 453-9022.

The SUMMIT HISTORICAL SOCIETY'S PUBLIC MUSEUM, 104 N. Harris St., is housed in the Romanesque Revival home of **William Harrison Briggle**, built in 1896. Briggle was cashier of Engle Bros. Exchange Bank for many years. The walking tours of the Historic District begin at the Briggle House. The Society also operates tours of the WASHINGTON GOLD MINE, located on the south side of Breckenridge, off Boreas Pass Rd., on County Rd. 518, 1.1 miles from Breckenridge's Main St. The Society also offers tours of the Lomax Placer Gulch at 301 Ski Hill Rd., two blocks west of the Town Hall. This tour allows participants to gain an appreciation of 1870s placer mining and try their hand at gold panning. The Washington Mine offers visitors the opportunity to explore Breckenridge's mining heritage, and observe the tools that shaped the lives of hard-rock miners.

The walking tour of the Historic District is scheduled at 10 a.m. Wednesday through Friday. The Washington Mine tours begin at 1 p.m. Wednesday through Friday. The tour of the Lomax Placer Gulch begins at 3 p.m. Wednesday through Friday. A combined walking tour and mine tour is scheduled for 10 a.m. on Saturdays.

Leadville

Back on I-70 six miles west of Frisco is the exit on CO 91 south leading to **Leadville** (pop. 3,879), county seat of Lake

The ore car above is a marker designating Leadville as a Registered National Historic Landmark. The historic marker below provides a brief history of Leadville.

County. It is a 24-mile drive to this historic mining town. Gold was discovered here by a small party of prospectors in mid-April 1860. The prospector who first washed a panful of gravel that contained gold is said to have exclaimed, "Oh, boys, I've just got California in this here pan." From that exclamation came the name of **California Gulch** where the first glimmerings of the future fame of Leadville began to appear.

The "Bylaws of California Mining District, California Gulch, Arkansas River" were adopted May 12, 1860. It described the boundaries of the District and spelled out the size of each claim and how the claims were to be worked. Within a few months more than 10,000 reached the gulch seeking their fortune. By the end of the Civil War the California Gulch placer gold had been worked out.

In 1868, the Printer Boy Lode was discovered in California Gulch. **W. H. Stevens** and **A. B. Wood** discovered silver in 1874 creating another mining boom. In 1877 the town of Leadville began to emerge as a mining camp. It was officially named on January 14, 1878, and incorporated on February 12, 1878.

During the boom years the population of Leadville was between 20,000 and 40,000. At one time Leadville was the second largest city in importance and population in Colorado.

One of the earliest arrivals to California Gulch was **H.A.W. (Horace) Tabor** and his wife, Augusta. They arrived in May 1860 and at the time Augusta was the first woman in the region. He was a storekeeper. In April 1878, **August Rische** and **George Hook** walked into Tabor's store and asked to be "grubstaked." Horace agreed and the return for his small investment was the beginning of a fantastic fortune which earned him the title of "Silver King." The two prospectors and Tabor struck it rich when the two men sunk a shaft about a mile up East 7th Street to find one of the richest silver lodes in Colorado. They named their mine the Little Pittsburgh.

Other famous personalities with ties to Leadville include **Margaret Tobin Brown**, who became noted as "The Unsinkable Molly Brown;" **Meyer Guggenheim**, the Swiss emigrant who found a fortune in the Y.A. and Minnie mines; **Charles Boettcher**, who gained his fortune in Leadville and went to Denver where he amassed an even greater fortune; and **David May**, one of the founders of the May D & F Department Store chain, who opened his first store in Leadville. The town gave Colorado three governors—**John L. Routt,** (1876-79); **James B. Grant,** (1883-85); and **Jesse F. McDonald,** (1905-07). Many noted personalities have made appearances in Leadville. Among some of these were three U.S. presidents, **Susan B. Anthony, Sarah Bernhardt, William F. "Buffalo Bill" Cody, John Henry "Doc" Holliday, J. B. "Texas Jack" Omohundro, Jefferson Randolph "Soapy" Smith,** and **Oscar Wilde. Charles Vivian,** founder of the Benevolent Protective Order of the Elks (BPOE) died in Leadville in 1880.

It was in Leadville on August 19, 1884, that Doc Holliday shot a local bartender over a small five dollar loan. The bartender, Billy Allen, had loaned Holliday the money and a short time later demanded he be repaid. He followed Holliday into a saloon threatening to "lick" him if the debt was not promptly satisfied. The belligerent Allen weighed 50 pounds more than the gunfighter who promptly drew his pistol and fired a shot wounding Allen in the arm. Holliday was taken into custody, tried and acquitted.

The fairyland **"Leadville Ice Palace"** was built on the block between 6th and 8th Streets of Capitol Hill in the west section of town, during the winter of 1895-96. The palace covered five acres and featured 95 foot towers at the front and 60 foot towers at the rear. It opened on January 1, 1896, and survived until July 1, 1896.

A historical marker on 2nd Street describes Leadville's so-called "red light" district. Originally called State Street, it was renamed 2nd Street in 1879 but this did not change its reputation. Notorious from the beginning, State Street was home for some of the most infamous of Leadville's early gamblers, "ladies of easy virtue," bunco artists, and various desperadoes. Violent death and unrestrained vice walked hand-in-hand on State Street. As late as World War II this area was off-limits to

Leadville known as "Cloud City"

Leadville is often called the *Cloud City* because at 10,200 feet above sea level it is the highest incorporated city in the United States.

222

military personnel. Fire destroyed most of the buildings but the history remains.

Leadville is the largest National Historic Landmark District in Colorado.

The HEALY HOUSE AND DEXTER CABIN, 912 Harrison Ave., are representative of the boom-and-bust era of the late 1870s and 1880s. The original two-story Healy House was built in 1878 by August R. Meyer. Daniel Healy gained ownership sometime after 1881. The Dexter Cabin was built in 1879 by the flamboyant James V. Dexter who acquired a fortune through mining and other business ventures. The cabin was originally located on West 3rd Street. The Colorado Historical Society operates these two buildings as public museums. Both are listed on the National Register of Historic Places. They are open 10 a.m. to 4:30 p.m. Monday through Saturday and 1 to 4:30 p.m. Sunday from Memorial Day weekend through Labor Day weekend. An admission is charged.

THE NATIONAL MINING HALL OF FAME & MUSEUM, 120 W. 9th St., depicts the history of the American Mining Industry from coal to gold and geology. Tours are conducted hourly from 10:30 a.m. to 4:30 p.m. For special group arrangements, call (719) 486-1229. An admission is charged.

HERITAGE MUSEUM & GALLERY, 102 E. 9th St., provides a view of Victorian Leadville through exhibits and artifacts. Dioramas of the area's mining history are also exhibited. Self guided tours are available. It is open daily and evenings during the summer months. An admission is charged.

HERALD DEMOCRAT NEWSPAPER MUSEUM, 717 Harrison, is open for self-guided tours of Colorado's last operating daily hot metal (lead) newspaper. The *Herald Democrat* has been published in Leadville since 1879. The newspaper was formed by the merger of four other publications including *The Leadville Daily Herald*, owned by Horace Tabor. The museum includes a 1900 era hot metal typesetting shop, a newsroom, and a pressroom with a flat bed letterpress. Also featured are displays of historic issues of the newspaper and early Leadville photographs. It is open 8 a.m. to 5 p.m. Monday, Tuesday, Thursday, and Friday the year-round and Wednesday, Saturday, and Sunday, noon to 6 p.m., during the summer months. An admission is charged.

THE TABOR HOUSE, 116 E. 5th St., was the home of **Aug-**

223

The Healy House and the Dexter Cabin in Leadville are listed on the National Register of Historic Places.

The National Mining Hall of Fame and Museum in Leadville.

The Heritage Museum and Gallery is located in Leadville's former Carnegie Library building.

usta and H.A.W. (Horace) Tabor. It was built at 312 Harrison Avenue c. 1877 and moved to its present location in 1879. Tabor was Leadville's first postmaster and mayor. They lived in Leadville until January, 1879 when they moved to Denver. The Tabors occupied this house and entertained former President Ulysses S. and Mrs. Grant in July 1880. Horace sold the house to Melvin L. Clark on March 31, 1881. Mrs. Clark was Augusta Tabor's sister. Mrs. Clark lived here for many years and Augusta returned several times to visit her. Horace abandoned Augusta in January, 1881 and they were finally divorced on January 2, 1883. In the meantime, Horace's romance with **Elizabeth McCourt Doe**, or Baby Doe, flourished and became an open secret. They were married in an elaborate wedding ceremony in Washington, D.C. March 1, 1883. Augusta Tabor died in Pasadena, California, February 1, 1895, leaving a $1.5 million estate. Her body was returned to Denver for burial. A self-guided tour of the home includes a taped 15-minute narration of the Tabor history. Memorabilia is also displayed. The 1877 Victorian home is open 9 a.m. to 5 p.m. daily. An admission is charged.

TABOR OPERA HOUSE, 310 Harrison Ave., was opened November 21, 1879, through the financial assistance of Horace Tabor who also helped to finance a hotel, a hospital and a post office. Florenz Ziegfield's "Mamselle Napoleon," starring Anna Held, was hailed as one of the greatest productions here. Among the many famous performers and entertainers to appear here were The Great Houdini and John Philip Sousa's Marine Band. Self-guided tours of the stage, dressing rooms, original sets and scenery are available at the Opera House. A taped narration is included. The length of these tours is 20-30 minutes. The Opera House is open 9 a.m. to 5:30 p.m. daily except Saturday from May 30 to October 1. An admission is charged.

The MATCHLESS MINE, two miles east on 7th St., was purchased by Horace Tabor for $117,000 in September, 1870. The mine's output until the crash of '93 is estimated at $7 million. Tabor lost everything after the crash of '93 as all of his assets were tied up in silver investments. The financial crash of 1893 was created by repeal of the Sherman Act, changing the dollar standard from silver to gold to make silver almost a worthless metal. Horace believed the Matchless would become valuable again and his admonition to Baby Doe at the time of his death was to hang on to the Matchless. In the meantime he

Horace Tabor was a sponsor of the Leadville Opera House that bears his name.

This was the Leadville home of Horace and Augusta Tabor. Tabor was Leadville's first postmaster and mayor. He became one of the town's benefactors.

Leadville's House with the Eye was originally built as a residence for a Canadian businessman in 1879.

H.A.W. Tabor was forced to sell the Matchless Mine at Leadville shortly before his death, however, Baby Doe's mother purchased it. When Horace died, Baby Doe returned to Leadville. She worked the mine for more than 30 years. She died here in 1935 in utter poverty. Some of Tabor's great wealth came from this mine.

was forced to sell the Matchless Mine which was repurchased by Baby Doe's mother in 1899. Baby Doe moved to the mine that year and worked it for 36 years. She became a recluse and destitute woman. The body of Baby Doe Tabor, frozen in the shape of a cross, was found at the Matchless Mine on March 7, 1935. She was last seen alive on February 20, 1935 by Elmer Kutzleb, a delivery man. She is buried with Horace in Mt. Olivet Cemetery in Denver. The Baby Doe Tabor Museum is open 9 a.m. to 5 p.m. daily during the summer months. An admission is charged.

The HOUSE WITH THE EYE, 127 W. 4th St., was built by Canadian **Eugene Robitaille** in 1879 as his residence. The stain glass window at the roof line represents the all-seeing eye of God.

The Leadville National Fish Hatchery, eight miles southwest on Mt. Massive Star Rt., is listed on the National Register of Historic Places.

Other Lake County Historic Districts are located in Twin Lakes and include Interlaken Resort District, east of Twin Lakes off CO 82, and Twin Lakes District, on both sides of CO 82.

A brochure entitled "Travel the Routes of the Silver Kings," with three self-guided tours of the famous Leadville Mining District, is available at the Leadville Chamber of Commerce office.

Vail

Returning to I-70, it is 22 miles to **Vail** (pop. 484). The history of Vail, 100 miles west of Denver, is brief in time. The town was named for State Highway Superintendent **Charles Vail** who was on the scene before World War II pushing the opening of U.S. Highway 6 over the pass that also bears his name. After the war it was home to sheep herders and lettuce farmers.

Three of the men who had served with the 10th Mountain Division during the war—**Peter Seibert, Bob Parker, and Bill Brown**—had fallen in love with the area during their service years here. They returned after the war, formed Vail Associates and developed a ski resort. They built the first gondola in the U.S. from the Vail Village area that helped to draw early attention to the area. The Town of Vail was incorporated in 1966. Interest continued to grow in the area as its reputation spread among ski enthusiasts. The success of World Cup Races

Exhibits in the Colorado Ski Museum and Ski Hall of Fame in Vail.

staged as part of the American Ski Classic in 1983, '84, and '85 prompted the FIS to name Vail the site of the World Alpine Ski Championships in 1989.

The COLORADO SKI MUSEUM/SKI HALL OF FAME, at the corner of Vail Rd. and East Meadow Dr., was founded in Vail in 1976 and is a public, non-profit, historical organization dedicated to preserving and interpreting Colorado's rich skiing heritage. The museum presents 120 years of Colorado's skiing heritage through photographs, artifacts, equipment and clothing. It features historical films, the latest ski videos and exhibits which include Aspen 1950-Vail/Beaver Creek 1989: "World Alpine Ski Championships," Skiing in War: "10th Mountain Division, Evolution of Ski Equipment and the role of the U.S. Forest Service." On display is a collection of black and white photos provided by Ski Magazine of the 10th Mountain Division: "Training, Combat and Post-War recreation." The museum is open 10 a.m. to 6 p.m. Tuesday through Sunday. It is open by appointment only during May and October. An admission is charged. The museum is available for receptions and private parties, for more information, call (303) 476-1876.

Eagle

Vail is one of several communities on I-70 located in Eagle County. The county seat is **Eagle** (pop. 950). There are several sites in the county listed on the National Register of Historic Places. These include the Archaeological Site, in the Basalt area; the waterwheel, southeast of McCoy at the Colorado River; the Red Cliff bridge on US 24, at Red Cliff; the Woods Lake Resort, 11 miles north of Thomasville at Woods Lake; and the state bridge over CO 131.

Aspen

Aspen (pop. 2,404), county seat of Pitkin County, is south of I-70 on CO 82, 172 miles from Denver.

Aspen began as a mining camp called **Ute** in 1879. **B. Clark Wheeler** arrived and platted the town in 1880 naming it Aspen. The new arrivals here found rich silver veins in the surrounding mountains. **Jerome B. Wheeler** is credited with bringing prosperity to Aspen in 1884-85 with the development of the mining interests. He opened a bank and purchased a smelter to provide a local market for silver ore. In 1885, Aspen boasted electric lights. By 1887 two railroads were servicing the community and during the first month of rail operations more than a million dollars of ore was shipped out of the town.

In 1889 a single silver nugget weighing 1700 pounds was removed from the Mollie Gibson Mine. By 1892 one sixth of all silver mined in the United States came from the Aspen area. By the next year the town reached its peak population of 12,000. It boasted four schools, four newspapers (two of which were dailies), eight churches, three banks, a hospital, nine hotels, five drug stores, six bakeries, nine restaurants, 31 saloons, and its own brewery.

Aspen's beginnings as a ski resort began in 1936 when the Highland-Bavarian Corp. was formed and built a lodge at the junction of Castle Creek and the Conundrum Valley. The following year a ski trail (Roche Run) was laid out on Aspen Mountain. This same year the Roaring Fork Winter Sports Club (today the Aspen Ski Club) was founded.

In 1941, the lodge and Ashcroft area were offered to the U.S. Army for ski troop training. The 10th Mountain Division was trained here during the war. **Camp Hale**, near Leadville, served as the division's headquarters.

In 1946, the Aspen Skiing Corporation was founded and began operation of Aspen's first single and the world's longest chair lift. Aspen hosted the FIS World Alpine Championships in 1950 to give the community international recognition and status.

Walter Paepcke, one of the town's benefactors after World War II, organized the **Goethe Bicentennial Convocation** in Aspen. **Dr. Albert Schweitzer** (1875-1965), recipient of the 1952 Nobel Peace Prize, delivered the dedicatory address here in his only visit to the U.S.

WHEELER-STALLARD HOUSE MUSEUM, 620 W. Bleeker St., began as the residence for Jerome B. Wheeler in 1888. He opened the Hotel Jerome and Wheeler Opera House, each costing $80,000, in 1889. The museum is open for tours from 1 to 4 p.m. June through September. An admission is charged.

Listed on the National Register of Historic Places in Aspen are the Armory Hall/Fraternal Hall, 130 S. Galena St; Aspen Community Church, 200 N. Aspen St.; Hotel Jerome, 330 E. Main St.; Hyman-Brand Building, 203 S. Galena St.; Pitkin County Courthouse, 506 E. Main St.; Wheeler Opera House,

330 E. Hyman Ave.; and the Wheeler-Stallard House, 620 W. Bleeker St. Listed on the National Register (Multiple Resource Area) are the Bowles-Cooley House, 201 W. Francis St.; Matthew Callahan Log Cabin, 205 S. 3rd St.; Collins Block, Aspen Lumber & Supply, 204 S. Mill St.; the Dixon Markle House, 135 E. Cooper Ave.; the D. E. Franz House, 333 W. Bleeker St.; the Samuel L. Hallett House, 432 W. Francis St.; the Thomas Hynes House, 303 E. Main St.; La Fave Block, 405 S. Hunter St.; New Brick/The Brick Saloon/Red Onion, 420 E. Cooper Ave.; the Newberry House/Judge Shaw House, 206 Lake Ave.; the Pioneer Park/Henry Webber House, 442 W. Bleeker; Reide's City Bakery, 413 E. Hyman Ave.; the Shilling-Lamb House, 525 N. 2nd St.; the Smith Elisha House, 320 W. Main St.; the Davis Waite House, 234 W. Francis St.; and Smuggler Mine, on Smuggler Mountain. The Maroon Creek Bridge, off CO 82, and the Sheely Bridge, in Mill Street Park, are listed on the National Register (Theme Resources).

Thirteen miles up Castle Creek is the restored ghost town of **Ashcroft**. It is listed on the National Register of Historic Places. During the silver boom it was the home of 5,000 people and boasted a hotel and several saloons.

Independence, located near the summit of Independence Pass, reached its peak population of over 1,000 as a gold mining town in 1882. It was the main stop for three stagecoach lines operating between Leadville and Aspen. Independence and Independence Mill Site, on CO 82 in the White River National Forest, are listed on the National Register of Historic Places.

Glenwood Springs

It is 41 miles from Aspen to **Glenwood Springs** via CO 82.

Glenwood Springs (pop. 4,106), county seat of Garfield County, is 169 miles west of Denver via I-70.

Capt. Richard Sopris discovered the Yampa Hot Springs on July 23, 1860. The date and party names were carved on a cottonwood tree on the island of the Grand River where the Hot Springs Lodge stands today. The first settler was James Landis who arrived in the Roaring Fork Valley in 1879 to cut hay for Leadville horses and mules. A mining camp called Defiance was begun in 1880 and later became Grand Springs. Although the Ute Indians used the hot springs for its "miraculous healing powers" it was not until 1882 that white men dreamed of turning the springs into a health spa. One of these men was Isaac

Cooper. It was his wife, Sarah, who, in 1885, renamed the town Glenwood Springs for Glenwood, Iowa, her hometown. On August 25, 1885, Glenwood Springs was platted and incorporated. The original county seat for Garfield County, established February 10, 1883, was Carbondale but due to heavy snow storms at that high level the county records were brought to **Defiance** or **Grand Springs**. This was considered the county seat until formally declared so in 1885. The Denver and Rio Grande and Colorado Midland Railroads arrived in 1887 and it was on November 8 that year that Dr. John "Doc" Holliday, who became famous for his part in the gunfight at the O.K. Corral in Tombstone, Arizona, in 1881, died of tuberculosis in the Glenwood Hotel.

Glenwood Springs developed rapidly due to the rich coal veins in the surrounding mountains. Eastern and European investors developed the hot springs pool/spa and the Hotel Colorado, making the town an ideal resort site for wealthy Victorians from all over the world.

The Hotel Colorado, 526 Pine and 6th Sts., listed on the National Register of Historic Places, was officially opened June 10, 1893. The hotel originally cost $850,000 and was modeled after Villa de Medici in Italy. Many famous persons have been guests in the hotel. **President Theodore Roosevelt** arrived April 15, 1905, to begin a bear hunt on the Flat Tops. The hotel served as the "Little White House of the United States" until Roosevelt ended his hunt May 5th. **William Howard Taft** appeared here for an address off the Presidential Balcony during his presidency. Other famous visitors to Glenwood Springs include **Film Star Tom Mix, Baby Doe Tabor, Diamond Jim Brady, Drs. William and Charles Mayo, "Unsinkable Molly Brown,"** and **Author Clarence Day**. Among some of the infamous visitors have been **Legs Diamond** and **Al Capone** who were said to have entered through a special screened entrance so they could go unnoticed.

During his stay at the Hotel Colorado, President Roosevelt returned empty-handed from a hard day's hunt and was somewhat depressed. It is said that in order to lift his spirits, the maids stitched together a small bear out of scraps of cloth. A reporter of the day found this an amusing story and coined the phrase, "Teddy Bear." A toymaker nabbed onto the caption and

The Colorado Hotel in Glenwood Springs served as a headquarters for President Teddy Roosevelt during a bear hunt in the area in 1905. The hotel is listed on the National Register of Historic Places.

The Frontier Historical Society Museum in Glenwood Springs.

began making Teddy Bears.

The hotel was used as a Naval Hospital during World War II. The Navy modernized the plumbing and heating plant and re-wired the entire building. Graffiti still can been seen and is pre-served in the area of the Navy's old brig. The Navy closed their hospital operation February 28, 1946.

"Diamond Jack" Alterie, a Chicago gangster, operated the Sweetwater Lake Resort near Glenwood Springs in the 1920s and '30s. The resort offered a mountain getaway for underworld figures including the notorious Al "Scarface" Capone.

Doc Holliday was only 35 years old when he died in the Glen-wood Springs Hotel, the site of today's Bullock's Department Store. A frontier dentist, Holliday was a gambler, quick with his pistols and somewhat reckless. He was born in Georgia in 1852 and attended dental school in Baltimore. He was thought to be a gentleman in his early years. A victim of "consumption," he headed West where he gained his reputation as a gunfighter. He joined with Wyatt, Virgil, and Morgan Earp in the gunfight at the O.K. Corral with the Clanton gang. The brief but deadly shootout in Tombstone, Arizona, on October 26, 1881, drew a mixed reaction from the public. The participants literally hung up their guns after this episode. Holliday's grave is in Linwood Cemetery. He was originally buried in the basement of a house at 8th and Palmer because there was a fear his body may be spirited away by a midwest gang. It was several years later be-fore the body was moved to Linwood Cemetery. The cemetery can be reached from Bennett and E. 13th Sts. and overlooks the town.

Harvey "Kid Curry" Logan and two other outlaws held up an afternoon train near **Parachute**, 40 miles west, on June 7, 1904. Within a few hours a posse was closing in and by the next afternoon cornered the trio in a small canyon near Glenwood Springs. In the first exchange of shots Logan was wounded and crawled behind a rock for protection. His accomplices were able to escape when Logan shot himself in the head. Logan had been a member of Butch Cassidy's Hole-in-the-Wall gang and be-came one of the most wanted men in the country by 1901.

Other local buildings listed on the National Register of His-toric Places include Starr Manor, 901 Palmer Ave., and the Ed-ward T. Taylor House, 903 Bennett Ave. The South Canon Bridge, on RD 134, is listed on the National Register.

FRONTIER HISTORICAL MUSEUM, 1001 Colorado Ave., is housed in a home built in 1905 for **Dr. and Mrs. Marshall Dean**. The museum depicts life styles of an earlier era with primary emphasis on education. One of the interesting rooms is the Tabor Room with its carved walnut bed and dresser once belonging to H.A.W. and Baby Doe Tabor of Leadville. The crazy quilt made of silk, satin, and velvet swatches from Baby Doe's luxurious wardrobe is also on display. The museum's summer hours are 1 to 4 p.m. Monday through Saturday. The winter hours are 1 to 4 p.m. Thursday through Saturday. An admission is charged.

Carbondale—Redstone—Marble

South of Glenwood Springs on CO 133 are the towns of **Carbondale** (pop. 726), **Redstone** (uninc.), and **Marble** (pop. 30).

Carbondale was known as **Red Creek** and the site of the Yule brothers cattle camp in 1881 when William M. Dinkel and James Zimmerman arrived in the late summer. By the late 1880s the town of Carbondale had emerged with Dinkel one of the most prominent citizens. The town was incorporated January 31, 1888. The Roaring Fork Valley has been noted for its potatoes.

The Satank Bridge, on RD 106, is listed on the National Register (Theme Resource).

MOUNT SOPRIS HISTORICAL MUSEUM is located in the old two-cell jail at 76 S. 4th St. Archaeological artifacts and early legal and business documents are on display. Also featured are exhibits relating to local history. The museum is open by request. For information contact the library.

The **Redstone** historic community is 17 miles south of Carbondale.

There are three structures in this area listed on the National Register of Historic Places. These include the Osgood Kuhnhausen House, 0642 Redstone Blvd.; Redstone Inn, 0082 Redstone Blvd.; and Osgood Castle/Cleveholm, in the Redstone area. The Redstone Historic District covers a strip along the Crystal River from Hawk Creek to 226 Redstone Blvd.

On the highway, just outside Redstone, are the **Redstone Coke Ovens**. These "beehive" coke ovens were constructed in the late 1890s to carbonize, or "coke," the coal mines and coal basin for Colorado Fuel & Iron (CF&I). A narrow gauge railroad approximately 12 miles long, removed in 1941, brought the coal down grades exceeding four percent from mines to Redstone.

The historic coke ovens at Redstone are marked by this monument on the highway.

The Marble Museum is housed in this old schoolhouse building.

The coke then was shipped to Pueblo. Total coal production here was 1.1 million tons.

South of Redstone, off CO 133, is **Marble** and the MARBLE HISTORICAL MUSEUM, 412 W. Main St. This local museum is open 2 to 4 p.m. daily from May to Labor Day.

Four miles above Marble is **Marble Quarry** that supplied the marble for the Tomb of the Unknown Soldier and the Lincoln Memorial in our nation's capital.

New Castle

Back to Glenwood Springs and I-70 it is about a dozen miles west to **New Castle** (pop. 563) on US 6.

At Exit 105, off I-70, is a historical marker commemorating the lives of nearly 100 coal miners who lost their lives in the explosions in the Allen & Wheeler coal veins across the Colorado River. The "scar" can still be seen on the side of the coal ridge looking south. In this area 49 miners were killed in an explosion February 18, 1896. On December 16, 1913, 37 miners were killed and on November 4, 1918, another three lives were lost in the mines.

NEW CASTLE HISTORICAL MUSEUM, 116 N. 4th St., concentrates on local and regional history. It is open 1 to 4 p.m. Thursday through Saturday. Admission is free.

Silt

Less than 10 miles west on US 6 paralleling I-70 is **Silt** (pop. 923). Silt, named for the light, fine soil on which it is built, was originally called **Ferguson**. The area was developed by farmers who raised vegetables for the miners in Aspen, Carbondale, and Leadville beginning in 1879. The railroad reached the town in 1889 and that same year, 5,000 cattle were shipped from Silt on the new Colorado Midland Railroad.

President Teddy Roosevelt visited in 1905 when he hunted bear on Divide Creek. He also visited the Blue Goose School on that trip.

SILT HISTORICAL PARK, 707 Orchard Ave., is a local museum developed by the Silt Historical Society to preserve the history of the area by collecting, for exhibit, several buildings: a furnished 1914 handhewn log home, a 1914 school house with memorabilia, an 1895 log cabin furnished as a country store, and a 1932 log cabin. Old railroad cars on tracks are on display at the Park. Also exhibited are early pioneer tools and machinery, including a complete blacksmith and wheelwright shop.

The New Castle Historical Museum.

This monument just east of New Castle describes the hillside once heavily mined for coal. Several accidents occurred here causing the death of many miners.

The Sallee Home was built of hand-hewn logs by Leander (Bud) Sallee and his family on Divide Creek in the Silt area in 1914. Today it is located in the Silt Historical Park.

The Austin School, in the southwest corner of the Silt Historical Park, is furnished as a school in the early 1900s, with many items from the Silt schools including the pictures.

The Rifle Creek Museum.

Other collections include Indian artifacts and rubbings of picture writing, Silt High School graduation photos, needlework, a barbed wire exhibit, and more. It is open 1 to 4 p.m. Thursday through Sunday and anytime by appointment. Admission is free.

Rifle

It is seven miles west of Silt to **Rifle** (pop. 3,215), incorporated in 1905. There are several stories on how the town and valley got the name of Rifle.

The geologist, **Ferdinand Vandiveer Hayden**, who explored much of the West, noted in his 1876 geological report for this area that rushing water passing from the creek here poured through a gap making a roaring sound heard for miles. He was said to have labeled the area here "Rifle Valley." Another story claims the area gained its name when one of the soldiers in a company laying out mileposts for a road between the Colorado and White Rivers left his rifle on the banks of the river that empties into the Colorado. When he returned to retrieve the rifle the stream was named Rifle Creek. Still another story claims that Hayden's survey party found a rusty rifle leaning against a tree on the banks of the creek and decided to call it

Rifle Creek. The town was named from the creek which flows through it.

In 1882 **Abram Maxfield** arrived and staked out a claim on a site in today's Rifle. He and his son, Clinton, built the first log cabin here. After the rest of his family moved from Battle Mountain in 1883, several other families arrived and settled here. One of the first successful enterprises in Rifle was that of horse trading. Wild mustangs were rounded up from the Road Plateau in the fall and taken to market. The need for horses became important during the Spanish-American War and World War I. Coal became an important resource and later vanadium was mined. Tailings from vanadium mines were rich in deposits of uranium and both are mined in the area today.

The Havemeyer-Willcox Canal Pumphouse, in the Rifle area, is listed on the National Register of Historic Places. The Rifle Post Office, Railroad Ave. and 4th St., and the Rifle Bridge, one mile south of Rifle off the I-70 approach, are listed on the National Register (Theme Resource). Elsewhere in Garfield County, Battlement Mesa Schoolhouse, 7201 - 300 Rd., is listed on the National Register of Historic Places.

RIFLE CREEK MUSEUM, 337 East Ave., features local history including the mining aspects of the area. It is open 10 a.m. to 4 p.m. weekdays. An admission is charged.

Grand Junction

Grand Junction (pop. 76,000), county seat of Mesa County, is 60 miles west of Rifle. Grand Junction, founded in 1881, received its name from its location at the junction of the Gunnison and Grand Rivers. The name of the Grand River was changed to the Colorado River in 1921. More than 30 dinosaur species, including the world's largest and smallest adult dinosaurs, have been discovered in Mesa County.

George Crawford, a Kansan, is credited with the founding of Grand Junction. The arrival of the Denver & Rio Grande Railroad in November, 1882 aided the growth of the community and area almost immediately. Construction of extensive canal and ditch systems helped agriculture grow as an area industry. By the early 1900s the Grand Valley was known as one of the best fruit and sugar beet growing regions in Colorado.

Grand Junction is an industrial trading center for western Colorado and eastern Utah. The area is rich in coal, livestock,

244

oil, peaches, and vegetables. **Mesa College** was founded here in 1921.

The community made national headlines in the 1950s during the uranium boom. The radioactive material used in the first atomic bombs was mined and processed in the region. After the war the U.S. government offered an attractive subsidy for more uranium. Thousands of prospectors and their families flocked to the deserts and canyons of Western Colorado and Eastern Utah, hoping to strike it rich. While a few did locate some promising uranium lodes, most didn't. By the late 1950s the government had enough uranium on hand, and the subsidies were lowered. The prospectors and miners eventually drifted away, causing an economic downturn in many towns, including Grand Junction.

The past was repeated in the late 1970s and early 1980s when major U.S. oil companies announced plans to process oil-bearing rock called oil shale. Construction began on large plants that would extract oil from the rock found in the Bookcliffs northeast of Grand Junction. A major boom developed but it lasted only a few years as the price of imported oil continued to drop.

Colorado National Monument is located five miles west of Grand Junction.

There are 17 structures listed on the National Register of Historic Places in the four-and-a-half blocks that make up Grand Junction's North Seventh Street Historic Residential District. Thirty five structures are included in the District and with the 17 listed on the NRHP, 11 others are classified as "contributing buildings" and the remaining seven buildings are categorized as "intrusions." A self-guided tour begins at the "Doc" Shores house, 327 N. 7th St., and proceeds north to Hill Ave. Cross N. 7th St. at Hill, and complete the tour by walking south to R-5 school. None of the buildings in the District are open to the public. A guidebook to the North Seventh Street Historic Residential District is available through the Grand Junction Visitors and Convention Bureau.

Grand Junction High School graduate **Dalton Trumbo**, author of the novel "Eclipse," was one of several personalities questioned by the House Committee on Un-American Activities and as a result was sentenced to prison for a year and blacklisted by the film industry. Trumbo was a screenwriter and was

The Museum of Western Colorado is housed in this building at 4th and Ute in Grand Junction.

involved in the films "Hawaii," "Exodus," and "Papillon."

Dr. Geno Saccomanno, a Grand Junction pathologist, developed the technique used world-wide to diagnose lung cancer.

Jim Petty of Grand Junction made it into the Guinness Book of World Records when he rode his 40 foot tall unicycle in 1976.

Dr. E. F. Eldridge, who practiced medicine in Grand Junction between 1890 and 1915, wrote the words to the song, "My Rocky Mountain Home."

Between 1896 and the 1920s, Grand Junction hosted the Chicago Symphony, New York Philharmonic Orchestra, Ballet Russe, and famed bandmaster John Philip Sousa.

MUSEUM OF WESTERN COLORADO, 248 S. 4th St., is located in the former Whitman School building and features Western Colorado history and archaeology. This building includes a mirrored decadal "Timeline," a local firearms displays, the world's tallest unicycle, and the Placerville Post Office. It is open 10 a.m. to 4:45 p.m. Tuesday through Saturday. Donations are accepted.

DINOSAUR VALLEY, 4th St. and Ute Ave., is a permanent

This photo of Ouray, chief of the Uncompahgre Utes, and his wife, Chipeta, c. 1880 is displayed in the Museum of Western Colorado in Grand Junction.

exhibit of Dinamation creatures. Noteworthy are specimens from Western Colorado's Jurassic layers, a working paleontological laboratory and six half-size animated dinosaurs, scientifically exact. These replicas move, roar and howl. Visitors may also observe the operation of the paleontological laboratory where scientists are restoring and preserving fossils of other huge creatures found in nearby quarries. Dinosaur Valley is operated by the Museum of Western Colorado. It is open 10 a.m. to 4:30 p.m. Tuesday through Saturday, October to Memorial Day; 9 a.m. to 5 p.m. Sunday through Tuesday and 9 a.m. to 7 p.m. Wednesday through Saturday, Memorial Day through September 20. An admission is charged.

Other Museum of Western Colorado exhibit sites include:

RIGGS HILL, at the intersection of Meadow Ways and

Shown are members of a local school group, thousands of which tour the Museum of Western Colorado's Dinosaur Valley in Grand Junction each year. The computerized dinosaur is a Corythosaurus.

Harley Armstrong, Museum of Western Colorado paleontologist, leads a tour of Dinosaur Hill interpretive trail. Dinosaur Hill is one of four outdoor sites jointly managed by the Museum of Western Colorado. It is co-managed by the Bureau of Land Management and the City of Fruita.

Kids of all ages enjoy the displays at the Museum of Western Colorado's Dinosaur Valley Exhibit in Grand Junction. This unique museum, entirely devoted to regional paleontology, features half-size animated dinosaurs furnished by Dinamation International Corp. of San Juan Capistrano, Calif., and a working paleontology laboratory.

South Broadway (CO 340 west of Grand Junction), was the site of the 1900 discovery of the first known Brachiosaurus altithorax, at the time considered the world's largest dinosaur. The quarry site was excavated under the direction of **Elmer S. Riggs**, Assistant Curator of Paleontology at the Field Museum of Natural History in Chicago.

DINOSAUR HILL, one and a half miles south of Fruita on CO 340, was the site of Elmer Riggs' excavations in 1901 and where he discovered the rear two-thirds of an Apatosaurus (Brontosaurus) excelsus. The Fruita Apatosaurus is a major exhibit in Chicago's Field Musuem. The quarry area became known as Dinosaur Hill. It takes approximately 45 minutes to walk the mile long trail here.

CROSS ORCHARDS LIVING HISTORY FARM, 3073 F (Patterson) Rd., is an outdoor museum, a division of the Museum of Western Colorado. Listed on the National Register of

Among the delights awaiting visitors at the Cross Orchards Living History Farms are freshly baked cookies hot out of the oven, baked by volunteers such as Phyllis George. Open seasonally, May-October, the Farm recreates with authentically garbed volunteers the era in which the National Register Site was one of the largest fruit producing operations in Western Colorado, 1909-23.

251

The Cyrus "Doc" Shores house at 327 N. 7th Street in Grand Junction is listed on the National Register of Historic Places.

Historic Places, Cross Orchards Living History Farm features daily "living history" demonstrations, as well as many seasonal events such as the "Spring Day on the Farm" held in May, the Apple Harvest Festival on the first Saturday in October, and Cross Orchards Country Christmas held during the first week in December. The museum complex interprets the social and agricultural heritage of Western Colorado. It is open 10 a.m. to 4 p.m. Wednesday through Saturday from mid-May to November 1st and selected days in conjunction with special events. An admission is charged.

The U.S. Post Office/Wayne N. Aspinall Federal Building/U.S. Courthouse, 400 Rood Ave., is listed on the Na-

The Diplodocus-like femur mold on Dinosaur Hill just outside of Fruita is clearly seen on this large rock near the parking area. This discovery of the Apatosaurus skeleton was made in 1901 by Paleontologist Elmer S. Riggs with the Chicago Field Museum at the turn of the century.

tional Register of Historic Places. The Fifth Street Bridge, on US 50, and Black Bridge, on 25.30 Rd. over the Gunnison River, are also both listed on the National Register (Theme Resource).

There are two structures listed on the National Register of Historic Places in nearby **Clifton**. These are the Clifton Community Center and Church, F and Main Sts., and the Kettle-Jens House, 498 32nd Rd.

East of Grand Junction, in **Molina**, Convicts' Bread Oven, W. of Molina on CO 65, is listed on the National Register of Historic Places.

Fruita

Fruita (pop. 3,492) is 11 miles west of Grand Junction. This area was opened to settlers through a treaty with the Indians in 1881. Apples and other fruit trees were planted here by the early settlers and these orchards produced World's Fair prizes, thus the city was named Fruita (a Spanish word for "fruit"). The town was platted and incorporated in 1884. The coddling moth infestation of 1916 destroyed most of the orchards at that time.

Michael Perry Photo, Museum of Western Colorado
The plaque commemorates the excavation of an Apatosaurus by the Field Museum of Natural History in 1901. The plaque was placed by Elmer S. Riggs, Al Look, and the Grand Junction Chamber of Commerce in the late 1930s. The plaque is located on the interpretive trail on Dinosaur Hill.

Fruita lies at the western edge of Mesa County's Grand Valley, a valley rich in prehistoric treasures. Remains of the world's largest and smallest dinosaurs have come from Mesa County. Two dinosaurs actually bear Fruita's name as part of their own scientific names.

Dinosaur Hill, site of a dinosaur dig-in-progress, lies just a mile south of Fruita. Less than two miles southwest is the **Fruita Paleontological Area**, where scientists have recovered skeletons of early mammals and of extinct lizards which were contemporaries of the more famous giant dinosaurs. Among the

"The White House" at 337 N. 7th Street in Grand Junction is another Grand Junction home listed on the National Register of Historic Places.

finds here have been the partial skull of a sphenodontid, a small extinct lizard related to an existing species in New Zealand. The sphenodontid has a third eye atop its skull, which scientists theorize was used to view the skies for flying predators. Also found here was a small crocodilian abundant during the age of the dinosaur. It was named Fruitachampsa callisoni, signifying the location and its discoverer, **Dr. George Callison** of California State University at Long Beach.

Fruita Bridge, on RD 17.50 over the Colorado River, is listed on the National Register (Theme Resource).

It is 20 miles west on I-70 to the Utah state line.

Colorado Notes

STONE ARTIFACTS BAFFLE SCIENTISTS

An unknown people, who remain a tantalizing mystery to scientists, roamed the eastern part of Colorado and some believe as far back as 20,000 years. Spearheads of these early hunters have been found with bones of prehistoric buffalo that date back more than 10,000 years. Two types of stone artifacts traced back to this vanished race have been found in Colorado. The Folsom point, ranging from one and a half to four and a half inches long with a long wide groove along both sides from the base of the point, and the Yuma point, longer and narrower than the Folsom point and without the grooves, have been found in abundance in eastern Colorado. The Folsom point was first found in Folsom, N.M.; the Yuma point in Yuma County in the northeastern Colorado.

HELEN HUNT JACKSON SUPPORTED INDIAN CAUSES

Helen Hunt Jackson, who spent many years in Colorado Springs, became best known for her efforts to achieve justice for the American Indians. In "A Century of Dishonor," written in 1881, she documented the government's mismanagement of Indian affairs. She presented a copy of her book to every member of Congress. Her best known work was her novel "Ramona," published in 1884, and it dramatized the mistreatment of the Indians. Probably one of her best known poems is "Cheyenne Mountain." She was born in Massachusetts.

Chapter 8

Across Colorado on US 40

US 40 crosses Colorado beginning at Cheyenne Wells just across the Kansas state line in the east to Brown's Park Hole at the Utah state line in the west. Nathan Meeker and several civilian employees at the Ute Agency in the northwest corner of Colorado were massacred in 1879 and their story is told, along with others, in this chapter.

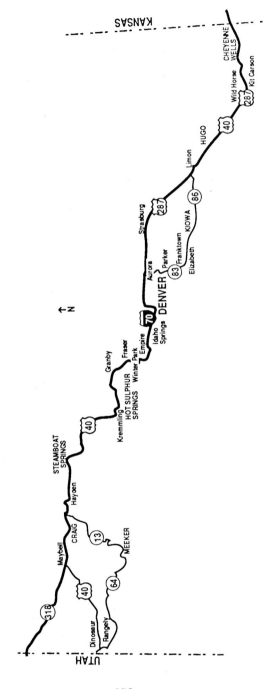

Chapter 8
Across Colorado on US 40

US 40 covers 102 miles from the Kansas state line to Limon. It runs together with I-70 from Limon to the turnoff to Empire, 42 miles west of Denver. From here the route runs northwest through Hot Sulphur Springs, Kremmling, Steamboat Springs, Craig and on to the Utah state line.

Cheyenne Wells

Cheyenne Wells (pop. 950), county seat of Cheyenne County, is 16 miles west of the Kansas state line. The Cheyenne County Courthouse in Cheyenne Wells was built in 1908 at a cost of $25,890. It is typical of the plains architecture at the turn-of the-century.

THE CHEYENNE COUNTY MUSEUM is housed in the old Cheyenne County jail built in 1892. The old jail is listed on the National Register of Historic Places. It contains the original cellblock as well as hundreds of items relating to the county's early history. It is open 2 to 5 p.m. Sunday, Memorial Day through Labor Day. An admission is charged.

Seven and a half miles west of Cheyenne Wells, on the north side of US 40, is a monument commemorating the **Smoky Hill Trail** and the **Old Cattle Trail**. Both ran just north of US 40 to Denver. The Smoky Hill Trail split just east of Kit Carson and also ran parallel on the south side of US 40 to Hugo and then west. Historical monuments have been erected in the area paying tribute to the pioneers, gold seekers and soldiers who traveled these trails. One of these monuments honors **Billy Comstock**, an early scout, who was killed by the Indians. Legend claims he wasn't scalped by the Indians in tribute to his courage.

Kit Carson

It is 25 miles west of Cheyenne Wells to **Kit Carson** (pop. 278). The town grew up two and a half miles southeast of the site of a trading post established by the famed frontiersman, **Christopher "Kit" Carson**, in 1838. It was a flourishing town even before it became a terminus of the Kansas-Pacific Railroad in 1870. A number of historical incidents occurred here.

On May 14, 1870, 46 railroad workers were killed by Indians.

Cheyenne County Jail Museum in Cheyenne Wells.

The Lincoln County Museum in Hugo.

This monument seven and a half miles east of Cheyenne Wells marks
the route of the famous Smoky Hill Trail emigrant and stage road from
Westport, Missouri, to Denver via Fort Riley, Fort Hayes and Fort
Wallace. It also was the route of Butterfield's Overland Despatch
launched in 1865. The Union Pacific Railroad replaced the Smoky Hill
Trail in 1870.

Kit Carson Museum in Kit Carson is dedicated to the famous fron-
tiersman.

Three days later, the Indians tore down a railroad water tower east of town. Three companies of cavalry under **Lt. Col. George Custer**, commanding the 7th U.S. Cavalry, arrived in the area to keep the peace. With the growing Indian problems additional troops were sent to this area. The Army had 100 troops stationed here by 1872.

Kit Carson became an important shipping point for cattle in the early 1870s. It was a boisterous town with saloons, gambling and dance halls drawing patrons from the cattle business. Almost every adult male packed a pistol or two. On July 30, 1870 **Milton H. Straight** was hanged by a lynch mob. His "crime" remains a mystery. Justice was swift if not always accurate.

On December 7, 1871, Kit Carson was surrounded by thousands of buffalo. The **Grand Duke Alexis of Russia** arrived in Kit Carson on January 20, 1872 to hunt buffalo. Among the Army brass accompanying the Duke were Custer and **Gen. Phil Sheridan**. In the hunt here Alexis killed five buffalo, Custer, three, and Sheridan, two.

The first community of Kit Carson was burned by the Indians. Later, the townspeople burned the town because of a rat infestation.

KIT CARSON MUSEUM, located in a park on the north side of US 287, focuses on the area's history. Among the exhibits is a pistol said to have been owned by Kit Carson. It is open from 9 a.m. to 5 p.m. Monday through Sunday, Memorial Day through Labor Day. An admission is charged.

Thirteen miles west is the unincorporated town of **Wild Horse**.

Hugo

Hugo (pop. 776), county seat of Lincoln County, is 48 miles west of Kit Carson.

LINCOLN COUNTY MUSEUM, 617 3rd Ave., Hugo, is housed in an old family residence. It has been restored with period furniture and features an exhibit of clothing dating back to the 1800s. It is open only by appointment. Admission is free.

It is 13 miles from Hugo to Limon and 86 miles from Limon to Denver (See Chapter 2).

An alternative route to Denver is the 83 mile trip on CO 86 and CO 83. These are two-lane highways.

Kiowa—Elizabeth—Franktown—Parker

West of Limon, Exit 352 off I-70 on CO 86, it is 38 miles to

ERECTED BY
PIONEER WOMEN OF COLORADO
1920 A. D.
IN MEMORY OF PIONEERS
MASSACRED BY INDIANS
1864 A. D.
HUNGATE
NATHAN W. AND ELLEN
AND CHILDREN
LAURA V.
FLORENCE V.

1868 A. D.
DIETEMANN
HENRIETTA
AND SON
JOHN

LOUIS ALAMA

JOSEPH BLEDSOE

This historical marker on the front lawn of the Elbert County court-house in Kiowa commemorates those killed by Indians in 1864 and 1868. Four members of the Hungate family were killed in 1864. Henrietta Dietemann and her son, John, and two other men were killed by Indians in 1868.

264

This statue in Casey Jones Park in Elizabeth is dedicated to the pioneer families who settled western Elbert County in the late 1880s.

Kiowa (pop. 206), county seat of Elbert County. A monument on the front lawn of the courthouse in Kiowa commemorates the several persons killed by Indians in this area. In 1864, **Nathaniel W. Hungate**, his wife, Ellen, and their two daughters, Laura and Florence, were killed by Indians. The victims in 1868 were **Henrietta Dietemann**, her son John, and **Louis Alama** and **Joseph Bledsoe**.

South of Kiowa on a county road is unincorporated **Elbert**, home of St. Mark's Presbyterian Church. This church was founded in the 1880s and is a National Historic Landmark.

Seven miles west of Kiowa on CO 86 is **Elizabeth** (pop. 789). A monument in Casey Jones Park, on the eastern edge of town, is dedicated to the pioneer families that settled western Elbert County in the late 1880s. It was donated by the artist Walter Way and the Elizabeth Park Recreation District.

Nine miles further west is **Franktown**. A monument on CO 83, just south of the intersection of CO 86, provides a brief history of the town. Franktown was named for **J. Frank Gardner**, a pioneer who settled here in 1859. First known as "California Ranch" it was a way station on the stage line between Denver and Santa Fe. In a stockade built here neighbors found refuge from the Indians in 1864. Franktown became the first county seat of Douglas County in 1861.

Nine miles north of Franktown on CO 83 is **Parker**. The 20-Mile House monument is located on the north side of Mainstreet 0.1 miles east of the intersection of Mainstreet and Parker Rd. (CO 83). The 20 Mile House (20 miles from Denver) stood a quarter of a mile west of this site. This was the first house built in Parker in 1864 on the Smoky Hill Trail, the emigrant road that was dotted with unmarked graves of pioneers. Parker was the junction of the Smoky Hill & Santa Fe Stage Lines and a refuge for early settlers against Indian attacks. Hostelry was established here and was operated at various times by **Nelson Doud** and **James S. Parker**, for whom the town of Parker is named.

From Denver it is 42 miles to the turnoff to Empire and from here US 40 becomes the northern route west to Utah.

Winter Park

US 40 is routed over 11,315 foot Berthoud Pass before arriving at **Winter Park** (pop. 480). Just north of Winter Park on the east side of the road is the white two-story house that was

This monument just outside of Franktown briefly relates the early days of this town named in honor of J. Frank Gardner, one of the earliest settlers.

The 20-Mile House was located just west of this monument. This one-time stage stop on the Smoky Hill Trail is in Parker.

the original home of the **William Zane Cozens family**, dating back to 1874. Cozens homesteaded here in 1872 and ran a stage coach stop, hotel and blacksmith shop. In 1876, Cozens was appointed postmaster of Fraser located at the ranch. Today the Cozens Ranch belongs to the Grand County Historical Society and is being developed into a museum. It is listed on the National Register of Historic Places.

Just south of Winter Park is the entrance to the **Corona Pass, or Moffat Road**, the so-called "hill route," which was the original roadbed of the Denver and Northwestern Railway Company. Construction on the railroad from Denver to Hot Sulphur Springs began in April 1903, and was completed in June 1905. The construction crews had to bore 33 tunnels on a two percent grade up South Boulder Creek and on a four percent grade over Rollins Pass. A four percent grade was the maximum slope up which a "standard adhesion locomotive" could pull a loaded train. The route was constructed to provide access to a proposed 2.6 mile tunnel under Rollins Pass at the 9,960 foot level to escape the hard and hazardous winter conditions

The imprint of the original railroad ties on the Moffat Road or "Corona Pass Road" can still be seen. This road over the Continental Divide was the original "hill route" of the Denver, Northwestern & Pacific Railway built by David H. Moffat.

on top of the Continental Divide. The tunnel was never built and the "temporary" line over the Divide was used until the 6.2 mile Moffat tunnel was completed in 1928. The first train over Rollins Pass was on June 23, 1904.

The Denver, Northwestern Railway Company was the inspiration of **David H. Moffat**, pioneer Denver banker, mine owner, and railroad builder, who dreamed of building a railroad from Denver to the West Coast. He organized the Denver, Northwestern & Pacific Railway Company on July 18, 1902. The railroad suffered financial problems from the outset even though there was an increase in its use during World War I because of the demand for coal from the Yampa Valley coal fields. The tunnel idea was strongly opposed until 1922 when the Moffat Tunnel District bill was passed by the state legislature. The 6.2 mile tunnel was built during 1923-27 at a cost of $18,000,000 and 19 lives. It is the second longest railroad tunnel in the U.S. The tunnel made the 23 mile, two and a half hour passenger train trip over Rollins Pass unnecessary and took only 12 minutes. David Moffat did not see his dream come true; he died in 1911. However, he served as president of the railroad from 1902 to the time of his death.

The DN&P Railroad was forced into receivership in 1912 and was reorganized in 1913 as the Denver & Salt Lake Railroad Company. In 1947, it became part of the present Denver & Rio Grande Western Railroad Company.

The Corona Pass, or Moffat Road, is open to high clearance four-wheel drive vehicles for those hardy souls interested in the history and view of the old railroad line. A two-wheel drive vehicle can traverse the road as far as the top of Corona. A self guided tour of the Moffat Road is available at the Winter Park Chamber of Commerce office and other locations in the area. This brochure lists 26 "points of interest" on the tour. The tour from the east starts at Rollinsville at the junction of CO 119 and RD 117. The tour starts on the west side off US 40. (Note: This is a very rough, one lane road and the going is slow regardless of the type of vehicle used. Persons travel at their own risk.)

The Denver, Northwest & Pacific Railroad Historic District (Moffat Road), at Rollinsville and Winter Park, are listed on the National Register of Historic Places.

Once a favorite hunting ground for the Ute and Arapaho Indians, the Fraser Valley was discovered by early pioneers around 1820. Development of the area began in earnest with the arrival of the railroad after the turn of the century. Recreational skiing was first introduced to Grand County in 1883, but a ski boom did not occur until 1911, when early jumping and skiing hills were built in Hot Sulphur Springs. The Winter Park ski area was opened in 1940.

Fraser

It is three miles west of Winter Park to **Fraser** (pop. 470). Fraser was the site of a German POW camp during World War II. The camp was located just to the north of the present elementary school.

Granby

It is 15 miles west to **Granby** (pop. 953). The community was founded in 1905 when the Moffat Railroad reached into Fraser Valley. It was incorporated in 1906 and named for U.S. District Attorney for Colorado, **Granby Hillyer**, in appreciation of his services.

Grand Lake

It is a mile west of Granby to the junction of US 34 and 15 miles north on US 34 to **Grand Lake** (pop. 382). There are several buildings in the Grand Lake area listed on the National Register of Historic Places. These include the Kauffman House, Pitkin and Lake Ave., Grand Lake; Dutchtown, on Ditch Rd. in the Rocky Mountain National Park; Shadow Mountain Lookout, southeast of Grand Lake in the Rocky Mountain National Park; and Grand River Ditch/Specimen Ditch, in the Grand Lake area. The Holzwarth Historic District is also in Grand Lake.

Grand Lake Historical Society has opened a museum in the historic KAUFFMAN HOUSE. The Kauffman House was built by Ezra Kauffman in 1892 and operated as a hotel until his death in 1921. It was operated as a summer tourist hotel by Ezra's widow and daughters until World War II. The museum is open from 1 to 5 p.m. daily from June through Labor Day. Admission is free.

The Lulu City Site, north of Grand Lake on Trail Ridge Road, is listed on the National Register of Historic Places.

Hot Sulphur Springs

Back on US 40 it is eight miles to **Hot Sulphur Springs** (pop. 405), county seat of Grand County. The Ute and Arapaho

271

The Kauffman House (above) in Grand Lake is listed on the National Register of Historic Places. A plaque on a group of buildings just east of the Kauffman House (below) identifies the site of the County Clerk's office in Grand Lake. This community served briefly as the county seat of Grand County.

The Grand County Museum complex is located on US 40 in Hot Sulphur Springs.

Indians used the springs area as a summer camping site. Later, the springs were called Boiling Springs by Francis M. Case, a government surveyor.

When John C. Fremont made his 1853 expedition into Colorado's Middle Park area, he camped at Hot Sulphur Springs as did other explorers after him. Hot Sulphur Springs' first serious entrepeneur was William N. Byers, best remembered as the founder of the *Rocky Mountain News* but who was as much a land speculator as a newspaper man.

The original Winter Carnival, the first serious competitive

skiing competition in Colorado, was held in 1911. Skiing here faded after the development of the larger Winter Park Ski Area following completion of the Moffat Tunnel in 1928.

GRAND COUNTY MUSEUM, at the east end of town on US 40, is housed in the old Hot Sulphur Springs School built in 1924. The exhibits portray the lives and times of the early settlers and businesses of Grand County. It features permanent and rotating exhibits on life typical of the West in the late 19th century. There are several other buildings on the museum grounds including a blacksmith shop and the old jail with original graffiti and its bars still in place. The old court house's interior has been restored to its c. 1890 appearance. The museum is open 10 a.m. to 5 p.m. daily Memorial Day through Labor Day. During the winter months it is open by appointment. Admission is free.

Kremmling

West, it is another 17 miles to **Kremmling** (pop. 1,296). The town was platted in 1891 and incorporated in 1904. The town was first called **Kinsey City** and did not become Kremmling until 1895. The railroad arrived in 1896 and remained the end of the line until 1908.

KREMMLING MUSEUM is located in the Town Square

The museum in Kremmling is located in the town square.

and concentrates on area history. It is open 9 a.m. to 5 p.m. Tuesday through Sunday, spring through fall, and 10 a.m. to 4 p.m. weekends during the winter months. Admission is free.

The E.C. Yust Homestead, south of Kremmling off CO 9, is listed on the National Register of Historic Places.

Steamboat Springs

It is 52 miles north to **Steamboat Springs** (pop. 5,098), county seat of Routt County. The community was founded in 1875 and incorporated in 1907. When the French trappers arrived they could hear the spring making a sound like a steamboat laboring upstream. Surprisingly this sound could be heard from as far as 200 yards away. It is said the trappers, upon hearing the sound exclaimed, "A steamboat, by gar!" Although the sound was lost when the railroad bed was cut through, the name remains.

The Ute Indians, native to this area, referred to Steamboat as "The Stinking Springs." A band of them summered here regularly, reveling in the warm spring waters of the Heart and Bath Springs.

The Moffat railroad line reached Steamboat Springs on December 18, 1908. The depot was completed in 1909 and was used until 1968 when rail service came to an end. Today, the depot is home of the Steamboat Arts Council.

The stage coach placed on the grounds of the County Court House is the actual stage last used in 1909 on the run from Steamboat Springs to Wolcott.

The Steamboat Springs Depot, 39265 RD 33B, and the Four Mile Bridge, RD 42, are listed on the National Register of Historic Places. Elsewhere in Routt County, the Foidel Canyon School, northwest of Oak Creek; Hahn's Peak School House, on Main St., Hahn's Peak Village; and the Rock Creek Stage Station/Gore Pass Stage Station, on Routt National Forest RD 206, Toponas, are also listed on the National Register.

Carl Howelsen, a Norwegian stonemason, introduced the sport of skiing to Steamboat Springs in 1914. Howelsen Hill Ski Area on the south side of the river was named in his honor. The hill is the oldest ski area in continuous use in Colorado and has produced more Olympians than any other ski area in North America. It remains headquarters for the first registered ski club and oldest continuing Winter Carnival west of the Mississippi.

Steamboat Springs boasts of a long list of ski champions. **Gordon Wren** was the first American to qualify in all four Olympic ski events—slalom, downhill, cross country and jumping—in 1948. Wren made the first jump of over 300 feet in the United States. **Billy Kidd** won the Olympic Slalom Silver Medal in 1964. Among Steamboat Springs' international skiers are **John Steele, Paul and Keith Wegeman, Katy Rodolph, Crosby Perry-Smith, Marvin Crawford, Skeeter and Buddy and Loris Werner, Jon and Jere Elliott, Jim "Moose" Barrows, Hank Kashiwa, Jeff Davis,** and **Chris McNeill.**

The Werner Memorial Library in Steamboat Springs is a final tribute to **Wallace "Bud" Werner** the three-time Olympic skier who was killed in 1964 in an avalanche in Switzerland while filming a ski movie. The 28 year old Olympian was the first American to win a major European downhill and was two-time Roche Cup winner. The library holds Werner's trophies and scrapbooks.

The Tread of Pioneers Museum in Steamboat Springs was moved and was being remodeled in 1989-90. It is housed in an old Victorian house. For more information on its reopening and schedule, call (303) 879-2214.

A one-mile walking tour of Steamboat Springs has been mapped out and introduces visitors to the community's Western heritage and architecture. It is suggested that, after acquiring the tour pamphlet, visitors begin the tour at the depot where ample parking is available. (Remember that most of the sites are private residences and are not open to the public.)

From Steamboat Springs it is 24 miles north to the village of **Hahns Peak**, via US 40 west and RD 129 north. Available for visitation here is the 1911 Little Green Schoolhouse and the museum with the Bear Cage jail. For information, call (303) 879-6781.

Hayden

Hayden (pop. 1,720) is 25 miles west of Steamboat Springs. It was founded in 1876 and incorporated in 1906 and was named for **Prof. Ferdinand V. Hayden**, who explored, mapped, and surveyed the area for the U.S. government in 1873. It was the original county seat of Routt County.

HERITAGE CENTER MUSEUM is located in the former Denver & Rio Grande Western Depot. The brick depot was

The Hayden Heritage Center is housed in the old depot at 300 W. Pearl St. in Hayden.

built in 1918, five years after the "Moffat Road" pushed through Hayden on its way to Salt Lake City. Unfortunately, the line was never completed past Craig. The museum presently maintains a collection of photographs that records the pioneer, mining and ranching heritage of the area, as well as excellent displays of vintage clothing. House goods, saddles and a rock collection are among the exhibits. Admission is free.

Farrington R. Carpenter (1886-1980), of Hayden, was the first director (1934-38) of the Division of Grazing and implementor of the Taylor Grazing Act.

An incident occurred in the northernmost reaches of Routt County in 1841 which gave the name to **Battle Mountain**. Thirty trappers held off 500 Arapaho and Cheyenne attackers for two-days in a momentous battle. Only four trappers were killed before the Indians were finally driven off.

Craig

Seventeen miles west of Hayden is **Craig** (pop. 8,133), county seat of Moffat County. Craig was incorporated in 1908. The town was named in honor of the **Rev. Bayard Craig**, of Denver, the chief financial backer to **W. H. Tucker**, who founded the town.

Ann Bassett, a beautiful pioneer homesteader who defied the

David Moffat's historical railroad car is displayed at the entrance to the City Park in Craig.

cattle barons, was tried in Craig for allegedly branding and killing Two-Bar cattle. The wily "Queen Ann," as she became known, married the Haley foreman and when the trial opened he testified in his wife's behalf. Queen Ann was acquitted.

During a trip to Salt Lake City **Franklin D. Roosevelt** and two companions stayed overnight at The Baker House in Craig. Shortly after he was appointed as Assistant Secretary of the Navy in 1913 by President Woodrow Wilson.

"Marcia," the Pullman car owned by **David H. Moffat**, listed on the National Register of Historic Places, is located at 341 E. Victory Way, Craig. It is one of the few remaining luxury Pullman cars in existence.

MOFFAT COUNTY MUSEUM is located in the Moffat County Courthouse and focuses on county history. Admission is free.

WYMAN ELK RANCH AND PIONEER MUSEUM is located north of Hamilton off CO 13. Guided tours to view the elk in their environment are available. An admission is charged.

Meeker

There are three routes to choose from out of Craig driving west. The first is CO 13 south to **Meeker** (pop. 2,356), county seat of Rio Blanco County. It is 47 miles to this historic community, named for **Nathan Meeker**, the Indian agent killed by the Ute Indians on September 29, 1879.

The **White River Utes** settled here in a green valley on the banks of the White River where they raised racing ponies. This Indian land became known as Powell Park, named for **Major John Wesley Powell** who lived here with the Indians during his exploration of the area in 1868-69. Powell Park later became the site of the Indian Agency on the White River established in 1869 by **Major D. C. Oakes**. Of the three other agents to follow Oakes, **Rev. E. H. Danforth** in 1875, introduced farming to the Northern Utes. Nathan C. Meeker then was named as Indian agent for the area in 1878. Meeker had earlier founded the town of Greeley on the Front Range.

Meeker wanted to make farmers out of the Utes in his charge following in Danforth's footsteps. They were no longer allowed to hunt, fish, spend their hours in their games, or carry on the kind of life handed down to them through the ages. The agent threatened to cut off all food supplies and let them starve unless they plowed, irrigated and cultivated, fenced, harvested and did the work of the typical farmer.

Meeker ran an irrigation channel through the Ute race track. He plowed up the meadow they were saving for winter pasture for their ponies. He moved the Agency buildings against their wishes. He insisted their children go to school. He promised there would be no military interference, then requested a military guard on the reservation. Eventually and predictably, a white man was killed and an Agency employee was fired upon. Meeker's life was threatened.

Finally, on September 29, 1879, **Chief Douglass** led the massacre which took place at the Agency. Meeker and nine reservation employees were killed. Mrs. Meeker and her 19 year old daughter Josephine, another woman, Flora Ellen Price, and two small children were kidnapped by the angry Indians.

In the meantime the Army had been summoned when Chief Douglass and Meeker came to blows on September 10th. Responding was **Major Thomas T. Thornburgh**, commanding officer at Fort Fred Steele in Wyoming Territory 150 miles north of the Agency. The major, commanding the U.S. 4th Infantry, leading a force of nearly 200 soldiers and civilians, arrived at the mouth of Elkhead Creek on September 26th. Here the troops were met by **Captain Jack**, the other chief at the Agency, and **Colorow**, a sub-chief. The Indian leaders protested

The site of the White River Ute Indian Agency is pinpointed by this historical marker west of Meeker on CO 64. Nathan Meeker and his male employees were massacred here on September 29, 1879.

the Army's plans to enter the Ute reservation. Captain Jack assured the major that all was peaceful on the reservation.

Two days later, the Army reached a point on Deer Creek, just outside the Agency. Colorow appeared once again and warned Major Thornburgh not to cross the Agency boundary line at Milk Creek. The major ignored the warnings and continued to Milk Creek the next day. The troops were attacked from ambush by some 300 Indian warriors. The Indians were able to split Thornburgh's troops and he and nine troopers were killed in a futile attempt to close the breach. Twenty three troopers were wounded and four others were killed in the fighting that lasted four days as the Indians pinned the Army down. **Capt. Francis S. Dodge**, commanding a company of black "Buffalo Soldiers," was able to join Thornburgh's beleaguered command. Dodge's 35 cavalrymen had been stationed in Middle Park since July with orders to check the Utes and get to White River if needed. A relief force commanded by **Col. Wesley Merritt** finally arrived Sunday morning, October 5, and the Indians fled.

In the meantime at reservation headquarters, 20 miles away,

A military camp was established near the Indian Agency on the White River shortly after the Meeker Massacre in 1879. This historical monument on the Rio Blanco County Courthouse grounds marks the site of Col. Wesley Merritt's military post. The post became the beginning of the town of Meeker.

Meeker and his men were killed and the women taken captive. All fighting ceased on October 11th. The women captives were not released until later in the month.

Colonel Merritt established the **Camp on White River** immediately following the massacre and this garrison was not abandoned until August 1883. Part of the camp was situated on what is today the Rio Blanco County Courthouse grounds. This military camp was the beginning of the town of Meeker.

The Meeker Massacre led to the removal of the Utes from

Colorado. A reservation was established for them in Utah. The Uintah Reservation was a comparatively barren location and far from the Utes' traditional hunting grounds. The land they vacated was thrown open to white settlement.

A plaque currently on a large boulder on the courthouse grounds describes the Army camp established here after the massacre.

The massacre site is located about four miles west of town on CO 64. A historical marker provides the facts of the massacre. An arrow points to the flagpole marker on the actual site of the Agency buildings located in a hayfield. A copper ball sits at the top of the flagpole that can be seen at the base of the trees.

The site of the original White River Indian Agency is marked with a monument also. It is located seven miles east of Meeker on RD 8. The Agency buildings were taken down and floated down the river to Powell Park, west of Meeker, in 1878 by the Indian agent. He felt the new location would be better for farming.

The Thornburgh monument is located 20 miles northeast of Meeker on RD 15 off CO 13 north of town. Turn right on RD 15 and it is approximately 17 miles to the site where Major Thornburgh and his men were ambushed. Altogether 13 troopers were killed in this battle. This site is listed on the National Register of Historic Places.

Also listed on the National Register of Historic Places is the Hotel Meeker, 560 Main St.; St. James Episcopal Church, 368 4th St.; Hay's Ranch Bridge, on RD 127; and Duck Creek Wickiup Village, 36 miles south of Meeker. One of the most famous guests at the **Hotel Meeker** was **Theodore Roosevelt**, who visited here during the time he was Vice President. The original hotel on this site was purchased by Susan C. Wright from the U.S. Army in 1883.

The **Ute War of 1887** was the final struggle between the Indians and whites in this area. Although the Indians had been banished to the Uintah reservation in Utah after the 1879 Meeker Massacre, they continued to come back to the White River to fish, gather berries, and hunt, in spite of a prohibition in the treaty. Hostilities again broke out in August 1887 when a posse of white settlers discovered a band of Indians camped at the forks of the White River. The main body of Indians were picking berries, and only a few elderly men, women, and chil-

The Meeker Hotel, across from the courthouse, is listed on the National Register of Historic Places.

dren were in camp. The posse invaded the camp without warning and seized an Indian boy. When his father objected the posse shot him. The boy was released and the posse opened fire on the camp wounding three. The Indians fled, leaving behind their camp, sheep and goats. **Chipeta**, Chief Ouray's widow, and a few followers were camped near the Thornburgh Battle site when she was accosted by a white posse. The posse burned the camp and killed an Indian boy as Chipeta and her followers fled.

Governor Alva Adams, in the meantime, called out the state militia and sent them to Meeker. The Indians had begun to return to their reservation in Utah but were headed off momentarily at the mouth of Wolf Creek near Rangely. Colorado Scouts and the 1st Colorado Cavalry attempted to have them stay until the next day but the Indians, now thoroughly alarmed, continued their retreat to Utah. When the Indians crossed what they thought was the Colorado-Utah line, they stopped and made camp. They were so sure that they were safe they turned their ponies out to graze and did not send out any sentries. Early August 25, as the Indians were preparing breakfast, the militia surrounded the camp and without warning opened fire on the Utes. The Indians returned the fire and were

283

able to hold the militia at bay while the women, children and elderly made their way to the reservation. When the braves thought they were safe, they followed, abandoning all their property. In the fight the soldiers killed a brave and two small girls. A baby boy, two braves and a boy were wounded. The Indians killed three soldiers. The settlers in Meeker and Rangely were outraged over the actions of the militia. Following an investigation, several hundred head of horses were returned to the Indians, but the sheep and goats probably became the property of the first white men to get to them. Thus ended the last armed conflict between the Ute Indians and white men.

On Tuesday, October 13, 1896, three men from Brown's Hole, at times a hideout for Butch Cassidy and his Wild Bunch, attempted to rob the **Bank of Meeker**, part of J. W. Hugus & Company, a firm which operated a number of stores and banks in northwestern Colorado and southern Wyoming. The trio made up the so-called "Junior Wild Bunch." The would-be outlaws, **Jim Shirley**, about 45; **George Law**, about 35; and "The Kid" Pierce, about 21, entered the bank and in their enthusiasm fired two warning shots that attracted the attention of the townspeople. As the trio emerged from the bank they were

The White River Museum in Meeker is housed in one of the original officer's quarters in the Camp on White River. It is located at 565 Park St.

shot down. Several townspeople were wounded in the brief shoot-out. The three dead men were put on public display for several days as a warning to other would-be badmen. They were buried in Highland Cemetery in Meeker.

WHITE RIVER MUSEUM, 565 Park St., Meeker, is housed in one of the original Cavalry Officer's Quarters buildings built in 1879. This folk type museum contains Indian artifacts, pictures, and other items related to the White River Indian Agency. Among the displays is Colorow's peace pipe, the Meeker stagecoach, the guns used in the 1896 bank robbery, plus other items depicting frontier life of the area. It is open 9 a.m. to 5 p.m. daily during the summer and 10 a.m. to 4 p.m. weekdays and Saturday and 1 to 4 p.m. Sunday during the winter. Admission is free.

Rangely

It is 41 miles driving south on CO 13 to **Rifle** on I-70. From Meeker it is 78 miles west on CO 64 to the Utah state line. It is 57 miles to **Rangely** (pop. 2,113) on this route.

The Spanish explorers **Fathers Dominquez and Escalante** recorded the first historical notes on the Rangely area as they traveled through Douglas Creek Valley while searching for a route from Santa Fe to California in 1776. The area just south of Rangely was named **"Canon Pintado"** (Painted Canyon) for the numerous examples of native American rock art, still seen today just off the road.

The local Museum and Visitors Center is located at the west end of Rangely on CO. 64.

The pictograph in Canon Pintado, south of Rangely on CO 139, was discovered by the Dominquez and Escalante Expedition on September 9, 1776. The sign below points to the painting in the rocks.

The Dominquez and Escalante Expedition, seeking a route from Santa Fe, N.M. to California, traveled through western Colorado in 1776. This historical marker on CO 64 just east of Rangely briefly describes their trip through this area.

Rangely began in the late 1800s as an Indian trading post. It was not incorporated until 1940 with the development of the area oil fields. West of town is the Rangely oil field, one of the largest in the country.

Just east of town on CO 64 are historical markers briefly describing the Dominquez and Escalante expedition through this area. They were the first white men to examine much of Western Colorado.

RANGELY MUSEUM provides a view into the area's past and describes some of the points of interest. It is open 1 to 5 p.m. Wednesday through Sunday. Admission is free.

There are four sites in the Rangely area listed on the National Register of Historic Places. These include Canon Pintado, on CO 139; Carrot Men Pictograph Site, southwest of Rangely; Collage Shelter, and the Fremont Lookout Fortification Site.

Eighteen miles north of Rangely is the **Dinosaur National Monument**.

Maybell

Back at Craig, US 40 continues west 31 miles to unincorporated **Maybell**. The town was founded by the Rev. Jack Ellis and named in honor of the daughters of John Banks, May and Bell. The Two-Bar Ranch, off CO 318 in Brown's Park Wildlife Refuge, is listed on the National Register of Historic Places.

Dinosaur

Continuing on US 40 in a southwesterly direction it is 59 miles to the Utah state line. One can enter Dinosaur National Monument off US 40 at **Dinosaur**. There are several sites in Dinosaur National Monument listed on the National Register of Historic Places. These include Rial Chew Ranch Complex, the Early Douglass Workshop-Laboratory, the Denis Julien Inscription, the Jose Bassett Morris Ranch Complex, the Quarry Visitor Center, and the Upper Wade and Curtis Cabin.

The other route from Maybell west is CO 318. It is 50 miles via this highway to the Utah state line.

Brown's Park

Brown's Park, on the Colorado and Utah state line, was originally called **Brown's Hole**, named for **Ephraim Brown**, an early day trapper. H. H. Bassett, who settled here in the 1870s, did not care for the name "Brown's Hole" and began calling it Brown's Park. **"Davy" Crockett** (1786-1836), the famous hunter, scout, soldier, and Congressman, led a party of trappers into this area in 1837. **John C. Fremont** and his guide and scout, **Kit Carson**, explored the area in 1844. Brown's Park, or often referred to as Brown's Hole, for a period of time in the late 19th century, became famous as a hideout for outlaws. One of the first and finest formal affairs in Brown's Park was the Outlaws Thanksgiving Dinner held in 1895. The dinner was given and served by a gang of outlaws for Brown's Park families. One of the outlaw gangs that frequented Brown's

Hole after holdups was **Butch Cassidy** and his **Wild Bunch**.

There are two sites in Brown's Park listed on the National Register of Historic Places—the Old Ladore School, on Green River on CO 318, and the White-Indian Contact Site, in the Park.

Colorado Notes

SYMBOLS OF COLORADO

Colorado's motto is Nil sine Numine (Nothing without Providence). A. J. Flynn wrote the words and music for the State Song, "Where the Columbines Grow." The Rocky Mountain Columbine is the State Flower and the Blue Spruce, the State Tree. The Lark Bunting is the State Bird.

PIKES PEAK OR BUST

Colorado had few settlers until 1858 when gold was found near present-day Denver. Thousands of persons rushed into the area. "Pikes Peak or Bust" became their slogan as they traveled the long and hard trails to the Colorado gold fields. This gold rush reached its height by the end of 1859, when about 100,000 persons had reached the territory.

ROOF OF NORTH AMERICA

The Colorado Rockies have been called the *"Roof of North America"* because between 50 and 60 peaks reach 14,000 feet or more above sea level. These peaks are the tallest in the Rocky Mountain chain, which stretches from Alaska to New Mexico.

COHAN AUTHOR OF "SEVEN KEYS TO BALDPATE"

George M. Cohan (1878-1942) wrote more than 40 plays and musicals. Among his plays was "Seven Keys to Baldpate," written in 1913. His song," Over There," was the most popular American patriotic song of World War I.

NOTED PHYSICIST TAUGHT AT CU

Edward U. Condon (1902-74) was a physicist who became noted for his contributions to theoretical physics and, in 1928, helped apply new quantum theories to radioactive processes. He taught from 1963 until his retirement in 1970 at the University of Colorado.

BIG THOMPSON RECLAMATION PROJECT

It has always been known that the Continental Divide usually decides whether the precipitation that falls in the Rockies shall wend toward the Pacific or the Atlantic Ocean. This has held true until the completion of the Colorado-Big Thompson Reclamation Project that takes surplus water from the Colorado River Valley west of the Divide, flows it through a 13-mile tunnel underneath the towering peaks, and turns it into the valley of the South Platte in eastern Colorado.

LARGEST MOLYBDENUM MINE IN THE WORLD

The Climax mine, 13 miles northeast of Leadville, is the largest Molybdenum mine in the world. Leadville gained its name because of the large quantities of lead ore found in the area. Also mined in this region are silver, gold, iron, copper, bismuth, manganese, tungsten, and zinc.

A MAJOR RIVER IN THE UNITED STATES

The 5,450 mile Colorado River rises in the Rocky Mountains of Colorado, and flows southwest into Utah. It is joined by the Green River in eastern Utah, and continues southwestward into Arizona. The Little Colorado River merges with the Colorado in northern Arizona. Nevada's Virgin River joins the Colorado beyond the Grand Canyon. The Colorado empties into the Gulf of California in Mexico.

SOAPY SMITH CLEANED OUT MINERS

Jefferson Randolph Smith, Jr., a Georgian, became the king of mining camp rogues as Soapy Smith. With his infamous soap game he fleeced prospectors from Colorado to Alaska. Standing before a crowd, Smith would flash a roll of bills ranging from a dollar to $100. He would wrap, or so it appeared, the bills around bars of soap, cover them with paper and toss them in a basket. He then would invite persons from the audience to pick a bar of soap out of the basket for $5. No one ever won more than $2 in the scheme other than his decoys. Smith was killed in gunfight in Skagway in 1898.

HARVEY WINS A PULITZER

Mary Coyle Chase won the 1944-45 Pulitzer Prize for her comedy, "Harvey," an invisible white rabbit, six feet one and a half inches tall. Frank Fay played the part of the central figure, Edward P. Dowd who is "mildly potted all the time," on Broadway. In the movie version, James Stewart played the part of Dowd. Mary Chase was born in Denver in 1907.

Chapter 9
Across Colorado on US 50

US 50 begins in southeastern Colorado and covers such historic places as Camp Amache, Fort Lyon, Bent's Old Fort, Canon City, Royal Gorge, Gunnison, Alpine Pass, and Montrose. The stories of several early day characters, such personalities as William Bent, Kit Carson, George Washington Swink, Warden Roy Best, Capt. John Gunnison, and Chief Ouray, are told as well.

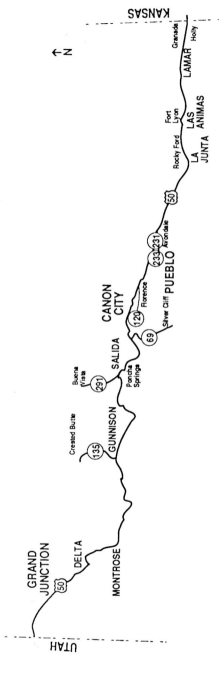

Chapter 9
Across Colorado on US 50

The Santa Fe Trail entered Colorado Territory at **Trail City**, on the present-day Kansas-Colorado line. Trail City began in 1886 as a cowtown serving the **Santa Fe and National Trails**. The first long stop on the dusty trail north was Trail City, and it was the first point where a trail boss paid off in cash. While this crossroads did not develop into another Dodge City, it did become "the hell hole of the Arkansas."

The Santa Fe Trail, dating back to 1822, followed along the general route of US 50 to La Junta where it turned southwest, along US 350 today, to Trinidad and then turned south along a route paralleling I-25 over Raton Pass into New Mexico.

Holly and Amity

From the Kansas state line into Colorado it is four miles to **Holly** (pop. 969), founded in 1903 and named for Hiram S. Holley, founder of a large cattle ranch. (When the town name appeared on early maps, the "e" had been dropped.)

The Towners-Holly Lions Club has erected a marker on the Towner road north out of Holly that commemorates those who died in the **"Towner Bus Tragedy"** in 1931 when a plains blizzard stranded a school bus at this site.

The outlaw **Henry Starr** robbed the bank at **Amity** in 1909. He was captured about a year later and sentenced to the penitentiary at Canon City for several years. Amity, started by the Salvation Army in 1898, was between Holly and Granada.

Granada

It is 11 miles from Holly to **Granada** (pop. 637), established in 1873 when the Santa Fe Railroad ended its line there. In 1885 **Fred Harvey**, founder of the Harvey House chain of restaurants, bought approximately 3,000 acres of land around Granada, later called the XY Ranch. Harvey did not want a town adjacent to his ranch and refused to grant title to more land to developers, so the town was moved to its present location in 1886. The town was incorporated in 1887.

The **Goodnight and Loving Trails**, used by cattle drovers, ran through the Granada area. Hundreds of thousands of cattle were driven over these trails northward.

Camp Amache, a relocation center for the Japanese residents moved from the Pacific Coast area during the early part of World War II, was located one and a half-miles southwest of Granada. The camp opened on August 1, 1942 and was named for **Amache Ochinee Prowers**, the Indian wife of **John W. Prowers** for whom the county is named. Several thousand Japanese were held here until the camp was closed in late 1945. Facilities at Camp Amache included a post office, fire and police departments, a 150-bed hospital, nursery through high school, and a camp newspaper, the *Granada Pioneer.*

The Douglas Crossing Bridge, on RD 28, at Granada is listed on the National Register of Historic Places.

Lamar

It is another 17 miles west to **Lamar** (pop. 9,000), county seat of Prowers County. Lamar began as **Blackwell**, a station on the Santa Fe Railroad. **A. R. Black,** a cattleman, owned the land on both sides of the railroad station and stock yards siding. Black refused to sell or give any of his land for a townsite. In 1886, the railroad moved its Blackwell Station three miles west where Lamar was born, May 24, 1886. The town was named for **Lucius Quintius Lamar**, Secretary of Interior under President Grover Cleveland.

BIG TIMBERS MUSEUM, on US 50 one mile north of Lamar, records the area's history and serves as a gallery for local artists. It is open 1:30 to 4:30 p.m. daily. Donations are accepted.

Lamar was one of 12 communities selected for a statue of **"The Madonna of the Trail,"** erected by the Daughters of the American Revolution to honor pioneer women who traveled the transcontinental trails coming West. The monument, dedicated September 28, 1928, is located on the east side of Main Street just south of the railroad.

On August 26, 1860, a military post was built in the vicinity of **Bent's Fort** on the Arkansas River near present-day Lamar. It was first called **Fort Wise**; then on June 25, 1862, it was designated **Fort Lyon**. In June, 1867, the original site was abandoned and a new Fort Lyon established about 20 miles upstream on the left bank of the Arkansas, two and one-half miles below the mouth of the Purgatoire River. The post was closed on August 31, 1889.

Col. John Chivington and the **3rd Colorado Cavalry** marched from Fort Lyon north late in November 1864 to a point on Sand Creek in Kiowa County. Here in the early morning hours of November 29th he and his troops attacked the Cheyenne camp of **Chief Black Kettle**, who had believed there had been an armistice. In the massacre that followed, 123 Cheyennes were killed, many women and children. The site of the **Sand Creek Massacre** is marked on County RD 96.

The marker and location of Fort Wise is found about one and a half miles east of Prowers Bridge.

Petroglyphs, referred to as "Indian writings," may be found along waterways and canyons in Hickland Springs.

The Davies Hotel/Payne Hotel, 122 N. Main St.; the Lamar Post Office, 300 S. 5th St.; and the Prowers County Courthouse, 301 S. Main St., in Lamar are listed on the National Register of Historic Places.

Fort Lyon

It is 31 miles west to **Fort Lyon** and the Fort Lyon Veterans Affairs Medical Center. It was here one of America's great frontiersman **Kit Carson** died on May 23, 1868 from an aneurism of the aorta in the home and office of Carson's friend and physician. Today this building serves as the Kit Carson Memorial Chapel. Admission to the chapel is free. A national cemetery is also located on the Fort Lyon VA grounds.

Las Animas

Las Animas (pop. 2,818) is the county seat of Bent County. Las Animas (Spanish for "The Spirits") was the name given to the river nearby that empties into the Arkansas. The name of the river was changed to El Purgatorio, the "River of Lost Souls," for the early Spanish explorers who lost their lives on its banks. Their souls were condemned to purgatory because they perished without the last rites of the church. Later, the French changed the spelling to the Purgatoire, as the name now appears on all maps. The early-day cowboys had trouble pronouncing the name and soon had Purgatoire corrupted to Picketwire, the name most commonly used today in the area.

Las Animas was established in 1869 and incorporated in 1886. Bent County, named for **William Bent**, was created in 1870. Early settlers were William Bent, **Thomas Boggs, John Prowers** and **Kit Carson**. The Bent County Courthouse, located at the corner of Carson and Bent, is listed on the National Register of Historic Places.

Tom Boggs arrived in the Arkansas Valley in 1840 and was associated with William Bent for about six years. When Fort

These two historical buildings on the Fort Lyon VA Medical Center grounds are listed on the National Register of Historic Places. Capt. E. B. Kirk, Army Quartermaster, signed his name in the stone building below in 1867.

The Kit Carson Memorial Chapel on the grounds of Fort Lyon VA Medical Center. The old scout was treated in this former Army hospital building erected in 1863. Carson died here in 1868.

Lyon moved to its present location in 1867, Boggs became a major food supplier to the military. He served as the first sheriff of Bent County and was elected to the state legislature in 1871. Kit Carson owned two tracts of land here given to him by Ceran St. Vrain. Carson, who had retired from the Army, and his family came to Boggsville at Christmastime 1867.

Mrs. Carson died in April 1868 and a month later her famous husband, Kit, died at the age of 56, leaving behind seven children. Mr. and Mrs. Boggs took the Carson children and raised them as their own. The Boggs family left Colorado in 1877 for New Mexico where Tom Boggs became territorial governor.

This historical marker identifies Boggsville named for early settler Thomas O. Boggs. Kit Carson and his wife died here in the spring of 1868. Thomas Boggs and his wife raised the seven surviving Carson children.

Boggsville, south of La Animas on CO 101, is listed on the National Register of Historic Places. It was a settlement which never grew to be a town. Tom Boggs introduced a new breed of sheep on his ranch here and John Prowers was the first to go into the cattle business on a large scale.

Las Animas is the hometown of **Ken Curtis**, who played the role of Festus in the long-running TV series, "Gunsmoke;" **Col. George M. Powell**, the attending physician to President Eisenhower at Fitzsimons Hospital in Denver and Gen. George

The Kit Carson Museum in Las Animas.

C. Marshall at Fort Bragg, N.C.; and **Llewellyn E. Thompson Jr.**, former ambassador to Russia. Llewellyn Thompson, Jr. (1904-1972) was born in Las Animas and received his education in the Bent County school system and the University of Colorado. He joined the U.S. Foreign Service in 1929 and was sent to the Soviet Union in 1940. He served as a valuable advisor on foreign affairs to Presidents Truman, Eisenhower, Kennedy and Johnson. His major achievement came during the Cuban Missile Crisis during the Kennedy administration. He played an important role in resolving the crisis in October 1962.

By the time he was 26 years old, **Clay Allison** had killed four men in as many gunfights. His last gunfight occurred on December 21, 1876 in Las Animas. Clay and his brother, John, were enjoying a drunken party in the Olympic Dance Hall when a deputy sheriff and the constable asked the brothers to check their guns. They ignored the request. A short time later, when the party was getting out of hand, the deputy, **Charles Faber**, and two other deputies returned to the dance hall. In the brief gunfight that ensued Faber wounded John and Clay shot and killed the deputy. Clay surrendered to the county sheriff and a short time later was released from jail.

KIT CARSON MUSEUM, 9th and Bent Ave., features exhibits of the area's early days. It is open 1 to 5 p.m. daily from Memorial Day to Labor Day. Admission is free.

The La Junta Post Office Building is listed on the National Register of Historic Places.

The Koshare Indian Kiva Museum and Dancers are housed in this building in the southern part of La Junta.

La Junta

Twenty miles west is **La Junta** (pop. 8,338), county seat of Otero County. La Junta, which translated means "the junction," began as a railroad settlement in 1873 but the railroad, the Kansas Pacific, went out of business just a few months later. The town began to emerge again in 1876 with the arrival of the Santa Fe Railroad. The first townsite map was laid out in 1876 and the town was incorporated in 1881.

La Junta was not unlike many frontier towns. Men wore guns, worked hard and drank hard, conditions that often meant trouble. In 1884 conditions were so bad, the town council hired **Bat Masterson** as their marshal. He served only five weeks. In August 1886 a mob of drunken cowboys terrorized the town firing off their six guns only to find themselves in the "Black Hole," as the town jail was called. The marshal and his deputies took 26 cowboys to jail that night to sober up. There were numerous shootings and several lawbreakers were sent to prison. At least on man, a tramp by the name of McNally, was convicted of murder and sent to Canon City where he was hanged.

Bent's Old Fort National Historic Site

Bent's Old Fort National Historic Site has been totally reconstructed by the U.S. Department of Interior National Park Service as accurately as possible to its appearance in 1845-46. The fort was completed in 1833 by Mexican laborers hired by **Charles and William Bent** and **Ceran St. Vrain**. It became the most important trading post on the Santa Fe Trail between Independence, Mo., and Santa Fe, N.M. It boasted a spectrum of cultures, races, and occupations; being exceptionally dependent on fur traders and buffalo robes.

The **Bent, St. Vrain Trading Company** operated their empire for some 17 years. In the mid-1830s, William Bent married **Owl Woman**, daughter of **Gray Thunder**, a powerful Cheyenne spiritual leader. Years later, when Owl Woman died, Cheyenne custom allowed him to marry her sister, **Yellow Woman**. He made every effort to encourage rival tribes to make peace with each other. In 1846, the federal government designated the adobe trading post as the advance base for Col. Stephen Watts Kearny's invasion of New Mexico. With the conquest and annexation of the Southwest, the days of rich trading evaporated. In 1847, Gov. Charles Bent, who had been appointed governor

Top photo shows a group of artisans entering Bent's Old Fort. Bottom photo is an inside shot of the historic old fort.

Costumed interpreters are scattered throughout Bent's Old Fort during a rendezvous.

Scenes inside the walls of Bent's Old Fort, one of Colorado's premier historical sites.

A volunteer at Bent's Old Fort takes time out for a breather during the busy tourist season.

One of the interpreters at Bent's Old Fort teaches two youngsters, in period costume, the finer points of the game of checkers during a break.

of New Mexico Territory by Colonel Kearny in 1846, was killed in a revolt in Taos, N.M. Ceran St. Vrain, who had become a Mexican citizen, lived in New Mexico and only occasionally visited the fort and eventually relinquished his stock in the fort leaving William the sole owner. As the fort was a business, William had a manager for when he was away on trading expeditions which was about 60 percent of the time. It is said that Charles's death greatly upset him. On August 21, 1849, amidst a cholera epidemic, William Bent loaded his goods and belongings in wagons and rumor had it he set fire to his trading post. He had tried to sell the fort to the government, but they would not give him his asking price. He may have been concerned that if simply he abandoned the fort the government or possibly a competitor might move in for free. For whatever reason the fort was destroyed it is probable that we will never know.

BENT'S OLD FORT NATIONAL HISTORIC SITE, located eight miles east of La Junta and 15 miles west of Las Animas on CO 194, is operated by the National Park Service. The reconstructed trading post on the Arkansas River was once the frontier hub from which American trade and influence radiated south into Mexico, west into the Great Basin, and north to southern Wyoming. The furnishings of the several rooms are both antiques and reproductions. Uniformed park employees and costumed interpreters are available to answer questions. It is open 8 a.m. to 6 p.m. daily during the summer and 8 a.m. to 4:30 p.m. daily during the winter. An admission is charged.

KOSHARE INDIAN MUSEUM, 115 W. 18th St., La Junta, is home of the world famous Koshare Indian dancers, all members of the Boy Scouts of America. The Koshares give an average of 50 performances a year in their own great Kiva and at conventions in their area. The museum is open 9 a.m. to 5 p.m. daily June through September and from noon to 5 p.m. from September to June. The Koshares perform at home Saturday nights, late June through July and August. Their Winter Show is held during Christmas Week. Admission to the museum is free. There is an admission charged to the Koshare performances.

OTERO MUSEUM, one block south of US 50 at 2nd and Anderson Sts., is dedicated to preserving the local heritage of Otero County and the surrounding area. The Scumbato Grocery Store and attached home at the museum complex date back to the turn of the century and is listed on the National Register of Historic Places. It is open 1 to 5 p.m. daily June through September. An admission is charged.

La Junta's post office, located at the corner of 4th St. and Colorado Ave., and Lincoln School Building, now Lincoln Square Professional Building, between Carson and Belleview Aves., are listed on the National Register of Historic Places. The entire east side of the 500 block of San Juan Ave. and 522 San Juan Ave. are also listed on the National Register of Historic Places as well as the Hart residence at 802 Raton Ave. These homes are private residences and not open to the public. Other structures on the National Register of Historic Places include the Dr. Frank Finney House, 608 Belleview Ave.; the Wilson A. Hart House, 802 Raton Ave.; the Eugene Rourke House, 619 Carson St.; and the Daniel Scumbato Grocery Store, 706 2nd St.

The **Comanche National Grasslands**, south of La Junta, occupy more than 400,000 acres of range lands.

Rocky Ford

Rocky Ford (pop. 4,804) is 11 miles west of La Junta.

307

The Rocky Ford Museum is housed in a former library building.

George Washington Swink, a native Illinoisan, arrived in the area in 1871. He filed a homestead claim and a timber claim. His timber claim was the first issued—Patent No. 1—November 3, 1887, signed by President Grover Cleveland.

Swink became famous for his development of cantaloupes. He shipped his first cantaloupes out of Rocky Ford in 1880. He began making a profit on this venture in 1882. By the turn of the century, millions of cantaloupes were shipped annually from Rocky Ford. Swink is credited with the success of this agricultural venture and is known as the father of the Rocky Ford melon industry. He served as the mayor of Rocky Ford for several terms and was elected to the state senate from southeastern Colorado.

ROCKY FORD MUSEUM, 400 S. 10th, features displays of area pioneers as well as extensive exhibits in archaeology, geology, military, anthropology, and ethnographic collections. It is 11 a.m. to 4 p.m. Tuesday through Saturday, May 1 to September 17. Admission is free.

Manzanola and Avondale

Manzanola (pop. 459) is nine miles west of Rocky Ford. The Manzanola Bridge, off CO 207, is listed on the National Register of Historic Places.

This marker on US 50 one and a half miles east of Avondale identifies the site of Fort Reynolds.

Twenty miles east of Pueblo, near **Avondale**, was the site of **Fort Reynolds**, identified by a historical marker on the north side of US 50.

See Chapter 4 for information about the Pueblo area.

Florence

Nine miles east of Canon City via CO 115 is **Florence** (pop. 2,987), incorporated in 1887, where the first oil field west of Pennsylvania was developed in 1862. The oil was said to have been shipped to Denver and sold for wagon grease. By 1901 Florence was an oil refining center with more population than Canon City. Three oil refining companies were operating here and the community boasted three railroads. Florence still has the oldest continuously producing oil well in the world.

The Florence Post Office, 121 N. Pikes Peak St., and Bridge No. 10/Adelaide Bridge, on Fremont County Rd. are listed on the National Register of Historic Places.

Canon City

Thirty-nine miles west of Pueblo is **Canon City** (pop. 13,037), county seat of Fremont County. Canon City was organized by the Canon City Claim Club March 13, 1860. The Canon City Claim Club was organized by six members to develop coal, iron, gysum, marble and granite in the area. Among the first settlers to arrive were **Mr. and Mrs. Anson Rudd**. The town was named **Canyon City** in 1861 but the reporter for the meeting used the Spanish spelling of canon (for canyon) and the name stuck. Canon City was incorporated in 1872.

The first territorial prison was built here and opened June 1, 1871. The first prisoner received was **John Shepler**, sentenced from Gilpin County to serve a one year sentence for larceny. Within six months 23 inmates were incarcerated here with U.S. Marshal of Colorado Territory, Mark Shaffenberg, acting as Chief Administrator. His staff included three guards. In April 1874 the penitentiary was officially transferred to the Territory of Colorado by the U.S. government and became known as the **Colorado State Penitentiary. Mary Salander**, No. 60, was the first woman sentenced to the penitentiary. She was sentenced March 12, 1873 for manslaughter from Boulder County. She was pardoned on August 8, 1873.

The first major prison break occurred in June 1874 when eight desperate convicts escaped armed with guns and knives. As a result of this break, a stone wall was built around the prison. It was 20 feet high and four feet thick and enclosed approximately five acres of prison property. One of the most infamous prisoners was **Alferd Packer**, No. 1389, who was convicted of killing five fellow gold prospectors in 1874 in the San Juan Mountains and eating them or living off their flesh until he escaped the snow storm. The famous "Cannibal" was sentenced to hang for murder but in a retrial was convicted of man-

One of the guard towers at the Colorado State Penitentiary in Canon City.

slaughter and sentenced to 40 years in prison. He entered prison in 1886 and was released in 1901 and died in 1907.

In 1929 there were numerous riots and uprising in U.S. prisons. Colorado State Prison was not spared and on October 3, 1929 a riot broke out and several prisoners, led by **A. A. "Danny" Daniels**, killed eight guards and wounded two others before the ringleader shot his fellow rioters and then killed himself. Severe damage was done to the prison and the loss was estimated to be $300,000.

The entrance to the Colorado Territorial Prison Museum in Canon City.

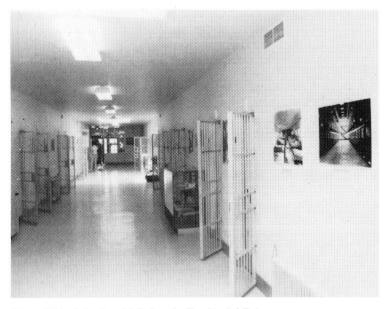

The cellblock in the old Colorado Territorial Prison.

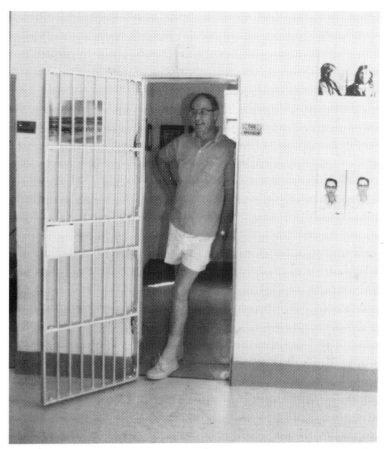

One of the many tourists visiting the Colorado Territorial Prison Museum in Canon City after inspecting one of the prison cells.

Until 1933, executions at the Colorado State Penitentiary were carried out by hanging. The first hanging occurred November 8, 1890 and the last recorded was December 1, 1933. Of the 45 inmates who were hanged, the youngest was 20 years of age, the oldest 58 years of age. The first execution in Colorado's gas chamber occurred June 22, 1934. The last to die in the gas chamber was **Louis Jose Monge** who was executed June 2, 1967. Thirty-two inmates have been executed in the gas chamber. No woman has ever been executed in Colorado.

Probably the most colorful warden at the Colorado State Penitentiary was **Roy Best**, who served in the post from 1932-52. During his 20 years, longer than any other warden, he built

The east wall of the state prison in Canon City. The Territorial Prison Museum is located at the rear of the building outside wall on the right.

Old photos such as the one above are displayed on the walls in the cellblock in the Colorado Territorial Prison Museum. This photo shows prisoners being moved by a single guard. The prisoners lined up and put their left hand on the shoulder of the inmate ahead of them, forcing them to walk in step. Cases along the wall in the museum are used to exhibit items pertaining to prison life and the life of certain individual prisoners.

new cell houses, industrial buildings, women's ward and others. He played in the motion picture "Canon City" based on the December 30, 1947 prison break in which two convicts were killed and two others wounded. The wife of a prison employee and a guard were seriously injured and four other guards were badly mauled when 12 inmates in Cell Block No. 6, an isolation cell block, tried their break. Warden Best was charged with violating the civil rights of inmates and suspended in May 1952. He died of a heart attack during the hearings on these charges.

COLORADO TERRITORIAL PRISON MUSEUM, 1st and Macon Sts., is open from 10 a.m. to 6 p.m. daily during the summer months and 1 to 5 p.m. Wednesday through Sunday during the winter months. An admission is charged.

In 1878 Alantasaurus fossil remains were discovered near Canon City. The femur is displayed in the Canon City Municipal Museum along with the footprint discovered in a coal mine in 1929. Complete fossils of several dinosaurs have been excavated and are now preserved in some of the country's leading museums.

CANON CITY MUNICIPAL MUSEUM, 612 Royal Gorge Blvd., was established in 1928 and contains three special wings —the DeWeese Wing, Historical Room, and Amick Wing. The DeWeese Wing, named for **Dall DeWeese**, nationally known hunter and world traveler, displays many of his outstanding exhibits. The Historical Room is based around the collection of **Bird Millman**, famous tight wire performer of vaudeville and circus fame. The Amick Wing, named for **Robert W. Amick**, features a variety of historical exhibits. It is open 9 a.m. to 5 p.m. weekdays and Saturdays and 1 to 5 p.m. Sunday from May 16 to September 16 and from 1 to 5 p.m. daily September 17 to May 15. Admission is free.

Just behind the museum is the HISTORIC RUDD CABIN AND STONE HOME. These were the early homes of Anson and Harriet Rudd who arrived in Canon City in 1859. The Rudds lived in the log cabin for 20 years before moving into the 10 room stone house where they lived for 23 years. Anson Rudd, a blacksmith by trade, was the first elected Lieutenant Governor of Colorado Territory (although he never served). He served as the first sheriff of the county, a county Commissioner, a provost marshal during the Civil War and the first warden of the penitentiary after it became Colorado Territory property. Rudd

The historic Rudd House in Canon City. Below is the Rudd Cabin, part of the historic complex at the rear of the Canon City Municipal Museum.

The historic Holy Cross Abbey in Canon City.

The Canon City Municipal Museum on Royal Gorge Boulevard.

was related to Zebulon Pike. The Rudds are buried in Fairmont Cemetery in Denver. The Rudd Cabin and Stone Home are open during the same hours as the museum. Admission is free.

Holy Cross Abbey, operated by the Benedictine Monks, was established in 1896 as St. Leander's Priory. The landmark Monastery building was completed in 1926 and has been placed on the National Register of Historic Places. The history of the Benedictines in Colorado began in 1886 when two monks from St. Vincent Archabbey in Latrobe, Pennsylvania, arrived in Breckenridge to assist in the local parish.

There are several other structures in Canon City listed on the National Register. These include the Downtown Historic District; Municipal Building, 612 Royal Gorge Blvd.; Post Office and Federal Building, 5th & Macon Ave.; First Presbyterian Church, Macon & 7th St.; Fourth Street Bridge; McClure House/Strathmore Hotel, 300 block on Main St.; and Robison Mansion, 12 Riverside Dr.

Canon City was the site of one of the earliest movie studios and between 1912-14 many of the early westerns were filmed here. **Tom Mix**, a local cowboy, began his movie career here and starred in several of the two reelers produced in Canon City. Many feature films have been shot on location in the area and among some of the stars who have been involved in these films have been **John Wayne, Jane Fonda, Zazu Pitts, Goldie Hawn,** and **Slim Pickens**.

The Royal Gorge Bridge is located in Royal Gorge Park owned by the City of Canon City. It is located eight miles west of Canon City. The construction of the Royal Gorge Bridge was proposed by **Lon P. Piper** of San Antonio, Texas, on April 15, 1929. Construction began on June 5, 1929 and was completed five months later without a single fatality and no major accidents. All the steel was manufactured at Colorado Fuel and Iron Corp. in Pueblo and each of the 4,200 wires in the suspension cables was pulled across the gorge one at a time. The bridge, the world's highest suspension bridge, is 1,053 feet above the canyon floor. The bridge and Incline Railway are listed on the National Register of Historic Places. The bridge is open daily and closes at dusk. There is an admission charge.

BUCKSKIN JOE, near the Royal Gorge bridge, is a 160-acre theme park often used as a set for western films. Among a few of the movies shot on location here were "Cat Ballou," "The Cowboys," "The Duchess and The Dirtwater Fox," "True Grit," and

The first Americans to view the Arkansas River canyon now known as Royal Gorge was Zebulon Pike and the members of his expedition in 1806. The Royal Gorge became the focal point of a bitter railroad dispute in 1878 as the Denver and Rio Grande and the Atchison, Topeka and Santa Fe railroads fought over routes into Colorado's rich mining country. Royal Gorge Park was ceded to Canon City in 1906 and in 1929 Canon City built the world's highest suspension bridge spanning the Arkansas River 1,053 feet below.

The Arkansas River is shown in the canyon below the Royal Gorge bridge.

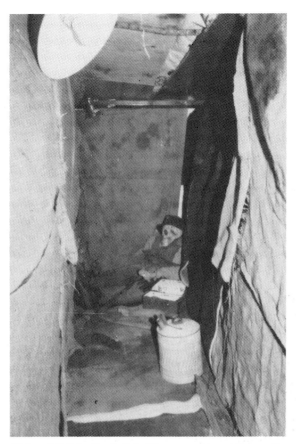

This exhibit in the Salida Museum shows the results of the hazards of mining in the early days.

"The Sacketts." A few of the stars who have made movies here: **James Arness, Vera Miles, Lee Van Cleef, Tom Selleck, John Wayne,** and **Lee Marvin**. The 100-year old buildings include general stores, print shop and blacksmith shop and others. It is open 8 a.m. to dusk from May through September. An admission is charged.

Salida

It is 57 miles from Canon City to **Salida** (pop. 4,870), county seat of Chaffee County. Salida is the Spanish word for "exit." Salida was founded c. 1880 and incorporated in 1891.

The movie actress **Jane Young** was born in Salida in 1910. She starred in such movies as "Horseman of the Plains" in 1928 with Tom Mix, "Vagabond Lover" in 1929 with **Rudy Val-**

The Salida Museum is located just off US 50.

The Poncha Springs Museum is housed in the City Hall.

The *Buena Vista Heritage Museum is located in the old Chaffee County Courthouse, listed on the National Register of Historic Places.*

lee, and "Little Accident" in 1930 with **Anita Page.**

SALIDA MUSEUM, 406 W. Rainbow Blvd., features early pioneer and railroad artifacts. It is open 11 a.m. to 7 p.m. daily from the last of May through Labor Day. Donations are accepted.

Listed on the National Register of Historic Places in the Salida area are the Chaffee County Poor Farm, 8495 RD 160; F Street bridge; Garret and Julia Gray Cottage, 125 E. 5th St.; Manhattan Hotel, 225 F St.; and the Ohio-Colorado Smelting and Refining Co. Smokestack/Smeltertown. Also listed as a National Historic District is the downtown area bounded by the Arkansas River, US 50, 3rd and D Sts.

Buena Vista

Twenty five miles north of Salida on US 24 is **Buena Vista** (pop. 2,075). Buena Vista is Spanish for "beautiful view." The town was founded and incorporated in 1879. It was once the center of a rich silver mining region.

BUENA VISTA HERITAGE MUSEUM, in the 300 block of Main St., is housed in the old Chaffee County Courthouse, listed on the National Register of Historic Places. It focuses on local and area history. It is open 9 a.m. to 5 p.m. daily from June to September. An admission is charged.

Other sites listed on the National Register of Historic Places in the Buena Vista area include Grace Episcopal Church, Main and Park Ave.; the bridge over the Arkansas River; Vicksburg Mining Camp, Pike & San Isabel National Forest; and Winfield Mining Camp, 15 miles north of Buena Vista on RD 390.

Other sites listed on the National Register of Historic Places in the county include the Hortense bridge, over CO 162, and St. Elmo Historic District/Forest City, bounded by Pitkin, Gunnison, 1st, Main and Poplar Sts. in Nathrop, eight miles south of Buena Vista. The Littlejohn Mine Complex on the north bank of Pine Creek in the Granite area is also on the Register.

Side Trip to Westcliffe and Silver Cliff

Another side trip that may be considered includes the 25 mile drive from Texas Creek on CO 69 to Westcliffe and Silver Cliff. **Westcliffe** (pop. 324) was founded in 1887 and is named for Westcliffe-by-the-Sea in England. Westcliffe has been the county seat of Custer County since 1928.

Several movies have been shot on location in this area including "Saddle the Wind," "Cat Ballou," "Duchess and the Dirtwater Fox," "Continental Divide," and "Comes A Horseman." The Westcliffe State Bank building, constructed in 1899, was used as a set for the movie "Comes A Horseman."

The Defender Mine Tipple is listed on the National Register of Historic Sites. The Hope Lutheran Church, built in 1917, houses one of the oldest Lutheran congregations in Colorado, first organized in 1872. It is listed on the National Register of Historic Places. Old Westcliffe School, c. 1891, is also listed on the National Register of Historic Places.

Silver Cliff (pop. 280), a mile east, served as the county seat of Custer County from 1887 to 1928. The first county seat was temporarily established in the now abandoned town of Ula. In 1877 Rosita was named the county seat.

SILVER CLIFF MUSEUM, 606 Main St., features local and area history. It is open 1 to 4 p.m. Thursday through Sunday. An admission is charged.

The Silver Cliff Museum is housed in this old fire-house.

Poncha Springs

Back on US 50 it is five miles west from Salida to **Poncha Springs** (pop. 321).

PONCHA SPRINGS MUSEUM is housed in the old two-story brick school house just off US 50 and 285. Displayed are exhibits depicting the area's early days. It is open 8 a.m. to 5 p.m. weekdays and at any other time by arrangement. Admission is free.

The Hutchinson Ranch buildings, three miles west of Salida but listed in Poncha Springs, are listed on the National Register of Historic Places.

Gunnison

It is 60 miles west to **Gunnison** (pop. 6.300), county seat of Gunnison County. The community and county are named in honor of **Capt. John Williams Gunnison** (1812-1853), an Army explorer who was assigned to the job of finding the safest and best route for a transcontinental railroad by President Franklin Pierce. Earlier, in 1849, he was assigned to an expedi-

These photos show some of the outside exhibits at the Gunnison Pioneer Museum.

tion into the the Great Salt Lake Valley of Utah commanded by **Capt. Howard Stansbury**.

Gunnison and his command arrived at **Fort Massachusetts** in mid-August 1853. On September 6 the explorers camped on what became known as the Gunnison River, near the present town of Gunnison. Weeks later the party reached their destination on the Sevier River in Utah. The trip had been successful.

The Fisher-Zugelder House and Smith Cottage, 601 N. Wisconsin, Gunnison, is listed on the National Register of Historic Places.

The Webster Building, 229 W. Main St., Gunnison, is listed on the National Register of Historic Places.

Not one of their 19 wagons was lost, and only two mules were lost.

On the morning of October 25, 1853, Captain Gunnison and a small detachment of men left camp for a reconnaissance of the area. They spotted several Indian signal fires and kept on the alert. The Indians, members of the Pah Vants tribe, attacked the camp the next morning, firing a volley of arrows. Captain Gunnison and all but four of his men were killed. Gunnison's body lies in an unmarked grave at Fillmore, Utah, and a monument has been erected at the scene of his death.

Denverite **Sylvester Richardson** organized the first town company and his small group arrived on May 21, 1874. Gunnison became the county seat in 1877 and was incorporated in 1880.

The gold rush was on and by 1878-79 mining had become important and the city began to grow. But it was also wild as were many mining towns in those early days. A railroad laborer employed on the Alpine Tunnel project was accused of killing contractors. He was taken to jail but in the middle of the night was taken from his cell and lynched on Main Street. **Bat Masterson** was a frequent visitor and it is said **Wyatt and Warren Earp** came to Gunnison to keep out of the "limelight."

Gunnison's "Red Light District" sported such establishments as the Red Lion Inn, Oyster House, and the Atlantic Gardens. The Adams House, at the corner of New York and Main Streets, was the site of the Red Lion Inn.

Horace A. W. Tabor, of Leadville and Denver, established the Bank of Gunnison (today the First National Bank of Gunnison) in 1880. He put up capital of $30,000 and served as president of the bank acting as a silent partner. This was the first bank established on the Western Slope and was located on the site of today's Toggery, from May 1, 1880 to June 4, 1881. The Tabor family were stockholders in the bank and its successor, the Iron National Bank, until 1898.

Alferd Packer's second trial was held in Gunnison in 1886. The confessed cannibal was found guilty of manslaughter and sentenced to 40 years in the state penitentiary in Canon City. He was pardoned on January 10, 1901. (See Chapter 12 for the Alferd Packer Story).

Cyrus "Doc" Wells Shores arrived in Gunnison in 1880 where he operated a freighting business. In 1884, he was elected sheriff of Gunnison County and served for eight years. He also served as a deputy U.S. marshal and as a railroad detective for the Denver and Rio Grande. In 1915 he was appointed chief of police in Salt Lake City. Shores was involved in a shooting in October 1880 while in his cabin. Two desperadoes, **Jack Smith** and **Tom Lewis**, began shooting up the streets of town, wounding a bystander. Shores grabbed a Winchester and started to pursue the fleeing men. He exchanged shots with the pair before a 15-man posse arrived on the scene and was fired upon by them. He returned to Gunnison with the posse not too far behind with Smith and Lewis. The lawman died in Gunnison on October 18, 1934 at the age of 90.

Western State College was founded in 1901 as the Colorado State Normal School. The large "W" on the side of Tenderfoot mountain was the brainchild of the late **Dr. John C. Johnson**, who is primarily responsible for the world's largest collegiate emblem. Dr. Johnson had been responsible for the large "N" built on Smelter Hill just back of the college in 1915 when the school was still known as a State Normal School. When the name was changed to Western State College in 1923, he suggested the idea of building the "W". **WSC President Samuel Quigley** decreed a holiday, May 2, 1923, and most of the students and some of the members of the faculty climbed the mountain to build the "W". The dimensions of the emblem are approximately 320 x 420 feet.

PIONEER MUSEUM, on US 50 on the east edge of town, is a complex that includes the Paragon school house, completed in 1905; an old log post office; a narrow-gauge railroad engine, flatcar, caboose, and water tank, as well as other historical items. It is open Memorial Day through Labor Day. An admission is charged.

There are three sites in this area listed on the National Register of Historic Places including the Curecanti Archaeological District, west of Gunnison; the Fisher-Zugelder House and Smith Cottage, 601 N. Wisconsin St.; and the Webster building, 229 N. Main St.

Crested Butte

Crested Butte (pop. 959) is 28 miles north of Gunnison via CO 135. The town has been designated a Historic District.

Before the first miners arrived in the 1870s, Ute Indians used this area, and the surrounding Elk Mountains, as a summer hunting grounds. They were gradually pushed out by the gold and silver booms of the 1880s which saw Crested Butte's birth. The town was incorporated in 1880, the same year that the Denver & Rio Grande laid out their narrow gauge railway from Gunnison. Crested Butte served as a supply center for the outlying mining camps until the mid-1890s.

Coal was discovered in the late 1880s and sustained the town for the next 60 years. The Colorado Fuel and Iron Company operated the largest mines. In 1952, the last mine (Big Mine) was closed.

In December 1891, coal miners struck the mines in Crested Butte. Sheriff Cyrus "Doc" Shores and two dozen deputies were called in from Gunnison to preserve order. Upon their arrival, the lawmen were met by a charge from 150 angry miners who opened fire. Shores and his men returned the fire and 36 miners were wounded, only one seriously hurt. None of Shores's men were hit, and the strikers soon retreated and disbanded.

Thirty miles northeast of Gunnison, in the **Gunnison National Forest**, is the **Alpine Railroad Tunnel** built in 1880-81. Abandoned in 1910, the tunnel bore through the Continental Divide at an elevation of 11,523 feet to make it the highest railroad station in the U.S. The tunnel is 1,805 feet in length. Persons driving to the tunnel are warned that it is not safe to enter. Persons who visit are asked to sign the register in the Alpine Tunnel Station, built about 1890.

Montrose

It is 65 miles west to **Montrose** (pop. 10,125), county seat of Montrose County. The townsite which included 320 acres was secured in late 1881 by **O. D. Loutsenhizer** and **Joseph Selig**. Loutsenhizer was a member of the the famous Alferd Packer party who came through the area that year. Because winter was setting in when the party decided to push on, he decided to remain here with Chief Ouray while the Packer expedition continued its journey toward Lake City. (For the story of Alferd Packer, the Colorado cannibal, see Chapter 12). The town was then known as **Pomona**, after the "Roman Goddess of Fruit."

The town was platted in 1882 and the name changed to Montrose for one of the characters, the Duchess of Montrose, in a Sir Walter Scott novel. Montrose was incorporated in May, 1882.

Chief Ouray and his wife, **Chipeta**, owned a farm south of Montrose. Ouray was the best-known chief of the Ute Indians

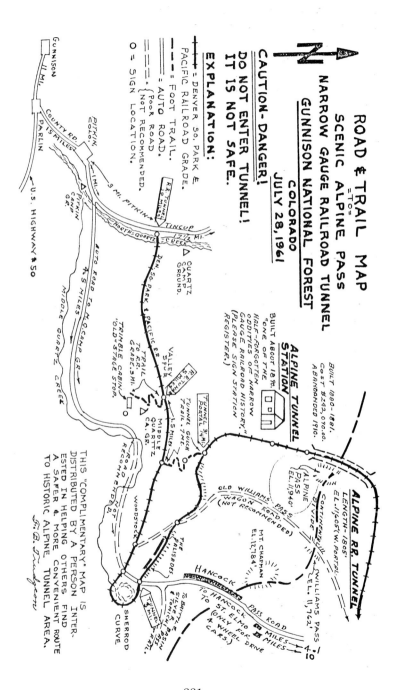

ROAD & TRAIL MAP
=TO=
SCENIC ALPINE PASS
NARROW GAUGE RAILROAD TUNNEL
GUNNISON NATIONAL FOREST
COLORADO
JULY 28, 1961

CAUTION-DANGER!
DO NOT ENTER TUNNEL!
IT IS NOT SAFE.

EXPLANATION:
▭ = DENVER SO. PARK &
    PACIFIC RAILROAD GRADE.
—— = FOOT TRAIL.
=== = AUTO ROAD.
--- = { POOR ROAD
        NOT RECOMMENDED.
O = SIGN LOCATION.

GUNNISON
11 MI.

COUNTY RD.
PARLIN
15 MILES

← U.S. HIGHWAY #50

PITKIN,
COLO.

1 MI.

PITKIN
CAMP
GR.

AUTO ROAD TO N. CAMP GR.

3 MI. PITKIN

R.R. TUNNEL

TINCUP
(7½ MI.)

NORTH QUARTZ CREEK

DEN. SO. PARK & PACIFIC R.R.

△ QUARTZ
  CAMP
  GROUND.

4.5 MILES

MIDDLE QUARTZ CREEK

TRIMBLE CABIN.
"OLD"STAGE STOP.

TRAIL
TO R.R.
GRADE.3 MI.

VALLEY
SPUR

R.R. GRADE

MIDDLE
QUARTZ
CA. GR.

TUNNEL GULCH
TRAIL .7MI.

TUNNEL 3/4 MI.
PORTAL

1.5 MILES

ALPINE TUNNEL
STATION

BUILT ABOUT 1890.
"ONE OF THE
HALF-FORGOTTEN
ODDITIES OF NARROW
GAUGE RAILROAD HISTORY."
(PLEASE SIGN STATION
REGISTER.)

BUILT 1880-1881.
COST $242,070.00.
ABANDONED 1910.

ALPINE RR. TUNNEL
LENGTH-1805'
EL.11,605'(W. PORTAL)

CONTINENTAL DIVIDE
EL. 11,940'

ALPINE
PASS
EL. 11,940'

WILLIAMS PASS
EL. 11,762'

ROAD NOT RECOMMENDED

WOODSTOCK

OLD WILLIAMS PASS
WAGON ROAD
(NOT RECOMMENDED)

DIVIDE EL. 11,762'

MT. CHAPMAN
EL.12,784'

THE PALISADES

HANCOCK

4 WHEEL
RR.

SHERROD
CURVE

To BRITTLE
SILVER PASS
& TOMICHI PASS
(ONLY FOR 4 WHEEL DRIVE CARS)

To ST. ELMO ...4
To HANCOCK...10

HANCOCK PASS ROAD

PASS ROAD

THIS "COMPLIMENTARY" MAP IS
DISTRIBUTED BY A PERSON INTER-
ESTED IN HELPING OTHERS FIND
A SAFER & MORE CONVENIENT ROUTE
TO HISTORIC ALPINE TUNNEL AREA.

F. B. Lindgren

331

The Ute Indian Museum is located two miles south of Montrose on land once part the farm of Chief Ouray. A monument on the grounds honors the memory of Chief Ouray and his wife, Chipeta. Just to the right of this monument is the tomb of Chipeta who died in 1924. Buried next to her is Chief John McCook who died in 1937.

and became prominent in the 1870s. He spoke and understood Spanish, English, and several Indian languages. He settled disputes between the Utes and white settlers and arranged the first treaty between the Ute Indians and the federal government. Under the provisions of the treaty negotiated in 1880 the Utes were assigned to reservations the following year.

Fort Crawford was established eight miles south of Montrose on the west bank of the Uncompahgre River in 1880. It was originally designated as the Cantonment on the Uncompahgre, but on December 15, 1886, its designation was changed to Fort Crawford, named for **Capt. Emmett Crawford**, killed that year fighting Geronimo's Apaches. The military post was established following the Meeker Massacre and ambush of **Major T. J. Thornburgh's** relief force in 1879 further north. Its mission was to defend settlers against any Indian raids and to pacify the Indians. The fort was abandoned on September 23, 1890.

The opening of the **Gunnison Tunnel** in 1909, one of the first Bureau of Reclamation projects in the United States, connected

The Montrose County Historical Museum is housed in the old railroad depot.

the Gunnison River with the Uncompahgre River to bring irrigation to the semi-arid Uncompahgre Valley. The contract for the project was let in 1904. **President William Howard Taft** dedicated the tunnel on September 23, 1909.

Among the personalities who have lived in Montrose have been **Jack Dempsey**, the heavyweight boxing champion of the world; **Otto Mears**, known as the Pathfinder of the San Juans; and **Thomas McKee**, discoverer of radium and early-day photographer of sites such as Mesa Verde. Both museums here have collections of his photos in and around the area. Dempsey trained and participated in a number of boxing matches here.

THE MONTROSE COUNTY HISTORICAL MUSEUM, located in the Denver & Rio Grande depot, focuses on all facets of early-day pioneer life. Highlights in this museum include a furnished homesteader's cabin, a country store with exhibits of household items needed for early-day living, a collection of tools, and a children's corner, containing collections of dolls, toys and baby furniture. Permanent displays include musical instruments, clothing items, and mining, farming, and medical equipment. The depot is listed on the National Register of Historic Places. It is open from 9 a.m. to 5 p.m. Monday through Saturday and 1 to 5 p.m. Sunday from May through October. An admission is charged.

UTE INDIAN MUSEUM, 17253 Chipeta Dr., two miles

The Thomas B. Townsend Home, 222 S. Fifth St., is listed on the National Register of Historic Places.

south of Montrose off US 550, commemorates the life and last residence of Ouray (1833-1880), famous chief of the Southern Ute Indian tribe and his wife, Chipeta. The two galleries, owned by the Colorado Historical Society, is the most complete exhibition of Ute Indian materials in the state. The nucleus of the Ute collection was purchased from Thomas McKee, a local photographer who lived with the Utes, photographed their lives, and acquired numerous traditional and ceremonial items over a 40-year period beginning in the 1880s. Included in the materials are dance skins, beadwork, feather bonnets, and leather garments. Many of these are documented to have belonged to Ouray and Chipeta as well as other famous Utes, among them

Ignacio, Colorow, and **Buckskin Charlie**. Colorow, who belonged to the White River tribe in the high Rockies, was one of the more colorful personalities. He played a major role in the 1879 Meeker massacre. Asked why the Indians had driven a barrel stave through agent Meeker's mouth, Colorow replied: "To stop his infernal lying." He was also in an incident in 1887 where he and a hunting party left their Utah reservation and crossed into northwestern Colorado. The militia was called out but the Indians relented and returned to their reservation before any shooting occurred. A second gallery features objects used and worn by Ute men, women, and children during the 19th century. Included is an explanation of the Ute religion. The museum is open from 10 a.m. to 5 p.m. Monday through Saturday and 1 to 5 p.m. Sunday from Memorial Day weekend to Labor Day weekend. The museum is also open during September under a modified schedule. An admission is charged. Included on the grounds is Chipeta's grave, Ouray Springs, and a marker commemorating the Dominguez-Escalante expedition of 1776.

There are several other sites in the Montrose area listed on the National Register of Historic Places. These include the Gunnison Tunnel, a half mile south of the Black Canyon Turn-off on US 50; the J. V. Lathrop House, 718 Main St.; the Montrose City Hall, 433 S. 1st St.; the Montrose Post Office, 321 S. 1st St.; the Thomas B. Townsend House, 222 S. 5th St.; and the Ute Memorial Site, two miles south of Montrose on US 550.

Delta

It is 21 miles via US 50 to **Delta** (pop.3,931), county seat of Delta County, founded on the site of a trapper's fort built in 1830. It was incorporated in 1882.

The notorious McCarty brothers, Tom and Bill, robbed the Delta bank the morning of September 7, 1893. **Bill McCarty** and his son, Fred, were killed in the botched holdup that netted Tom a mere $100. After entering the bank, **Tom McCarty** fired a warning shot when it appeared the cashiers were not cooperating fully. The shot was heard by a store owner and his son who grabbed rifles and opened fire on the robbers who ran through the rear of the bank where Fred was holding the getaway horses. In the hail of gunfire Bill and Fred were killed. Tom escaped.

Sites in this area listed on the National Register of Historic

Places include the Delta bridge, over US 50; the Delta Post Office and Federal Building, 360 Meeker St.; the Escalante Canyon bridge, RD 650R; and the Roubideau bridge, RD G50R.

North of Delta via CO 92 is **Austin** and **Hotchkiss** (pop. 849).

The Ferganchick Orchard Rock Art Site in the Austin area is listed on the National Register of Historic Places. There are two sites in Hotchkiss listed on the National Register and these are the Hotchkiss bridge, RD 3400R, and the Hotchkiss Hotel, 101 Bridge St.

From Delta it is 31 miles to Grand Junction and another 30 miles to the Utah state line.

The Great Seal of Colorado

The symbols of the State of Colorado are displayed in its Seal. On the seal, the triangular figure represents the "all-seeing" eye of God. The fasces (bound rods) are a symbol of power. The three mountains stand for the state's rugged land, and the pick and hammer for the importance of mining. The Seal was adopted in 1877.

Chapter 10

The Navajo Trail—US 160

This route covers the route from Walsenburg to the Four Corners, where Colorado, Arizona, Utah, and New Mexico meet. One of the most spectacular sites on this route is Mesa Verde National Park, east of Cortez. It was here the Anasazi, "the ancient ones," lived for 1,000 years in their cliff houses. A great mystery surrounds this civilization to this very day. Many other historic sites are found along this route through southern Colorado.

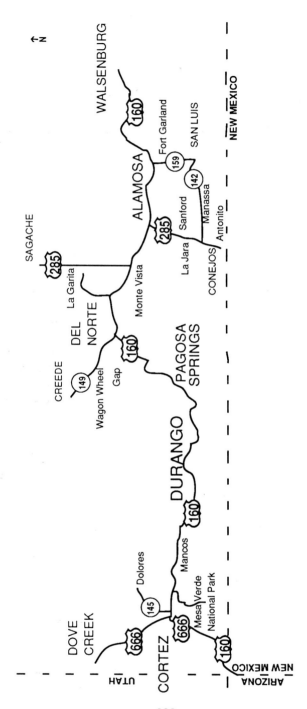

Chapter 10
The Navajo Trail—US 160

The trip from Walsenburg to the Four Corners (Colorado, Utah, Arizona and New Mexico) is 285 miles via US 160 (the Navajo Trail), however, several side trips on this historic route are included in this chapter.

Walsenburg is covered in Chapter 4.

La Veta

La Veta (pop. 611) is on CO 12, 14 miles west of Walsenburg. **Col. John M. Francisco**, a native Virginian, came west in 1839 and in 1851 settled at Fort Massachusetts. When the fort was moved and became Fort Garland he became the sutler for the fort. In 1862 he bought land in Cuchara Valley where he built Franciso Plaza, primarily as a defense from Indians. At different times his fort was a haven for settlers frightened by Indian raiders.

Today Franciso Plaza is home of the FORT FRANCISCO MUSEUM, featuring exhibits on early-day life in this area. It is open from 9 a.m. to 5 p.m. daily. An admission is charged.

The Francisco Plaza and La Veta Pass Narrow Gauge Railroad Depot are listed on the National Register of Historic Places.

Fort Garland

It is 47 miles west of Walsenburg to **Fort Garland**. Fort Garland replaced **Fort Massachusetts** on June 24, 1858. Fort Massachusetts was established six miles north on Ute Creek at an opening into the San Luis Valley on June 22, 1852 as a defense against the Utes and Apaches. It was abandoned in 1858 because of its vulnerability to Indian attack.

Fort Garland was then established to protect settlers in the San Luis Valley, a part of the Territory of New Mexico. The fort here was large enough to accommodate two companies of about 100 men and a handful of officers.

During its quarter century existence, Fort Garland was home to several different companies of infantrymen and mounted riflemen. One of the volunteer units occupying the fort was a regiment commanded by **Col. Kit Carson**, the legendary frontiersman. He was sent to command the fort in 1866 to keep the

Fort Francisco Museum in La Veta began as a trading post in 1862. It was built by Col. John M. Francisco who came from Fort Garland. The old Ritter school house (below) was built in 1876 and today is part of the museum complex.

Fort Garland replaced Fort Massachusetts in southern Colorado Territory on June 24, 1858. The fort was named in honor of Brig. Gen. John C. Garland. The fort was established to protect settlers and the roads south to Taos from renegade Ute and Apache Indians.

Several of the buildings in old Fort Garland have been restored. The old frontier Army post was once commanded by Kit Carson, commanding officer of a New Mexico Volunteer Regiment.

The San Luis Cultural Center and Museum is located in Colorado's oldest town.

The beautiful old Most Precious Blood Catholic Church is located in San Luis, Colorado's oldest town.

peace and negotiate with the Utes. He served in this position for a year. When his volunteers were mustered out, he became Colorado's superintendent of Indian Affairs. Fort Garland was abandoned November 30, 1883, nearly three years after the Utes had been removed from Colorado.

Fort Garland's history includes the gruesome story of the Espinosa bandits. After the infamous bandits had eluded capture by the Army, an old scout, **Tom Tobin**, was put on their trail. He returned to Fort Garland five days later with the Espinosas' heads in a sack across his saddle!

FORT GARLAND, located on CO 159 just off US 160, has been restored and features a re-creation of the commandant's quarters during the Carson period. Also featured are exhibits depicting the rugged military life of the period. Six original flat-roofed buildings comprise the museum. The fort has been listed on the National Register of Historic Places. It is open 10 a.m. to 5 p.m. Monday through Saturday and 1 to 5 p.m. Sunday from Memorial Day weekend to Labor Day weekend. An admission is charged.

San Luis

Sixteen miles south of Fort Garland, via CO 159, to **San Luis** (pop. 842), the oldest town in Colorado. Founded in 1851, San Luis was once a part of four Spanish land grants decreed by the King of Spain. Found here is the Vega, one of two remaining "commons" in the U.S., the oldest water right in Colorado and the oldest family-owned store in the state.

SAN LUIS MUSEUM AND CULTURAL CENTER, 402 Church St., houses colonial and post-colonial artifacts of the Hispanic cultural tradition. On display are santos, which are Hispanic religious items that include paintings on wooden tablets, or "retablos," and carved religious figures called "bultos." It is open 8 a.m. to 4:30 p.m. weekdays and 10 a.m. to 4 p.m. weekends from Memorial Day through Labor Day. It is also open during the off season from 8 a.m. to 4:30 p.m. weekdays. An admission is charged.

There are three sites in San Luis listed on the National Register of Historic Places. These include the Smith-Gallegos House, on Main St.; the Plaza de San Luis de la Culebra Historic District, on CO 159; and the San Luis Bridge, off CO 159.

Alamosa

Back on US 160 at Fort Garland it is 26 miles west to **Alamosa** (pop. 6,830), county seat of Alamosa County.

343

Alamosa is the Spanish word for cottonwood, once plentiful in the area.

Alamosa was established as a terminal for the Denver and Rio Grande Railroad and a trade center for the San Luis Valley in 1868. It was founded and incorporated in 1878.

Adams State College was established here in 1921. The **Luther E. Bean/E.S. Museums** are located on the college campus. The Luther Bean Museum, located on the second floor of Richardson Hall, contains one of the Southwest's most complete collection of santos. The archaeological and anthropological museum is located in the Education and Social Studies building. The displays feature artifacts including stone points and pottery by Pueblo Indians. The museums are open 1 to 5 p.m. weekdays and admission is free.

La Jara

It is 17 miles south of Alamosa, via US 285, to **La Jara** (pop. 858). The railroad depot, now housing the La Jara City Hall, is listed on the National Register of Historic Places.

The CONEJOS COUNTY AGRICULTURAL MUSEUM is located two miles south of La Jara on US 285 and is home to the largest Mormon hay derrick ever built in the United States. The museum features harvest equipment and restored farm tractors from the 1920s, '30s, and '40s. It is open 8 a.m. to 4 p.m. daily the year-round. Admission is free.

Sanford and Pike's Stockade

Five miles east of La Jara, via CO 136, is **Sanford** (pop. 687). Seven miles east of Sanford is Pike's Stockade erected in February 1807 by Capt. Zebulon M. Pike. This was the first fort built on Colorado soil. It was here Pike and his men were taken into custody by Spanish troops and taken to Santa Fe where they were held several months before their release. Pike, one of the most famous of the early-day American explorers, was born in Lamberton, N.J., in 1779. He was killed in the battle at York (Toronto), Canada, in 1813. It is extremely difficult to locate Pike's Stockade, owned by the Colorado State Historical Society. It is listed on the National Register of Historic Places. To reach this historic site, drive on CO 136 to Sanford but instead of turning into town drive straight east on the gravel road (6th St. North) to the end of the road (.7 of a mile). Turn north (left) on RD 20 and drive to RD Y (2.1 miles) and drive east (right) for four miles to RD 24. The entrance to the stockade is on the

La Jara City Hall is housed in the old depot at Broadway and Main. The depot and town hall are listed on the National Register of Historic Places.

The Agricultural Museum is located two miles south of La Jara. In the background is the largest Mormon haystacker.

This monument marks the site of Pike's Stockade several miles east of Sanford.

Pike's Stockade, built by Capt. Zebulon Montgomery Pike in 1807, was the first military base established on Colorado soil. The rudimentary fort has been designated a Registered National Historic Landmark.

This monument in Manassa describes the Mormon settlement that occurred here in the late 1870s. It salutes the Mormon settlers who arrived in 1878.

right. It is .8 of a mile from the entrance to the stockade driving along a heavily covered ranch road. The area is open during the daylight hours from May 1 to October 15. BE EXTREMELY CAREFUL OF SNAKES AT THE STOCKADE SITE.

Manassa

It is seven miles south from La Jara to Romeo via US 285. Three miles east of Romeo on CO 142 is **Manassa** (pop. 945). Mormon pioneers from the Southern states and Utah arrived in the area in 1878. They organized the town of Manassa in 1879. The San Luis Stake, comprised of several settlements including Ephraim, Richfield and Manassa, was organized in 1883.

Manassa is the hometown of **Jack, the "Manassa Mauler,"**

This small house in Manassa was the birthplace of the heavyweight boxing champion Jack Dempsey. Today it serves as a museum.

William Harrison "Jack" Dempsey became the heavyweight boxing champion of the world in 1919 when he knocked out Jess Willard. Dempsey, known as the Manassa Mauler, began his fight career in the Colorado mining camps starting in 1912. He was born in Manassa.

349

Our Lady of Guadalupe in Conejos is the oldest church in Colorado.

Dempsey, popular heavyweight boxing champion from 1919 to 1926. William Harrison Dempsey (1895-1983) began fighting in mining camps in 1912. He knocked out Jess Willard in July 4, 1919 to win the heavyweight title, but lost it in 1926 to Gene Tunney. Their second fight, in 1927, was climaxed by the famous "long count." Dempsey knocked Tunney down in the seventh round but the referee delayed the count because Dempsey did not go immediately to a neutral corner. Tunney got up at the count of 9 but it was estimated this was equivalent to a count of 14. Tunney went on to win the fight. During his career, Dempsey fought 81 bouts, winning 60, 49 by knockouts.

JACK DEMPSEY MUSEUM, 401 Main St., is a tribute to the Dempsey family and the champion with photographs, mementos and personal items. It is open 9 a.m. to 5 p.m. Monday through Saturday from Memorial Day to Labor Day. Admission is free.

Conejos, Home of Oldest Church

Back on US 285 it is five miles south to the unincorporated town of **Conejos**, home of Colorado's oldest church, **Our Lady of Guadalupe**. The site of the church was selected by Bishop Machebeuf. A jacal "picket" church was built and later replaced with a larger church. The first church was dedicated in 1863 by Bishop John B. Lamy, first bishop of Santa Fe. The church was operated by Jesuit fathers from 1871 to 1920. The church is located at the corner of RD G6 and RD 13 just east of town.

Antonito

Just south of Conejos is **Antonito** (pop. 1,103), headquarters for the **Cumbres & Toltec Scenic Railroad**, one of the last narrow gauge railroads. Depots are located in Antonito and Chama, New Mexico. It is listed as a Registered National Historic Site. Locomotive Engine 463 is also listed on the National Register.

The Cumbres & Toltec began in 1880 as the San Juan extension of the Denver & Rio Grande to serve the rich mining camps in the San Juan Mountains. The train operates daily from mid-June to mid October. Timetables and fare schedules are available at either depot.

Also in Antonito are the Warshauer Mansion at 515 River St. and the Costilla Crossing Bridge, on the county road over the Rio Grande River. Both are listed on the National Register of Historic Places.

The Labo Del Rio Bridge, RD F 50 over Piedra River, at Arboles, and the Chimney Rock Archaeological Area, in the San Juan Forest, both in Archuleta County, are listed on the National Register of Historic Places.

Monte Vista

Returning to Alamosa on US 160, it is 17 miles west to **Monte Vista** (pop. 3,902). The Monte Vista Post Office and Federal Building are listed on the National Register of Historic Places.

MONTE VISTA HISTORICAL SOCIETY MUSEUM, 1st Ave. and Jefferson St., just off US 160, is housed in the area's first library, c. 1895. This mini-museum features city history in its displays. It is open 2 to 5 p.m. daily. Admission is free.

The Cumbres & Toltec Scenic Railroad is a Registered National Historic Site. It began in 1880 as the San Juan extension of the Denver & Rio Grande to serve the rich mining camps in the San Juan Mountains.

The Warshauer Mansion in Antonito is listed on the National Register of Historic Places.

Saguache

From Monte Vista it is 35 miles north via US 285 to Saguache (Sawatch is a Ute word meaning "water at the blue earth"). **Saguache** (pop. 656) is the county seat of Saguache County. Alferd Packer, Colorado's infamous cannibal, was held here briefly in 1874 in a log cabin outside of town before his escape during that summer. At the time of his arrival in April 1874, this was the Los Pinos Indian Agency. Further information on the Alferd Packer story is found in Chapter 12.

SAGUACHE MUSEUM, on US 285, is a Registered National Historic Site. The museum is housed in an adobe building (c. 1880s) with seven rooms of memorabilia including a school room, pioneer kitchen, parlour, mineral room, Wesley DeCamp cowboy room, Indian and Spanish room, Memorial room which houses one of the largest Indian artifact collections in Colorado. Beside the house is the Saguache county jail built in 1908 and used until 1958. The yard is filled with mining and ranching displays along with a blacksmith shop. It is open 10 a.m. to 5 p.m. daily from Memorial Day through Labor Day. An admission is charged.

The Saguache Flour Mill is listed on the National Register of Historic Places.

La Garita

Driving back south on US 285 to RD 412 is La Garita comprised basically of a store and a handful of residences. There are two historic sites.

The La Capilla de San Juan Bautista Church here is listed on the National Register of Historic Places. Nearby are ruins believed to once be part of a convent. Today the old church houses the San Juan Art Center.

Indian pictographs are located on a wall in El Carnero Canyon, across the Carnero Creek, on the L-Cross Ranch. This is on private property therefore permission must be obtained to cross the ranch property. Permission and directions are available at the La Garita Store. These **Carnero Creek Pictographs** are listed on the National Register of Historic Places.

Back on the road west of La Garita about a mile is a dirt road on the right leading to wagon ruts cut 12 to 14 inches deep into solid rock intermittenly for almost a mile. No one knows exactly how these tracks got here but there are several theories including a road to bypass a swamp, a wood haulers road, or a short-

The Saguache County Museum is listed on the National Register of Historic Places. In the photo, below, is the old county jail now part of the museum.

The La Capilla de San Juan Baptista (the Church of Saint John the Baptist) today houses the San Juan Art Center. The old La Garita church building is listed on the National Register of Historic Places.

This partial wall is all that remains of a convent constructed near La Capilla de San Juan Baptista Church in La Garita.

The pictographs in El Carnero Canyon just outside La Garita are listed on the National Register of Historic Places. These pictographs have been featured in the Denver media on several occasions.

Wagon ruts cut deeply into the soft sandstone west of La Garita.

cut to the Gunnison area. These wagon tracks can be found about a mile and a half off the road. A small sign, easily missed, on RD 38A points the way to the wagon ruts.

Approximately four miles southwest of La Garita on RD 38A, on the right, is RD A32 leading to **La Ventana Natural Arch**. To get there follow RD A32 for six miles to the arch. From Del Norte take CO 112 3.2 miles east to RD 38A and then drive north for 6.1 miles on RD 38A to RD A32 to Rio Grande National Forest and La Ventana Arch.

In this same area are **Round Rocks**, also called **Elephant Rocks**, and **Penitiente Canyon**, one of America's newest and most diversified rock climbing areas. Maps and other information are available at the Del Norte Chamber of Commerce office.

Del Norte

Del Norte (pop. 1,709) is the county seat of Rio Grande County. It is only 31 miles via US 160 between Monte Vista and Del Norte.

The history of the area dates back to 8000 B.C. as confirmed by finds. Artifacts of the Folsom Man were discovered in the county between 1935 and 1940. Fossilized human bones and fluted points of the Yuma culture have been found. It is known that Yuma occupation appears to have ceased after 5000 B.C. Various inhabitants have included the Upper Rio Grande Culture (B.C.); the Utes (800 A.D.); the Hogan Builders (1100 A.D.); and the Pueblo Indians (1300 A.D.). **Francisco Vasquez de Coronado** was the first European explorer to pass through the area in 1540-42. **Don Juan de Onate** took possession of the area for Spain in 1598 and the next 200 years were marked by fighting between the Ute and Comanche tribes and the Spanish.

In 1859 a plaza-farm was founded at **La Loma de San Jose** two miles from the present day Del Norte. In 1870 gold was discovered at **Summitville**. Del Norte was platted in 1871 and incorporated in 1872. Del Norte itself was never a mining town, but rather the supply and commercial center for mining areas.

It is believed that the Utes came to the San Luis Valley in about 1300 A.D., and that the Valley was a special homeland to the Moache Band in the southern valley, and the Tabeguache in the northern valley. The Utes remained in this region until they were forced to move to the Uintah Reservation in Utah in

357

The Natural Arch (La Ventana) is one of the many unusual rock formations in the San Luis Valley. La Ventana is located between Del Norte and La Garita in the Rio Grande National Forest.

The Rio Grande County Museum and Cultural Center in Del Norte.

358

1880. **Gov. Juan Bautista de Anza** traveled through the San Luis Valley in 1779 with 700 troops and 200 Ute-Apache allies from Santa Fe.

In the late 19th century, **Tom Bowen**, a flamboyant mine owner, proposed another state of the Union, separate from Colorado. The name of the new state was to be the **"State of San Juan,"** with its capital, Del Norte. It is claimed the proposition lost by a single vote. Bowen later defeated **H.A.W. Tabor** for a GOP Senate seat in 1883.

RIO GRANDE COUNTY MUSEUM, 580 Oak St., offers a glimpse into the cultural and natural history of the area from the Indians and Hispanic settlers, the mountain men fur trappers and traders, to the later settlers who came in search of gold and silver. It is open 10 a.m. to 5 p.m. Monday through Saturday through the summer months. It is open during the fall on a limited basis. An admission is charged.

The **Barlow-Sanderson Stage Station** has been moved to the Centennial Park three blocks north on Spruce Street off US 160. The station was one of the original stage stations that was discovered being used as an outbuilding garage and was headed for the wood stove. Local citizens obtained it and reconstructed it. It is open during the summer on a limited (by request) basis.

There are two bridges, the Sutherland and Wheeler, both off US 160 which are listed on the National Register of Historic Places.

The **Stone Quarry**, east of town off US 160, provided the stone used for the Governor's Mansion in Denver, the Rio Grande County Courthouse, the Stone Quarry restaurant in Del Norte, and several other buildings in the Del Norte area. This site may be difficult to locate and directions should be obtained at the Chamber of Commerce office in Del Norte.

Summitville

Summitville, one of the state's largest gold camps in the 1870s, is located about 27 miles south of Del Norte. The town boomed again in 1934 and was the second largest mining camp in the state. In 1976, a 114 pound boulder containing $350,000 in gold was found along the road. Some of the original buildings are still standing in the town. To reach Summitville, take RD 14 (turns into Forest Service RD 330 in the Rio Grande National Forest) south from US 160 at the west end of Del Norte.

Continue south to the "Chicken Fork," a three road fork, and take the right fork (FS 332) to the first road that turns left. There is a sign here with directions to Summitville.

In 1847-48 **John C. Fremont** was commissioned to search for a central route through the mountains for the railroad. On December 11, 1848, the party crossed the Rio Grande River near Del Norte and headed into the San Juans to find a pass through the mountains. A heavy snow storm struck while they were high in the mountains and they could not continue their trip. The weather was bitter cold and soon their food supply was exhausted and they were forced to eat their mules. Several members of the party lost their lives. The survivors finally were able to get out of the mountains and returned to Santa Fe. The area where they were snowbound is known today as Fremont's Christmas Camp Site. It can be reached by driving west on US 160 for about nine miles to Embargo Creek access road (green forest service sign). Turn right and continue across the river to an intersection, turn right and then left on FS 650 (about 1/4 mile) and follow to the junction with FS 640. A sign provides directions to Cathedral Campgrounds. Take FS 640 past the campground to the dead end. From this point it is about three miles via a foot path to Fremont's camp. Still seen here are the stumps of trees that were cut for firewood and other signs of the almost disastrous expedition.

Creede

It is 17 miles west to South Fork. From here, via CO 149, it is 22 miles northwest to **Creede** (pop. 610). The Masonic Park Bridge off CO 149 at South Fork is listed on the National Register of Historic Places.

Creede, county seat of Mineral County, was one of the wildest and unruly mining towns in the West. It was incorporated on March 19, 1892 and named for **Nicholas C. Creede** who discovered the Holy Moses Mine. The last two lines in a poem written by Cy Warman, editor of *The Chronicle* in 1892, perhaps best describes this mining camp during its heyday: "It's day all day in the daytime. And there is no night in Creede."

Enroute to Creede, via CO 149, is **Wagon Wheel Gap**, scene of several early Indian battles. It is said **Tom Boggs**, a brother-in-law of **Kit Carson**, farmed at Wagon Wheel Gap in 1840. The Wagon Wheel Gap Railroad Station is listed on the National Register of Historic Places.

The train depot in Wagon Wheel Gap, between South Fork and Creede, is listed on the National Register of Historic Places.

The **Bachelor Townsite** is northwest of Creede on Bachelor Road. This is a historic suburb of Creede in its boom years. **North Creede**, or the original townsite, is located in East Willow Creek Canyon. During the height of the mining era some 10,000 persons lived in this area. Below Creede other towns sprang up with such names as **Stringtown, Jimtown** and **Amethyst**. Others were **Spar City, Stumptown** and **Weaver**. The Commodore Mine Workings are located north of town along Willow Creek. These old mine remains tell the story of the 19th century silver boom.

Bob Ford who killed the famed outlaw **Jesse James** on April 3, 1882 in St. Joseph, Missouri, arrived in Creede a few years later and opened a saloon and gambling parlor. On June 8, 1892, Ford suspected and accused **Edward O. "Red" Kelly** of stealing a ring and Kelly entered his saloon to protest. Ford had him thrown off the premises at which time Kelly obtained a shotgun. He returned to Ford's saloon and again confronted him. In a brief encounter he shot Ford, killing him almost instantly. He was arrested in Pueblo, tried for murder, convicted and sentenced to life imprisonment. His life sentence was commuted and he was released in 1900. He managed to attract trou-

361

Robert Ford's grave site in Creede. Ford shot and killed the outlaw
Jesse James in St. Joseph, Missouri, in 1882. He was shot and killed
in his Creede saloon and gambling house in 1892 by Edward Kelly.
Ford's body was later reinterred in Richmond, Missouri.

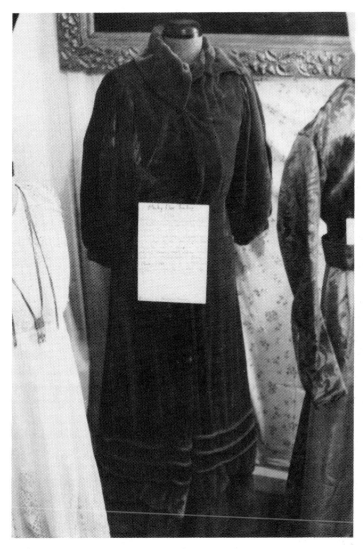

One of Baby Doe Tabor's dressing gowns is displayed in the museum at Creede.

ble again and was killed January 13, 1904 by an Oklahoma City police officer. Ford was buried just outside the Creede cemetery. Later his body was moved to his hometown of Richmond, Missouri.

CREEDE MUSEUM is housed in the old Denver and Rio

Grande Railroad Depot. Exhibits feature Creede's first hand-drawn fire wagon, a horse-drawn hearse, early mining tools, pioneer utensils, gambling devises, historic photographs, early newspapers and other memorabilia of Creede's past. It is open 10 a.m. to 4 p.m. Monday through Saturday from Memorial Day through Labor Day. An admission is charged.

Pagosa Springs

Back to South Fork and US 160, it is 42 miles southwest to **Pagosa Springs** (pop. 1,331), county seat of Archuleta County. Pagosa Springs was incorporated in 1891 and is the only incorporated municipality in the county. The county was formed in 1885.

The Ute Indians who hunted in this area made use of the mineral hot springs which they called "Pagosah" or "Healing Waters." Members of a topographical survey party commanded by Capt. John N. Macomb arrived in 1858 and are believed to be the first Americans to see and describe the hot springs.

Fort Lewis was established at Pagosa Springs on October 15, 1878 to guard the Ute Indian Reservation. It was named Camp Lewis on October 26, 1878 and gained fort status in December, 1878. The fort was manned by troops from the 9th Cavalry and 15th Infantry. On August 30, 1880 a new Fort Lewis was established on the La Plata River, about 12 miles west of Durango. The original post was then called **Cantonment Pagosa Springs** until it was soon abandoned. The new Fort Lewis was abandoned on October 15, 1891.

Jack Buchanan was living near Fort Lewis in 1882 when he was attacked and wounded by Indian raiders. Frank and George Coe, who lived nearby, chased the Indians, and after firing several shots routed the raiders and recovered Buchanan's livestock which was being driven off.

Fred Harman, creator of the comic strip "Red Ryder," called Pagosa Springs home. The prolific artist began his Red Ryder comic strip in 1938 and continued it until 1964. Several Red Ryder movies and serials were made featuring the cowboy hero and his Indian friend, **Little Beaver**. Many Hollywood celebrities visited Harman including the Duke, **John Wayne**. Harman died January 2, 1982 at the age of 79.

FRED HARMAN ART MUSEUM, on US 160 west of town, features original Western paintings by the artist. Included are several of his Red Ryder and Little Beaver strips. Movie and western memorabilia are also on display. It is open 10:30 a.m. to

Howdy ~ YOUR FRIEND "RED RYDER" FRED HARMAN

5 p.m. daily, 10 a.m. to 4 p.m. Saturday and 12 noon to 4 p.m. Sunday. An admission is charged.

UPPER SAN JUAN HISTORICAL MUSEUM, on US 160 on the east side of town, offers a fascinating and extensive display of the early day Pagosa Springs area. It is open 11 a.m. to 5 p.m. Tuesday through Saturday. Admission is free.

Among the most notable geographic features in the county is **Chimney Rock**, the site of Anasazi ruins called **Square Top**. The Chimney Rock Indian ruins are located 17 miles west of CO 151.

Just west of Pagosa Springs on the right hand side of the highway going west is a historical marker. It marks a site near the spot where **Col. Albert H. Pfeiffer**, famous frontiersman

The Upper San Juan Historical Museum is located in Pagosa Springs.

The Animas Museum is located in this old school house in Durango.

The famous Durango-Silverton Narrow Gauge Railroad is seen here shortly before leaving Durango for the trip to Silverton.

representing the Ute Indians, killed a Navajo in a knife fight in 1872. The prize in this duel was the Pagosa Hot Springs, and since Pfeiffer represented the Utes they won possession of the coveted springs.

Durango

It is 60 miles west to **Durango** (pop. 11,649), county seat of La Plata County. It was founded in 1880 when the Denver & Rio Grande Railroad platted the site a mile and a half south of **Animas City**, founded in 1861 by **S. B. Kellogg**. The D&RG depot was built at this new site and Animas City was soon out of business. Within a year after it was platted, Durango boasted of 20 saloons, a red light district along its western edge, and 134 businesses. Some 2,000 settlers had poured into the area in response to newspaper advertisements that hailed Durango as the "Denver of the Southwest."

Durango was not always a quiet and peaceful town. The Peter Keegan family, who lived at 622 3rd Avenue, was caught in a crossfire in a gunfight between Farmington and Durango cowboys over cattle rustling. Henry Moorman was lynched on West 9th Street, just off Main Avenue, on Sunday, April 10, 1881, when he walked into a saloon, declared he was going to kill

367

someone and then carried out his threat. He was hanged the same day. George Woods was hanged for killing an unarmed man May 23, 1882 in the Pacific Club Saloon. Justice was swift and his legal hanging was carried out one month later with some 300 persons witnessing the execution. An attempt was made to rob the Bank of San Juan (today the 1st National Bank) in 1883 but the would-be robber was foiled by alert citizens. A posse was formed and the culprit quickly captured.

The new town was named after a Mexican town named Durango. It is home of **Fort Lewis College** founded in 1911.

The Animas River running through the town was called the Rio de las Animas Perdidas or "River of Lost Souls." The late **Louis L'Armour**, who became one of the most prolific authors of the Western novel, owned a mountain home in Durango.

ANIMAS MUSEUM, 31st St. and W. 2nd Ave., features exhibits on local history, archaeology, and natural history. It is open 10 a.m. to 6 p.m. weekdays and 11 a.m. to 4 p.m. weekends from Memorial Day through the end of September. An admission is charged.

There are two historic districts in Durango listed on the National Register. These include the Main Avenue Historic District and the East Third Avenue Historic Residential District. Also on the National Register of Historic Places are the Colorado Ute Power Plant, 14th St. and Animas River; the Newman Block/Kiva Building, Main and 8th Sts.; the Durango-Silverton Narrow Gauge Railroad; the Durango Rock Shelters Archaeology Site; and Ute Mountain Mancos Canyon.

Some 11.7 miles from the 32nd Street junction, the road takes a series of abrupt turns that lead to a one-lane bridge spanning a chasm created by the churning Animas River. Baker's Bridge, site of Animas City No. 1 (1860-61), remains a landmark in the area. The Baker's Bridge chasm provided the setting for Paul Newman and Robert Redford to make their famous leap from the cliff into the river for a scene in the 1969 movie, "Butch Cassidy and the Sundance Kid." It also was the background for several scenes from "The Naked Spur," a 1953 movie starring James Stewart, Janet Leigh, and Robert Ryan.

Ute Mountain Mancos Canyon Historic District, in Durango, is listed on the National Register of Historic Places.

Ignacio

The **Southern Ute Indian Cultural Center** is located at **Ig-**

368

The Museum of the Mesa Verde Cowboys is housed in the George Bauer mansion in Mancos.

nacio southeast of Durango on CO 172. The CULTURAL CENTER MUSEUM features exhibits and a multimedia production depicting the early history of the Utes. There are many artifacts of Anasazi origin. The museum is open 9 a.m. to 6 p.m. daily and 10 a.m. to 3 p.m. Sunday. An admission is charged.

Mancos

It is 19 miles west of Durango via US 160 to **Mancos** (pop. 870). There are two sites in Mancos listed on the National Register of Historic Places. These include the Mancos Opera House, 136 W. Grand, and the Lost Canyon Archaeological District.

The MUSEUM OF THE MESA VERDE COWBOYS, one and a half blocks south of US 160 on N. Main St., is housed in the old George Bauer mansion. The house, built by Bauer in 1890 who was the founder of Mancos, is a big three-story house that sits in the middle of a spacious lawn. Bauer also founded the first bank in Mancos in 1888 and remained as president as well as mayor of the town for many years. The museum is open 1 to 4 p.m. Monday through Saturday.

Two Quaker cowboys from the Alamo Ranch southwest of

Mancos, discovered the ruins that became Mesa Verde National Park in 1906.

Mesa Verde National Park

It is eight miles to the entrance of Mesa Verde National Park, the first national park set aside to preserve the works of man. The park, which occupies a large plateau rising high above the Montezuma and Mancos Valleys, preserves a spectacular remnant of their thousand-year-old culture. These people are called the **Anasazi**, from a Navajo word meaning "the ancient ones." The first Anasazi settled in Mesa Verde (Spanish for "green table") about A.D. 50.

They were known as Basketmakers because of their skill at that craft. Formerly a nomadic people, the Anasazi began leading a more settled way of life. Farming replaced hunting-and-gathering as their main source of livelihood. They lived in pithouses clustered in small villages. These were usually built on the mesa tops but occasionally in the cliff recesses. They soon learned to make pottery, and they acquired the bow and arrow, a more effective weapon for hunting than the atlatl, or spear thrower.

These were prosperous times for the Basketmakers. Their population began to grow and about 750 A.D. they began building their houses above ground with upright walls made of poles and mud. They built these houses against one another in long, curving rows, often with a pithouse or two in front. These pithouses were probably the forerunners of the kivas that came into existence later. From this period, these people are known as Pueblos, a Spanish word for "village dwellers."

By 1000 A.D. the Anasazi had become skilled stone masons. Their walls of thick, double-coursed stone often rose two or three stories high and were joined together into units of 50 rooms or more. Pottery also changed and their designs became more artistic. Farming provided more of the diet than before, and much mesa top land was cleared for that purpose.

The years from 1100 to 1300 were Mesa Verde's classic period. The population had grown at a rapid rate and the population may have reached several thousand. The compact villages included many rooms with the kivas often built inside the walls. Round towers began to appear and there was a rising level of craftsmanship in masonry work, pottery, weaving, jewelry, and tool-making.

370

Two of the several cliff dwellings in Mesa Verde National Park. Cliff Palace (above) and Spruce Tree House (below) were built by the Anasazi, "the Ancient Ones." The Anasazi inhabited this area between A.D. 1 to 1300.

About 1200 there was another major population shift. The Anasazi began to move back into the cliffs that had sheltered their ancestors centuries before. The reason for this move remains a mystery. Whatever the reason or reasons, it gave rise to the cliff dwellings for which Mesa Verde is famous.

Most of the cliff dwellings were built in the middle decades of the 1200s. They range in size from one-room houses to villages of over 200 rooms (**"Cliff Palace"**). The masonry work varied in quality; from rough construction to walls made of well-shaped stones. Many rooms were plastered inside and decorated with painted designs.

The Anasazi lived in their cliff houses less than 100 years. By 1300 they had left Mesa Verde which has created another mystery. Why did they leave for New Mexico and Arizona where did they settle next? Scientists know that the last quarter of the century was a time of drought.

It is 21 miles from the park entrance to **Chapin Mesa ruins.** The major cliff dwellings here are **Spruce Tree House, Cliff Palace,** and **Balcony House.** An archaeological museum interprets the life of the ancient Anasazi. Ranger tours through some cliff dwellings are available. Two hiking trails lead into Spruce Canyon. The Petroglyph Point Trail, 2.8 miles, and Spruce Canyon Trail, 2.1 miles, begin at points on the Spruce Tree House Trail. Hikers must register at the ranger's office before attempting these trails.

Spruce Tree House is the third largest cliff dwelling in the park and is open all year long. The museum here is open every day of the year and maintains a full range of artifacts uncovered in and near Mesa Verde over the years.

Mesa Verde National Park is a MUST for visitors to Southwest Colorado. It is listed on the National Register of Historic Places. An entrance fee to the park is charged.

Cortez

Back on US 160 it is another 10 miles to **Cortez** (pop. 7,095), county seat of Montezuma County, founded in 1887 and incorporated in 1902. Cortez is an ideal base of operations to explore the ancient Anasazi culture.

Other Indian points of interest include the **Hovenweep National Monument (Colorado/Utah), Ute Mountain Tribal Park, Crow Canyon Archaeological Center, the Lowery Ruins,** and **the Anasazi Heritage Center and Escalante**

Ruins and the **Cortez CU Center** in downtown Cortez. Detailed information about these historic sites are available at the Cortez Visitor's Center, 808 E. Main in Cortez.

Crow Canyon Archaeological Center near Cortez is committed to creating a greater understanding of the pre-historic Anasazi people. The Center offers students and adults with no previous experience to participate in its research and educational programs. Among its sponsors have been the Smithsonian Institute, the Denver Museum of Natural History, the Heard Museum in Phoenix, and other museums across the country. Crow Canyon charges tuition for all of its programs.

The museum in the Cortez CU Center in downtown Cortez displays interpretive exhibits on the Basketmaker and Pueblo periods of the prehistoric Anasazi civilization and exhibits from Yellow Jacket Pueblo and the Anasazi Heritage Center. Also featured are displays from the Mountain Ute Tribe. A very popular feature of the Center is its enrichment lecture series four nights per week in the summer and bi-monthly in fall and winter. These illustrated talks feature archaeology, astronomy, Native American arts, culture and history, ornithology, entomology and other topics. The Center is operated through a unique partnership between the University of Colorado and the community of Cortez and all programs are free of charge.

The Ute Indian tribe has set aside their Tribal Park to preserve the prehistoric Anasazi culture. Hundreds of surface ruins and cliff dwellings, some which are stabilized for visitation, are found in the Park. Also found here are a number of historic Ute wall paintings and ancient petroglyphs. Full day tours are offered to the main ruins area in Johnson Canyon beginning at approximately 9 a.m. Arrangements for these tours may be made at the Ute Mountain Pottery Plant, 15 miles south of Cortez on US 666.

Hovenweep National Monument (Colorado/Utah) was established in 1923 by Presidential proclamation. The Square Tower Ruins and campground complex are located 45 miles west northwest of Cortez in Utah. The ruins of Hovenweep (a Ute word meaning "deserted valley") are characterized by their unique square, oval, circular, and D-shaped towers.

The Monument consists of six groups of ruins. In Utah there are the Square Tower Ruins and the Cajon Ruins. In Colorado are the Holly, Hackberry Canyon, Cutthroat Castle, and Good-

The Lowery Pueblo Ruins date back to the late 11th century. The pueblo was constructed by pre-historic farmers, the Anasazi. These farmers raised corn, beans, squash, tobacco and turkeys. It is believed that at its height the Lowery Pueblo housed about 100 persons.

man Point Ruins. All of the roads to Hovenweep are unpaved and under certain conditions may be impassable. Since there is no telephone service to the Hovenweep Monument, visitors should call Mesa Verde National Park, (303) 529-4461 or 4465, for the latest information on weather and road conditions. The Monument is listed on the National Register of Historic Places.

The Lowery Ruin is just off Rd CC west of Pleasant View on US 666 northwest of Cortez. The Lowery Pueblo at one time housed about 100 people. The presence of a great kiva here suggests that Lowery Pueblo was a regional, urban and ritual center. The main pueblo was built in stages on top of abandoned pit houses. Initially it consisted of only four rooms but over a 30 year period was expanded to include over 40 rooms and eight kivas, or ritual rooms. The pueblo was abandoned about A.D. 1150. The Lowery Ruin is listed on the National Register of Historic Places.

There are two sites in the Pleasant View vicinity listed on the National Register of Historic Places. These include the James A. Lancaster Site/Clawson Ruin and the Pigge Site.

Dove Creek

Returning to US 666 it is 15 miles northwest to **Dove Creek** (pop. 826), county seat of Dolores County. It is in the center of seven National Parks or Monuments: Mesa Verde National Park, Arches National Park, Canyonlands National Park, Hovenweep National Monument, Four-Corners National Monument, Monument Valley National Park, and San Juan National Park.

Back to Cortez there are two other historic sites in the area listed on the National Register of Historic Places including the Mud Springs Pueblo and the Yucca House National Monument, 12 miles south of Cortez via US 666.

Dolores

From Cortez it is 11 miles north to **Dolores** (pop. 802) via CO 145. The Dolores River was named by the two Franciscan priests in honor of feast day of Our Lady of Sorrows, August 13, 1776.

Three miles west of Dolores via CO 184 is the ANASAZI HERITAGE CENTER, a new museum opened by the Bureau of Land Management in 1988. The Center houses records, samples, and artifacts from the Dolores Archaeological Program (survey and excavation in advance of McPhee Dam and Reservoir construction), as well as other archaeological material from southwest Colorado. Exhibits include a "hands-on" Discovery Area with a loom and corn grinding tools, a holographic image, microscopes, a test-trench profile, interactive computer programs, a cutaway reconstruction of a furnished pithouse, and other exhibits on the Anasazi, archaeology, and public lands in the Four Corners. An 18-minute orientation film is shown hourly, and temporary and traveling exhibits are scheduled in the Special Exhibit Gallery.

In front of the museum is the **Dominquez Ruins**, a 12th century AD Ansaszi ruin named for **Father Atanasio Dominquez** who led a Spanish expedition through this area in an unsuccessful attempt to reach California. On August 13, 1776, **Father Escalante** discovered the ruin that now bears his name, located on the hilltop above the Center.

The Escalante Ruin is the first prehistoric structure in Colorado to be described in writing. Also a 12th century AD Anasazi ruin, it shows affinities with the Anasazi of the Chaco Canyon

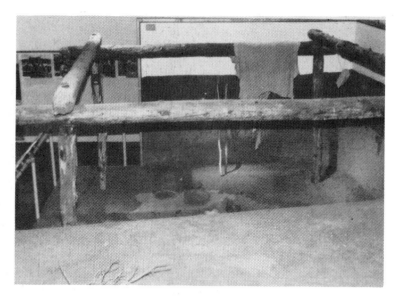

Two exhibits in the Anasazi Heritage Center near Dolores. Above is a full-sized cutaway replica of an Anasazi pithouse. The Hopi man below is carrying corn home in a manner the Anasazi may have used.

The Escalante Ruin (above) and the Dominquez Ruin (below) are at the Anasazi Heritage Center near Dolores. The ruin bearing his name was discovered in 1776 by Father Silvestre Velez de Escalante, member of a Spanish expedition led by Father Atanasio Dominquez in search of a route from Santa Fe to Monterey, California.

The old Southern Hotel in Dolores is listed on the National Register of Historic Places.

area in New Mexico, whereas the Dominquez Ruin is more typical of the Northern San Juan Anasazi. Escalante Ruin is reached via a half-mile long paved trail from the vicinity of the Center's parking lot; it affords the visitor an excellent panoramic view of the Montezuma Valley, perhaps more heavily populated in Anasazi times than it is now.

The Escalante Ruin is listed on the National Register of Historic Places.

The DOLORES MUSEUM is located at S. 4th and Center Sts. The Southern Hotel, 101 S. 5th St., is listed on the National Register of Historic Places.

Galloping Goose Historical Society

The Galloping Goose Historical Society of Dolores owns one of the two Galloping Goose trains, still in the area, used from 1931 to 1951 by the Rio Grande Southern Railroad to serve several of the San Juan Mountain mining towns. It is displayed in the Dolores City Park. The other is in Telluride. Three are in the Colorado Railroad Historical Museum in Golden, near Denver.

The Dolores group plans to put their Galloping Goose in operation and offer tours. For more on the story of this unusual "train" see Chapter 11.

Chapter 11
Mining Towns in the San Juans

The stories of several historic mining towns in the San Juan Mountains are recounted in this chapter. Among two of the most colorful mining communities were Telluride and Ouray. Also included are stories of some of the unusual people who played special roles in the history of the region.

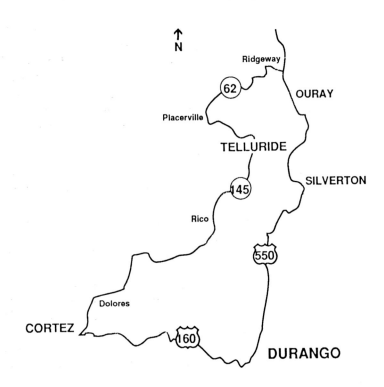

Chapter 11
Mining Towns in the San Juans

This chapter covers the mining towns that sprang up in the San Juan Mountains during the late 19th century. The focus is on Rico, Telluride, Ouray, and Silverton. (Nearby Lake City is covered in Chapter 12).

The area can be reached over several routes. From US 50, Ouray and Silverton can be reached directly on US 550 from Montrose. Telluride can be reached via this route by turning off at Ridgway on CO 62 to CO 145. Rico is south of Telluride on CO 145. US 550 runs between Montrose and Durango so this route can be used from the south to Silverton and Ouray. Rico and Telluride can be reached from the south via CO 145. The mountain drive is beautiful.

Rico

Rico (pop. 76) is 44 miles north of Cortez and is located in Dolores County. At the north end of the small community is the **Atlantic Cable Mine. R. C. Darling** discovered the mine property in March 1878 and two years later filed the Atlantic Cable Load Mining claim. The ore mined here was concentrated in a blanket deposit within the Leadville Ouray limestone. The formation contained lead, zinc, copper, and silver in mineralized beds. These mineralized beds assayed at approximately 20 percent lead, 22 percent zinc, one and a half percent copper, and 10 to 15 ounces of silver per ton. The Atlantic Cable Load was patented in March 1883 as mineral land survey No. 1136. The mine was a large producer of lead and zinc ore during World War II. The mine is currently owned by the Anaconda Minerals Company.

There are two buildings in Rico listed on the National Register of Historic Places and these include the William Kauffman House, Silver St. off Mantz Ave. and Rico City Hall, Commercial and Mantz Sts.

Telluride

Telluride (pop. 1,200), was named for tellurium, a rare gold bearing ore found in the San Juan Mountains, and is the county seat of San Miguel County. The old miners and railroaders cried "to hell you ride," emphasizing the boisterousness

The old Atlantic Cable Mine, at the north outskirts of Rico. The mine was discovered by R. C. Darling in 1878.

of the 1880s mining town with its gaming parlours and infamous brothels. The town has been designated a National Historic Landmark.

Telluride came into being in January 1878, as **Columbia**. Columbia was incorporated on July 13, 1878. The name change came about on June 4, 1887 at the postal department's request because of the confusion with the mining town, Columbia, California.

Silver first dominated the Telluride scene but after the crash of 1893, the "gold boom" kept Telluride a bustling, busy town. **John Fallon** recorded the area's first lode claim on October 7, 1875. He called the claims the Emerald, Ausboro, Ajax, and Sheridan in the Marshall Basin which collectively became

Telluride's "Sporting House Row" is described and identified in this plaque in the downtown area. Several brothels operated for several decades in the mining town.

known as the Sheridan. **J. B. Ingram** discovered that the adjoining Sheridan and Union mines had each claimed 500 feet over the legal limits so he claimed this property and called it the Smuggler. **James Carpenter** and **Thomas Lowthian** discovered the famous Pandora Mine two miles from town in 1876. The first placer claim in the San Miguel Mining District was recorded on August 23, 1875.

By mid-summer 1890, Telluride consisted of 90 businesses including two banks, hardware stores, blacksmith shops, jewelry stores, drug stores, grocery stores, livery stables, barber and bath shops, seven laundries, 11 saloons and a brewery.

L. L. Nunn, a mine operator in Telluride, is credited with the first use of the alternating current generator to provide electricity for his Gold King Mine. This plaque describes this event.

By 1890, most of the timber around the Gold King Mine had been cut. Coal was transported on the backs of horses and mules at prohibitive costs to power the winches and pumps at the mine. When **L. L. Nunn** was elected president of the Gold King Mining Company he quickly surmised he needed to develop his own power source. He and his brother, Paul, decided to build a water-powered generator to produce high-voltage alternating current and transmit it over lines from the river to the mine. A team of engineers from Cornell University was called in and in 1891 they began building the new generator. They used a 3,000 volt Westinghouse generator and had it working two

This is one of several historical markers in Telluride. This one briefly describes the labor strikes in the mines at the turn of the century.

months before the world's next high-voltage AC generator was put into service in Germany.

Nikola Tesla (1856-1943) invented the alternating-current induction motor. He invented a motor with coils arranged so that when alternating current energized them, the resulting magnetic field rotated at a predetermined speed. He patented his motor in 1888 and sold it to George Westinghouse, who introduced it through his company.

L. L. Nunn was given most of the credit for building the world's first alternating current power station. Electrical power was carried over a line from the river to the Gold King Mine three miles away. By 1894, most of the mines and the Town of Telluride were powered by electricity. The site of the world's first alternating current power plant, built by Nunn, is at **Ames**. To reach Ames, first drive south on CO 145 to "National Forest Access Illium" located across from Ophir, another old, interesting mining town, then west (right turn) one and a one-quarter miles to Ames.

On June 24, 1889 the **Tom McCarty gang** robbed the San Miguel Valley Bank, located on the site of the Mahr Building on Colorado Ave. (Main St.). It has been reported the robbery

This monument provides a brief history of the famous old Sheridan Hotel in Telluride. The hotel was built in 1895.

netted the four men involved a little over $20,000. One of the members of the gang was **George Leroy Parker**, later who took on the alias **"Butch Cassidy."** While it is often reported this was the first bank robbery Cassidy was involved in, this is not the case. McCarty's gang robbed the First National Bank of Denver on March 30th of that same year. The gang also robbed the Denver & Rio Grande express train near Grand Junction in 1887. Cassidy is believed to have been involved in both Colorado robberies. Actually he did not take the name Butch Cassidy until 1894 after he was arrested for stealing horses in Wyoming. He earned the sobriquet "Butch" while working in a

Wyoming butcher shop in 1892. He took the name "Cassidy" for Mike Cassidy who taught him the fine art of rustling and stealing horses. The Telluride bank burned not too long after the robbery and the Mahr Clothing Store replaced it.

Badman Jim Cummings Clark, who, during the Civil War, had ridden with William Quantrill's guerrillas, served as a Town Marshal of Telluride. He was fired because of his tough tactics in dealing with ruffians. Although he threatened to kill the members of the town council, he never carried out the threat. The night of August 6, 1895, Clark was shot in the back by a stray bullet as he was passing the Colombo Saloon. He died in his cabin about an hour after being wounded. One of the theories was that he was assassinated by the town government because they were afraid to tell him that he was fired as Town Marshal.

The Rio Grande Southern Railway reached Telluride on November 15, 1890. The right-of-way used by the railroad was the Otto Mear's toll road over the Dallas Divide. Another toll road from Silverton to the Red Mountain diggings was built in 1884 and became known as Mears' "Million Dollar Highway."

Otto Mears, known as the "Pathfinder of the San Juans" for his road building to the remote mining camps, was one of several colorful and influential figures in Colorado's early history. A Russian Jew, he came to the United States as an orphan at the age of 12. He emigrated to California where he was to have met an uncle but failed to find him. The youngster was thrown to his own devices and began selling newspapers and doing odd jobs. At the outbreak of the Civil War, he enlisted in Company H, 1st California Volunteers and saw action in the New Mexico Indian campaigns. When his enlistment expired he became a store clerk in Santa Fe, then opened a business in Conejos in 1865. With a partner he built a sawmill and a grist mill.

To reach the mining camps and the other markets for his flour that sold as high as $20 a hundred pounds, Mears constructed a toll road over Poncha Pass to the Arkansas Valley. Eventually he built about 300 miles of toll roads in the San Luis Valley. Several of these roads were later utilized as railroad beds, notably the route over Marshall Pass. His roads in the San Juans made it profitable to work low-grade ores and increased mining activities throughout the Ouray-Silverton-Telluride district. To aid in promoting the district he published newspapers at Saguache and Lake City.

The talented Mears learned to speak the Ute language and was a friend to **Chief Ouray**. After the Meeker Massacre of 1879, he assisted in the rescue of the women captives. He then accompanied an Indian delegation to Washington where a treaty was negotiated. The Utes in Colorado at first refused to accept the treaty, but Mears won them over by paying each Indian two dollars. He was charged with bribery but the charge was dismissed by the Secretary of the Interior and Mears was reimbursed the $2,800 he had paid to the Indians.

He continued his toll-road building and operated freighting outfits and pack trains. Then he became involved in the construction of railroads and built the Rio Grande Southern and Silverton Northern railroads in southwestern Colorado. He also invested in mining and smelter properties in the district. In 1884 he was elected to the Colorado legislature and became influential in the Republican party. He lost much of his fortune in the Crash of '93 and spent his last years in California where he developed ranch and hotel property. He died in Pasadena, Calif., June 24, 1931 at the age of 91. His portrait appears in one of the stained glass windows of the Colorado state capitol and a historic marker is set in the granite wall of the mountain beside one of his picturesque pioneer roads near Ouray.

The **Sheridan Hotel**, at the corner of Colorado Ave. and Oak St., in Telluride was built in 1895 and once rivaled the Brown Palace in Denver in food and service. Those early day menus offered vichyssoise, fresh strawberries, pork tenderloin, steak, and an excellent selection of California and European wines. **William Jennings Bryan**, presidential candidate, delivered his famous "Cross of Gold" speech on July 4, 1903 on a platform in front of the famous hotel.

The "sporting district" or "red light district" in every mining town flourished in the early days. Since prostitution was not illegal in Telluride's early days, the town council actually taxed the madames to help with the town's budget. The bordellos depended upon a large mining population and their affluence, so when mining slowed in the 1920s, the brothels eventually closed.

Telluride supported 26 saloons and over two dozen bordellos by 1905. The bordellos were located primarily in the area of

East Pacific Ave. These "pleasure palaces" included the Senate, Pick 'n Gad, Cozy Corner, Silverbell, Gold Belt and many others. The women who were not connected with a large brothel worked out of two room structures called "Cribs." Approximately 175 women operated "on the line." Understandably, the district was constantly bustling with activity. Many famous madames ruled Telluride's bordellos "Diamond Tooth Leona," "Big Billy," "Jew Fanny," and "Nigger Margaret" were among the more flamboyant.

Some of the buildings on **"Popcorn Alley"** can be seen today on Spruce St. between Colorado Ave. and Pacific Ave. Three cribs, little Victorian houses standing in a row on Pacific St., are all that remain of similar structures that lined both sides of the street all the way to the edge of Town Park. The Telluride Housing Authority saved these last houses by renovating them in 1983. The exterior restoration was carefully done saving each salvageable board and using the same colors of the period. Other remaining buildings of the "sporting district" still standing include the sedate Pick 'n Gad, the Silver Belle, and the Senate.

A man named **Jack Dempsey** washed dishes for awhile at the Senate and was a bouncer at the Pick 'n Gad. These were humble beginnings for the future heavyweight boxing champion of the world!

The **Telluride Brewery** bottled Telluride beer and distributed it in the mining towns of the area.

Between 1901 and 1904, Telluride was besieged with serious labor disputes. The first labor strike occurred at the Smuggler Union Mine to protest the newly instituted contract system which resulted in longer hours for less pay. On July 3, 1901, tension between union and non-union workers escalated into an armed confrontation. After suffering a number of casualties, the non-union miners abandoned their posts. The angry strikers unceremoniously expelled them from town. A temporary agreement was reached between the union and mine owners. Within weeks, however, the assassination of the manager of the Smuggler Union Mine touched off new hostilities.

In 1903, mill workers called a strike demanding a reduction in the workday from 12 to eight hours. Union miners soon joined the strike. Afraid of continued violence, mine owners requested that Colorado **Governor James H. Peabody** send in the Colorado National Guard. Five hundred soldiers were posted at Telluride as a peace keeping force. As a further precaution martial law was declared and union activists were expelled from town. Within a few days all mines were in partial operation with nonunion workers. Believing the conflict resolved, Governor Peabody recalled the troops and suspended martial law.

This action proved to be premature. On March 12, 1904, about 100 armed Telluride area vigilantes supporting nonunion labor organized themselves as the Citizen's Alliance and took the law into their own hands. They forced about 60 union men and sympathizers out of town on a special train, which dropped the men at the top of Dallas Divide minus shoes and coats. The renewed violence prompted the return of the National Guard and martial law restrictions. Eventually all union sympathizers were expelled from the community. Union organization returned to Telluride in 1948 and remained until major mining activity ceased in 1978.

Smuggler-Union Hydroelectric Power Plant built in 1904 sits at the top of **Bridal Veil Falls**, Colorado's highest waterfall. Tram lines from the valley floor brought ore down from the upper basin. Beyond the base of the falls four wheel drive vehicles are required. The plant is listed on the National Register of Historic Places and is currently (1990) being renovated for use.

The center of the town of Telluride has been designated a National Historic District. When the Crash of 1929 brought the **Bank of Telluride** to near collapse **Charles D. Waggoner**, bank president, bilked New York banks out of about a half-million dollars. In the attempt to save his bank, Waggoner swindled the New York banks and eventually served three years of a 15-year prison sentence. It is claimed that Waggoner testified at his trial, "I would rather see the New York banks lose money, than the people of Telluride, most of whom have worked all their lives for the savings that were deposited in my bank." Depositors in the Telluride bank collectively were able to retrieve only about thirty percent of their monies. Waggoner did not return to Telluride after his release from prison. He died in Reno, Nevada.

The first **Galloping Goose**, an odd-looking locomotive, was built in 1931 by the Rio Grande Railroad to provide an economical method of transporting mail and passengers in the area.

The Galloping Goose No. 4, powered by a Buick motor, was first put into use on June 1, 1931. It was developed as an economical means of rail transportation between Telluride and Ridgway. Altogether eight of these unusual railroad contraptions were built. The service on the Galloping Goose was ended on October 26, 1951.

Eight Geese were built, using Pierce Arrow or Buick engines to power them. The first Galloping Goose went into service on June 1, 1931, powered by a Buick engine. On October 26, 1951, the Galloping Goose ended service, the last train running from Telluride to Ouray. Goose No. 4, built in 1932, is one of seven that remain and is located next to the San Miguel County Courthouse on Colorado Avenue.

Mining began to fade after World War II. Telluride Mines, Inc., purchased many of the mines in the area, producing lead, zinc, and copper. These operations proved unprofitable and the company was finally forced to close down. In 1952 the Idarado Mining Company bought many of these mines and claims in the region and connected them by a series of tunnels 350 miles long. Millions of dollars in gold, lead, silver, copper, and zinc were mined until operations ceased in 1978.

Beverly Hills entrepreneur **Joe Zoline** arrived in Telluride in 1968 to establish a winter recreation area second to none. In April, 1971, **Governor John A. Love** dedicated the **Telluride Ski Area**. Since that time, summer recreation has boomed and Telluride has become known as the "Festival Capital of The Rockies."

The San Miguel County Historical Museum is located at the north end of Fir St. in Telluride.

The three buildings shown here on Pacific Ave. in Telluride were once used as "Cribs" by prostitutes. They have been restored and are now used as housing by the Telluride Housing Authority.

SAN MIGUEL COUNTY HISTORIC MUSEUM, at the north end of Fir St., is housed in the 1893 stone building that once served as a miner's hospital. Its focus is on the early days of Telluride when mining flourished. The exhibits and artifacts are displayed on three floors and each room in the museum features a different subject. There is also an extensive display of historic photos. The museum is open 10 a.m. to 5 p.m. daily from Memorial Day to mid-October. An admission is charged.

The Telluride Chamber Resort Association has included a walking tour in their seasonal vacation guide. It includes 14 historic sites and other information about the town.

A shortcut from Telluride, called **Tomboy Road**, requires a four wheel vehicle over 13,000 foot Imogene Pass to Ouray. For the adventuresome it is suggested to obtain directions and conditions of this possible route which passes through the old ghost town of Tomboy.

For others traveling to Ouray from Telluride take CO 145 west 13 miles to **Placerville**, then northeast 25 miles to Ridgway, and then south 11 miles on US 550.

Ridgway

Ridgway (pop. 369) began as a railroad town and became an important junction, track yard and roundhouse on the Rio Grande Southern Railroad line. It connected with Durango, 175 miles south. The Denver & Rio Grande railroad took over the road after the Silver Panic of 1893. The original railroad buildings burned to the ground in 1906. Today, Ridgway is a ranching community.

Ouray

Ouray (pop. 684) is the county seat of Ouray County. The town was incorporated in the fall of 1876 and named for **Chief Ouray**, the influential Ute leader who encouraged peace between the whites and his people. Prospectors came into the area in the mid-1870s and after discovering rich lodes of silver and gold throughout the area began building a town, originally called **Uncompaghre City**.

Perhaps one of the most significant persons connected with Ouray was **Thomas Walsh**, who purchased 103 claims on 900 acres to develop **Camp Bird**, one of the state's richest mining operations. The discovery was made when Walsh and an associate, **Andy Richardson**, found a rich gold strike in an abandoned tunnel of the Gertrude mine. The three-foot vein of quartz contained gold tellurium that had been missed by previ-

The Beaumont Hotel in Ouray is listed on the National Register of Historic Places.

ous owners who were looking for silver ore in various forms.

Walsh, who emigrated from Ireland, had settled in Deadwood, South Dakota. He was offered a half-interest in the **Homestake Gold Mine** when it was discovered and turned it down. The Homestake, largest gold mine in the U.S., has since produced over $500 million. Walsh moved his family to Ouray and had been looking for flux ore for his smelter in Silverton when he and Richardson made their find in Imogene Basin.

Returning to his home in Ouray that night, Walsh whispered his secret to his 10-year old daughter, Evalyn, "Daughter, I've struck it rich!" In the first year of operations the Camp Bird produced two million dollars and a million was put back into the development of the mine and mill. During the first 20 years of operation the mine returned the highest rate of profit shown by any mine in Colorado history, 65 percent.

Walsh built accommodations for miners unheard of in mines of that period, and especially in one located at the timberline in the midst of a wilderness. The three-story boarding house was equipped with electric lights, steam heat, telephone, running hot and cold water, marble tiled bathrooms with porcelain fixtures, a library, and incomparable meals offered free to any traveler who stopped at the mine. The building had hardwood floors, tongue and groove wainscotting, and marble panels.

In six years Walsh realized about $4,000,000 from the mine and sold it in 1902 for $6,000,000 to **John Hays Hammond**, representing London interests. He received $3,500,000 cash plus $2,000,000 from future production and $500,000 in stock. The English firm, Camp Bird Limited, leased the property for many years, and it has been Ouray's steadiest producer.

In the meantime, the Walshes moved to Denver. In 1902 they moved to Washington, D.C., where they built a 60-room, five-story, million dollar mansion with 23 servants. Today it would cost $10 million or more to build. It had a ballroom, a theatre, and a roof garden. The Walshes became part of Washington's high society.

King Leopold of Belgium became a close personal friend of Tom Walsh and visited him in Ouray. According to an unconfirmed story, on one visit to the Beaumont Hotel, and after a number of drinks, Leopold decided to demonstrate mountain climbing on the balcony above the lobby. He lost his balance and fell off the balcony, but luckily landed on an over-stuffed sofa.

Tom Walsh died of cancer in 1910 at the age of 59. **President William Howard Taft** attended his funeral as did the Chief Justice of the United States. The Walsh family was intimate friends of five presidents, William McKinley, Theodore Roosevelt, William Taft, Warren G. Harding, and Calvin Coolidge.

Daughter Evalyn married **Ned McLean** whose parents owned the *Washington Post* and *Cincinnati Enquirer*. After the wedding they honeymooned in Europe. She bought the **Star of the East** diamond for $120,000. Later, she and Ned bought the **Hope Diamond**, a beautiful blue stone, for $140,000. It was and is the world's most famous jewel. It is valued at several millions of dollars today.

Unpredictable Evalyn developed a talent as an electrician and rewired two of her Washington homes. She was given a journeyman's badge by the local electricians' union and when she worked at the trade her badge was clipped to the Hope Diamond.

During her life time, **Evalyn Walsh McLean** gave fabulous parties, inviting Presidents, royalty, all the greats of Washington, New York and Palm Beach society. She once gave a dinner for 40 people at a cost of $40,000. Her garden parties were given

The Ouray Historical Museum is located at 420 6th St.

The historic Wright's Opera House in Ouray.

for hundreds of guests and costs often ran to several hundred thousand dollars.

Despite her wealth, Evalyn's life was one of sorrow. Her brother, Vinson, died at the wheel of her red Mercedes roadster. He was sixteen. Her oldest son, also named Vinson, died in another auto accident at the age of nine. Her husband, Ned, was eventually confined to a mental hospital. Her daughter, Evalyn, died at the age of 25 of an overdose of sleeping pills. Less than a year later, grieving her daughter's death, Mrs. McLean died. When she died in 1947 in her Washington home, "Friendship," at the age of 61 she was almost broke except for her jewels and furs. She was survived by her sons, John, born in 1916, and Edward, Jr., born in 1918. Scattered about her bedroom were two million dollars worth of jewels. The entire collection was purchased by New York dealer **Harry Winston** who paid her estate $1,500,000 for the Hope Diamond. In 1958 he donated it to the Smithsonian Institute. It has become one of the national museum's outstanding attractions, drawing three to four million visitors a year.

OURAY HISTORICAL MUSEUM, 420 6th Ave., is housed in the old hospital that served the community for 77 years. Built in 1887 by contributions of the mine owners and businessmen, it was called the Miner's Hospital. The Sisters of Mercy operated the hospital which was supported through contributions until the Silver Crash of '93. The Sisters were forced to borrow $3,500 to keep the hospital open. Tom Walsh paid off the mortgage in 1899 when the hospital was threatened with foreclosure because of the overdue payment with the understanding the building would always remain a hospital and would be managed by the Sisters.

The promise to Walsh was kept until World War I when a shortage of nurses and money made it impossible for the Sisters to keep the hospital open. Tom Walsh had died, but thanks to Mrs. Walsh and her daughter, Evalyn, the Sisters were released from their management promise, and offered it for sale. It operated from 1919 to 1944 as the Bates Hospital and then another seven years as the San Juan Miners Hospital. The building was purchased for a museum in 1976 by the Ouray County Historical Society from St. Daniels Church. The museum features relics of pioneer days, mining history, log cabins, Indian history, Walsh room, photographs, hospital memorabilia and other items. It is open 9 a.m. to 5 p.m. Monday through Saturday, 1 to

5 p.m. Sunday during the summer and 1 to 4 p.m. Wednesday through Sunday during the winter (October through May). An admission is charged.

The Ouray chamber of commerce has prepared a walking tour including 16 historic sites in the community. A map and description of the tour is included in Ouray's annual vacation guide. The town itself is a National Historic District.

The **Wright Opera House** is the one of the largest remaining metal front buildings in the U.S. Several of the buildings on Main Street have metal fronts.

The Beaumont Hotel, the Ouray City Hall and Walsh Library, 6th Ave. between 3rd and 4th Sts., are among the many buildings in Ouray listed on the National Register of Historic Places. More than two-thirds of all the buildings in the community are listed on the National Register.

Silverton

It is 23 miles south on US 550 to **Silverton** (pop. 794), county seat of San Juan County. This mining town, listed on the National Register as a Historic District, is the terminus of the Durango and Silverton Narrow-Gauge Railroad, also listed on the National Register of Historic Places. Also listed on the NRHP is the Cascade Lodge in San Juan National Forest, between Durango and Silverton.

Silverton is located in an area originally called **Baker's Park**, named for **Charles Baker**, an early prospector-promoter. In 1870, three prospectors discovered the Little Giant and the Mountaineer, the first productive mines in Baker's Park. The ensuing gold rush precipitated negotiation of the **1873 Brunot Treaty**. At the time these mines were discovered, the land was on the Ute Indian reservation and the Indians controlled about 15 million acres of land in Colorado serving about 2,000 Utes which provided 12,800 acres per head of each Indian family. The Brunot Treaty ceded 3.5 million acres of Indian lands to white settlement.

It is 50 miles south on US 550 to Durango.

Chapter 12
The Alferd Packer Story

The story of Colorado's cannibal—Alferd Packer. He was charged with killing five companions in 1874 and eating their flesh but was not apprehended until 1883. A spectacular trial was held in Lake City where Packer was condemned to be hanged but his life was spared at the last minute. Later, in 1886, a second trial was held in Gunnison and Packer was found guilty of manslaughter and was given a 40-year prison sentence. After spending 14 years in prison he was paroled in 1901 by the Colorado governor. He died near Denver in 1907.

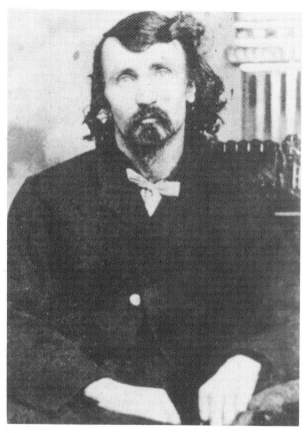

This is a 1880s file photo of Alferd G. Packer who was convicted of cannibalism in 1886. The bodies of his five victims were found near today's Lake City. The death sentence in his first trial was overturned and Packer was convicted of manslaughter in his second trial and sentenced to 40 years in the Colorado Penitentiary. He was released in 1901 after serving 14 years of his sentence and died in 1907.

Chapter 12

The Alferd Packer Story

Alferd Packer, a 42-year old harness maker plagued with epilepsy, and 20 other prospectors from the Bingham and Cottonwood mines left Provo, Utah, on November 21, 1873 for the newly discovered goldfields in the Breckenridge area of the Colorado Territory. Packer said later that he was familiar with the Breckenridge and Fairplay districts and believed at the time they were situated between the San Juan Mountains.

The weather turned bad by the time the party reached the winter camp of Ute **Chief Ouray**, near present-day Delta, in mid January, 1874. The chief's advice was to stay put until the weather was more favorable for travel.

Packer and five others—**Wilson Bell, Frank Miller, Israel Swan, George Noon** and **James Humphreys**—decided to push on February 9, 1874, against Chief Ouray's advice. They headed into the snowcovered San Juans bound for the Los Pinos Indian Agency via the government cow camp near what is now Gunnison, Colorado.

Little is known of Packer's companions. Israel Swan, a native of Missouri, was the eldest and may have been carrying as much as $6,000 in cash and notes. Frank Miller was a young German butcher. Wilson Bell was a native of Michigan and James Humphrey was from Philadelphia. The youngest was 19-year old George Noon from San Francisco.

Nothing more was heard from the six men until April 16, 1874 when an apparently well-fed and healthy Packer wandered into the **Los Pinos Agency** alone. According to the story his first request was for a drink of whiskey, not food.

Suspicion was aroused when Packer, who had little money when he left Utah, started spending large sums of money around **Saguache** for liquor and games at Larry Dolan's saloon. He also was in possession of a gun owned by one of his fellow travelers.

Packer told conflicting stories about the fate of his companions. He first told Agency officials that he had frozen his feet and the others had left him behind with the promise they would send someone to rescue him.

The Packer massacre site just south of Lake City. It was here that Alferd Packer was alleged to have killed five of his companions in 1874.
The tablet below lists the names of the five men who met their death
at the hands of the man who admitted he eventually lived off the flesh
of their dead bodies.

On May 4 he confessed that there had been trouble on the trail about 10 days out of Chief Ouray's camp. He claimed Swan died first and was eaten by the other five men. Four or five days later, according to Packer, Humphreys had died and was also eaten. Packer said he found $133 on Humphreys' body and kept it. Packer also explained that he was carrying wood when Frank Miller was accidently killed. Miller was also allegedly eaten. Packer claimed Bell shot Noon and he in turn shot and killed Bell in self defense. He covered the remains and took a large piece of human flesh with him. It took him 14 days to reach the Agency.

Later, in a confession made in Denver on March 16, 1883, Packer admitted that he covered his five companions up and tried for nearly two months to continue his journey to the Agency. He claimed at this time that the total amount of money on the five amounted to only $70. He admitted he lived on the flesh of his victims for this period of time and cooked some of the flesh before leaving his camp for the Agency. He carried this with him and ate the last of the human flesh the day before reaching his destination.

Packer was jailed in Saguache ("Sa-watch") but escaped in August 1874 when someone slipped him a key made from a knifeblade. He claimed to have made his way to a ranch 18 miles south of Pueblo where he worked the rest of the summer.

Sheriff A. P. Wall of Saguache offered an initial reward of $200 for his capture. Shortly after Packer's escape from Saguache **Capt. C. H. Graham** and a party of prospectors found the bodies of his companions in a dense grove of willows and trees beneath a bluff beside the Lake Fork. **Artist John A. Randolph**, on assignment for *Harper's Weekly*, was with the group and sketched the five bodies. This spot is two miles south of present-day Lake City on CO 149 just across the Lake Fork bridge heading up toward Slumgullion Pass.

Alferd Packer was recaptured at **Wagonbound** near Fort Fetterman, Wyoming Territory, on March 12, 1883. At the time he was using the alias John Schwartze. He was recognized by one of the original prospectors from Utah. He was arrested by **Deputy Sheriff Malcolm Campbell** and taken to Cheyenne where he was picked up by **Hinsdale County Sheriff Clair Smith**. He was first held in the Gunnison County jail before being moved to the Hinsdale County jail in Lake City.

Lake City had been incorporated in 1875 by miners and

The Hinsdale County courtroom today appears much as it did in 1883 when the Alferd Packer murder trial was held here. At the back of the courtroom is this encased record (below) of the trial heard by Judge Melville B. Gerry.

prospectors who had arrived to dig for gold. Today it is Colorado's largest National Historical Landmark.

Packer was brought to trial in Lake City, charged with the murder of Israel Swan, on April 6, 1883, before **7th Judicial District Judge Melville B. Gerry**. Fifty-six persons were interviewed before the jury, consisting of **John Bergen, J. C. Dubois, David Edgar, Charles Fenstermacher, William Hunt, Jack Henderson, Charles Randall, Henry Snyder** and **Charles Weinberg**, was impaneled.

John C. Bell was the prosecutor, assisted by J. Warner Mills. Gunnison attorneys **Aaron Heims** and **A. J. Miller** represented the defendant.

The jury returned a verdict of guilty on Friday, May 13, 1883, and Judge Gerry pronounced sentence that Packer be hanged in Lake City on May 19.

The trial was held in the court room on the second floor of the Hinsdale County courthouse, built in 1877. The transcription of the sentence handed by Judge Gerry is encased at the back of the small room that appears today as it did in 1883.

Alferd Packer memorabilia is displayed in the Hinsdale County Museum, 2nd and Silver Sts., in Lake City. It is open 11 a.m. to 4 p.m. Monday through Saturday and 1 to 4 p.m. Sunday.

One of the first persons out of the courtroom after the sentencing was **Larry Dolan**, who operated the Centennial Saloon in Lake City. He had been a key witness against Packer during his trial. Dolan's outlandish version of the sentence has gained much wider attention than Judge Gerry's original sentence. Dolan's version was repeated by Will Rogers years later.

Here is what Dolan is reputed to have said to his listeners at the Centennial Saloon:

"Well boys, ut's all over. . .Packer's t' hang.

"Th' judge says, says he, 'Stand up y' man-eatin' son iv' a bitch, Stand up!' Thin, p'intin his tremblin's finger at Packer, so ragin' mad he was, 'they was sivin Dimmycrats in Hinsdale County an' ye et five iv thim, God damn ye! I sintins ye t' be hanged be th' neck ontil ye're dead, dead, dead, as a warnin' ag'in reducin' th' Dimmycratic popyalashun iv th' state."

(NOTE: Judge Gerry was an ardent Southern Democrat.)

The following is the complete transcript of Judge Gerry's sentence:

"It becomes my duty as the judge of this court to enforce the

The Hinsdale County Courthouse where Alferd Packer's first trial was convened. The Hinsdale County Museum, in Lake City, houses some of the Packer memorabilia as well as other early-day exhibits.

verdict of the jury rendered in your case, and to impose on you the judgement which the law fixes as the punishment of the crime you have committed. It is a solemn, painful duty to perform, I would to God the cup might pass from me: you have had a fair and impartial trial. You have been faithfully and earnestly defended by able counsel. The presiding judge of this court, upon his oath and his conscience, has labored to be honest and impartial in the trial of your case and in all doubtful questions presented, you have had the benefit of the doubt.

"A jury of twelve honest citizens of the county have sat in judgement in your case and upon their oaths they find you guilty of willful and premeditated murder—a murder revolting in all its details. In 1874 you in company with five companions passed through this beautiful mountain valley where stands the town of Lake City. At that time the hand of man had not marred the beauties of nature, the picture was fresh from the hand of the Great Artist who created it.

"You and your companions camped at the base of a grand old mountain, in sight of the place you now stand, on the banks of a stream as pure and beautiful as ever traced by the finger of God upon the bosom of earth. Your every surrounding was calculated to impress upon your heart and nature the Omnipotence of Deity and the helplessness of your own feeble mind. In this goodly spot you conceived your murderous designs.

"You and your victims had had a weary march, and when the shadows of the mountains fell upon your little party and the night drew her sable curtain around you, your unsuspecting victims lay down on the ground and were soon lost in sleep of the weary; and when thus sweetly unconscious of danger from any quarter, and particularly from you, their trusted companion, you cruelly and brutally slew them all. Whether your murderous hand was guided by the misty light of the moon, or the flickering blaze of the campfire, you can only tell. No eye saw the bloody deed performed; no ear save your own caught the groans of your dying victims. You then and there robbed the living of life, and then robbed the dead of the reward of honest toil which they had accumulated; at least so say the jury.

"To other sickening details of your crime I will not refer. Silence is kindness. I do not say these things to harrow up your soul, for I know you have drunk the cup of bitterness to its very dregs, and wherever you have gone the stings of your conscience and the goadings of remorse have been avenging Nemesis which has followed you at every turn in life and painted afresh for your contemplation the picture of the past. I say these things to impress upon your mind the awful solemnity of your situation and the impending doom which you can not avert.

"Be not deceived. God is not mocked, for whatever a man soweth that shall he also reap. You Alferd Packer, soweth the wind; you must now reap the whirlwind. Society can not forgive you for the crime you have committed. It enforces the old Mosaic law of life for a life, and your life must be taken as the penalty for your crime. I am but the instrument of society to impose the punishment which the law provides. While society cannot forgive, it will forget. As the days come and go and the years of our pilgrimage roll by, the memory of you and your crimes will fade from the minds of men.

"With God it is different. He will not forget, but will forgive. He pardoned the dying thief on the cross. He is the same god today as then—a God of love and mercy, of long suffering and kind forbearance; a God who tempers the wind to the shorn lamb, and promises rest to the weary and heartbroken children of man; and it is to this God I commend you.

"Close your ears to the blandishments of hope. Listen not to its flattering promises of life; but prepare for the dread certainty of death. Prepare to meet thy God; prepare to meet the spirits of thy murdered victims, prepare to meet that aged father and mother of whom you have spoken and who still love you as their dear boy.

"For nine long years you have been a wanderer upon the face of the earth, bowed and broken in spirit; no home; no loves; no ties to bind you to the earth. You have been, indeed, a poor, pitiful waif of humanity. I hope and pray that in the spirit land to which you are so fast and surely drifting, you will find that peace and rest for your weary spirit which this world cannot give.

"Alferd Packer, the judgement of this court is that you be removed from hence to the jail of Hinsdale County and there confined until the 19th day of May, 1883, and that on said 19th day of May, 1883, you be taken from thence to a place of execution prepared for this purpose at some point within the corporate limits of the town of Lake City, in said county of Hinsdale, and between the hours of 10 a.m. and 3 p.m. of said day, you, then and there, by said sheriff, be hung by the neck until you are dead, dead, dead, and may God have mercy upon your soul."

Alferd Packer did not hang on May 19, 1883.

His death sentence was overturned on a technicality. The Territorial death sentence had been repealed after Colorado attained statehood and thus was not in effect for the murders which took place prior to 1876. The murders also had taken place on what was at that time the Ute Indian reservation, outside the jurisdiction of the Territory of Colorado.

Packer was jailed in Gunnison from 1883 to 1886 when a second trial was held in the Gunnison County courthouse. On the bench was Judge Harrison. The prosecution was handled by **Herschel M. Hogg**, assisted by **J. Warner Mills**, who had assisted the prosecutor in the first trial. **Thomas C. Brown** defended Packer.

The Gunnison trial was held August 2 through 5, 1886. This time Packer was found guilty on five counts of manslaughter. He received a 40-year prison sentence, eight years for each of his five victims. He spent the next 14 years in the State Penitentiary in Canon City.

In 1900, **Fred G. Bonfils** and **Harry Tammen**, co-editors of the *Denver Post*, decided to obtain a pardon for Packer as one of their famed promotional stunts. They sent one of their top writers, **Mrs. Leonel "Polly Pry" Ross Anthony**, to Canon City to interview the warden and Packer.

Polly eventually turned up **W. W. Anderson**, a lawyer who believed he could win Packer's release on a writ of habeas corpus on the grounds that the alleged crimes were committed on an Indian reservation which had not yet been incorporated in the then Territory of Colorado. The Los Pinos Agency had not been turned over by the U.S. government until 90 days after the day Packer admitted killing his companions. The lawyer believed that the state court that tried Packer had no jurisdiction over the Indian reservation as it was in United States territory.

It was discovered that Anderson had been before the Colorado Supreme Court on charges of general misconduct. Although the charge had been dismissed, the newspaper reporter and its editors decided not to let him represent them. Anderson in the meantime went to Canon City where he obtained Packer's power of attorney. He had obtained the power of attorney by stating he represented the *Denver Post* as a director. When Polly learned of this, she went to the prison and was able to convince Packer to revoke the power of attorney from Anderson. Anderson demanded a meeting with Bonfils and Tammen.

During their discussion in the *Denver Post* office Bonfils punched Anderson in the face when the lawyer raised his arm in a threatening manner. He then threw the angry Anderson out of the office but as he was heading back to his office the door flew open and two shots rang out. Bonfils was hit and Anderson, smoking gun in hand, leaped into the room where he shot Tammen twice. Anderson walked out through the crowd that had gathered at the sound of shots.

Anderson was arrested but released on $20,000 bond. He was tried on assault to kill charges but the jury refused to convict. Tammen was arrested on charges of trying to influence the jury when he induced a friend to pass a newspaper reciting Anderson's acts into the jury room. He served a nominal sentence for this misdeed.

The *Post* continued to crusade for Packer's release. In 1901 he was paroled by **Governor Charles S. Thomas**.

Packer left Canon City and settled on Deer Creek near Denver. He suffered a stroke and died on April 24, 1907 and was buried near Littleton. Although Judge Gerry said society would forget his unforgivable crime, the story lives on.

Chapter 13
The Fossil Beds and Fairplay

This chapter focuses on the Florissant Fossil Beds National Monument and the historic mining town of Fairplay. The first fossils were found in the Florissant lakebed in 1874 by Dr. A. C. Peale. The early history of Fairplay, the county seat of Park County, is typical of the 19th century mining settlements that sprang up overnight and died a short time later.

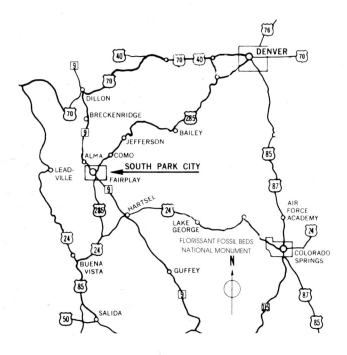

Florissant Fossil Beds National Monument is just south of the community of Florissant, four miles east of Lake George. South Park City is in Fairplay, 85 miles from Denver on US 285 and 85 miles from Colorado Springs on US 24 and CO 9.

Chapter 13
The Fossil Beds and Fairplay

West of Colorado Springs on US 24 are the Florissant Fossil Beds and 30 miles west of this National Monument on US 24 and 18 miles north is historic Fairplay.

Florissant Fossil Beds can be reached by taking US 24 west from Colorado Springs 35 miles away. In the town of **Florissant**, turn south toward Cripple Creek on unpaved RD 1. The park is a half mile from the center of town.

Florissant Fossil Beds National Monument

The **Florissant Fossil Beds National Monument** was established by Congress on August 20, 1969 and is administered by the National Park Service, U.S. Department of the Interior. The fossils here are preserved in the sedimentary rocks of ancient **Lake Florissant**, which existed in this valley during the Oligocene times, roughly 38 to 26 million years ago. Intermittent volcanic activity during a period of 500,000 years showered millions of tons of ash, dust, and pumice into the air. Much of this fragmented material, carried by the wind, settled over and around Lake Florissant, trapping a wide variety of plants and animals. Some of these life forms were carried into the lake and settled to the bottom, where they became embedded in layers of fine-grained ash. There they became fossilized as the ash compacted to form shale, a thinly layered sedimentary rock. During the same period of volcanic activity, mud flows buried forests that grew around the lake and petrified them in place.

Incredibly detailed and exquisitely beautiful impressions of insects and leaves exist in such profusion that the Florissant Fossil Beds form the most extensive fossil record of its type in the world. Impressions of dragonflies, beetles, ants, butterflies, spiders, fish, some mammals and birds, and innumerable insects that lived here 34 to 35 million years ago are almost perfectly preserved.

The fossils of the Florissant lakebed were first discovered by **Dr. A. C. Peale** of the U.S. Geological Survey in 1874. Since then, scientists from around the world have dug into the shale to remove over 80,000 specimens. More than 1,100 species of insects, including almost all the fossil butterflies of the New

Thousands of fossils have been discovered at the Florissant Fossil Beds west of Colorado Springs. Among these are (top) Pine Cone, Pinus and (bottom) Sequoia, Sequoia affinis.

World, over 140 plant species, and several species of fish, birds, and small mammals have been identified. Several petrified tree stumps have also been excavated.

Excavated petrified tree stumps may be seen in two places within the park. Visitors may view the petrified stumps and shale deposits by entering a nature trail two miles south of Florissant on RD 1. One of the largest known petrified sequoia stumps may be found here. It stands 11 feet high and 10 feet in diameter.

Judge Castello, who named the valley for his home town of Florissant, Missouri, established a Ute Indian trading post here after the Civil War. Among the early settlers was **Adaline Hornbek** and her three sons. Her homestead application was dated March 2, 1878.

A native of Massachusetts, Adaline was born in 1833. She married **George Harker**, an Indian agent in the Indian Territory (what is today Oklahoma), in 1859. In the early 1860s the family homesteaded on the South Platte River northeast of Denver. George Harker died in 1864, shortly after the Cherry Creek flood had all but wiped out the family property. Two years later, in 1866, Mrs. Harker married **Elliot Hornbek** of Denver and in 1872 she moved to Colorado Springs to continue ranching. She had borne three sons, Frank, George, and Elliot. Her second husband, Elliot Hornbek, abandoned the family in 1875.

Today, the Florissant homestead includes the main house, a bunkhouse, carriage shed, barn, and root cellar. Adeline Hornbek was not a typical homesteader in many respects. She was wealthy, largely due to real estate transactions in the Denver area. She built an unusually large house and furnished it from the Montgomery Wards mail order catalog. The buildings and exhibits in this homestead complex depict the settler's way of life.

The park is open 8 a.m. to 7 p.m. daily during the summer months and 8 a.m. to 4:30 p.m. daily during the other months of the year. It is closed Thanksgiving, Christmas Day, and New Year's Day. An entrance fee to the museum is charged.

Fairplay

From the town of Florissant it is about 30 miles west on US 24 to the intersection of CO 9. Seventeen miles north on CO 9 is **Fairplay** (pop. 421), the county seat of Park County. Fairplay is 18 miles from the geographic center of Colorado. It is 85 miles southwest of Denver via US 285 and 85 miles northwest from Colorado Springs via US 24 and CO 9.

The mining district known as **"Fairplay Diggings,"** in South Park, was established in 1859. The name Fair Play came from the idea that every man had an equal chance to stake a claim. The original settlement was known at various times as **Platte City, Fair Play,** and **South Park City.** Fairplay was the accepted spelling after 1874. It became the county seat in 1874.

There is a more colorful account of the name's origin known as the **Legend of Fairplay.** When gold was discovered on Tarryall Creek the discoverers guarded their find jealously and charged newcomers outrageous prices for mining ground. The Tarryall diggings became known as **"Graball."** The prospectors, forced out of the Tarryall diggings as a result, moved on to the Middle Fork of the South Platte River where they found gold also. Four prospectors from Leadville arrived and made a strike. They named one of their members as their banker, a man by the name of Hill. When the others wanted money to buy provisions, Hill refused them. **Tom Payne,** a member of the group, complained to the other miners in the camp, many who had been mistreated at the Tarryall diggings. The miners at the meeting ordered Hill to divide the gold in equal shares between the four members of the group. Hill made a run for it but was caught and forced to divide the gold. **Jim Reynolds,** later known as South Park's notorious leader of a band of highwaymen, was present during the incident and afterward exclaimed, "Thar b,gad, if one is the devil and t'other is Tom Payne they shall have Fairplay." The growing camp soon needed to become a legal mining district and rules were established. After the rules were posted it was decided the oldest miner of the camp should choose the name. The oldest miner, a Mr. Mills, who had also been involved in the Hill-Payne incident, recalled the words of Jim Reynolds. He also believed strongly that all persons living in the district should have justice and declared that "Fairplay" be the name of the town.

The "Tuesday Murder," on April 3, 1879, occurred in the lobby of the **Bergh House** (the Fairplay Hotel) when **John J. Hoover** shot and killed **Thomas M. Bennett** in a minor dispute over the cleaning of drainage ditch. Bennett was hired by the hotel to clean the ditch because the water ran onto Hoover's property next to the hotel. According to the story, Hoover took a

The Father John Dyer Memorial Chapel began as a Methodist Church in 1867. Dyer was known as the "Snow-Shoe Itinerant" and the story of his work is presented here. Today it is one of the many exhibits open in Fairplay's South Park City Museum.

A narrow gauge train is displayed in Fairplay's South Park City Museum. Exhibits here focus on the early mining days of the region.

The old lager beer brewery is in today's South Park City Museum in Fairplay. South Park Lager Beer was brewed and distributed from this building.

A diorama in the old brewery in the South Park City Museum shows miners using a sluice box in their mining operation. The Fairplay Diggings district was established in 1859.

The Park County Court House in Fairplay is listed on the National Register of Historical Places.

large drink of whiskey, walked into the hotel and confronted Bennett. A few moments later Hoover shot and killed Bennett. Before the authorities could take control of the situation, Hoover was hanged from an upper window in the old court house.

The **Fairplay Hotel** is worth a visit for refreshments or simply a view. It began in 1873 as the Valiton Hotel. Over the years it has had many owners. The original building was destroyed by fire in 1921 and was rebuilt by the Fairplay Hotel Corporation.

South Park is a broad valley covering over 900 square miles and is surrounded by the Mosquito and Park ranges. In 1859 gold was discovered in a stream bed in South Park and the rush was on. Towns quickly sprang up all over the Park; now most are ghost towns.

Old Mining Towns

One of the most delightful Colorado legends is about **Buckskin Joe**, the name of the mining camp, 1.7 miles from **Alma**. As often happened, disease ran rampant in these early times, and this mining camp was no exception. Smallpox hit and everyone who could, left town. Everyone that is but "Silverheels," a beautiful dancehall girl, who stayed to nurse the miners after all the other women had fled. Later, when the grateful miners came to offer a reward for her heroic services, she could not be found. It was discovered "Silverheels" had fallen victim to smallpox herself and had simply disappeared. In memory, **Mount Silverheels** was named for her. The town was named for **Joseph Higganbottom**, a mountaineer who discovered gold here in 1859. Because he wore buckskin clothing he was nicknamed "Buckskin Joe."

The town of **Leavick** is unique because it existed for 16 years as a settlement without a name. From 1880 to 1896 up to 200 miners lived in the shadow of Horseshoe Mountain close to the Last Chance and Oldtop mines and their mill. Finally, when the narrow gauge railroad arrived in 1896 the settlement needed a name. The town was named for **Felix Leavick**, a prominent mining man from Leadville and Denver, who owned properties in the Mosquito Range. Most of the town's buildings have been moved to South Park City.

Early French trappers called this area **"Bayou Saldo"** or "Salt Creek." It was a favorite summer camp of the Ute Indians for trapping and hunting. In 1866, one of the first industries of Colorado, the Salt Works, was established. It produced salt both for domestic use and to aid in the smelting process. By the mid 19th century, ranchers occupied the South Park valley where they raised cattle and sheep.

The SOUTH PARK CITY MUSEUM in Fairplay is an outdoor museum representing a Colorado mining town during the 1870-90 period. It includes 32 authentic buildings, along with some 60,000 artifacts, that portray the economic and social aspects of a mining boom town. The log, batten, clapboard and stone buildings contain authentic period room settings. Exhibit areas illustrate the professions, trades, and industries that contributed to a 19th century mining town in Colorado. Also included here are remnants of such once-bustling places as **Mudsill, Dudley, Garo, Buckskin Joe, Eureka, Horseshoe, Alma,** and **Como.**

One of the industries in the early days was the local brewery where **South Park Lager Beer** was brewed and distributed. The brewery is one of the sites in the outdoor museum. The museum is open 9 a.m. to 7 p.m. daily from Memorial Day to Labor Day. From May 15 to Memorial Day and from Labor Day to October 15 the hours are from 9 a.m. to 5 p.m. An admission is charged.

The South Park Community Church/Jackson Memorial Chapel in Fairplay is listed on the National Register of Historic Places.

There are four sites in Fairplay listed on the National Register of Historic Places. These include the Park County Court House, 418 Main St.; the South Park Community Church/Jackson Memorial Chapel, 6th and Hathaway; the South Park Lager Beer Brewery, 3rd and Front Sts.; and the Summer Saloon, 3rd and Front Sts.

Alma

North of Fairplay 6.2 miles, on CO 9, is **Alma** (pop. 132). The town was named for **Alma James** whose husband established a store here in 1873.

Como

North of Fairplay 11 miles, on US 285, is **Como** which has two sites on the National Register. These include the Como Roundhouse/Railroad Depot and Hotel Complex, just off US 285, and the Estabrook Historic District, bound by Estabrook, Platte Canyon, Rivercliff and Rivercliff Ranch.

Of interest in historic Como is the **Mountain Man Gallery**, located in an 1880s miner's cabin on US 285. **Artist Jack Portice** has carved numerous characters and wildlife from bristlecone, the oldest living thing known to man. He specializes mostly in Western Art, carving Indians, mountain men, and wildlife. On occasion he carves other types of characters. The gallery is open daily and if no one is home, someone at the Como Mercantile will open the gallery for visitors. It may be wise to call before visiting, (719) 836-2403.

Bailey's McGraw Memorial Park

There are several historic exhibits in **Bailey's McGraw Memorial Park**. This is located in the far northeastern corner of Park County. Among these exhibits is the Entriken cabin, an old school house, the Keystone bridge, and a narrow gauge railroad caboose. The cabin, one of the oldest in the Platte Canyon area, is named for **Elizabeth L. Entriken**. It was built by her brother, the **Rev. John Dyer**, the "Snow-Shoe Itinerant." **William Louis Bailey**, for which **Bailey** was named, was Father Dyer's brother-in law. The cabin is open weekends during the summer. The Keystone bridge was once part of the Colorado & Southern Railroad and was rebuilt on its present site by the U.S. Army's 52nd Engineering Battalion from Fort Carson. Also in the park is the old Shawnee school house and a 50-year old Burlington caboose.

Glenisle and Tarryall

Glenisle, off US 285, is listed on the National Register of Historic Places. The Tarryall School, 31000 RD 77, **Tarryall**, is also listed on the National Register. It is between Como and Bailey.

Prince of the Gold Hunters

He became famous as a $100 a month frontier scout and guide for John Charles Fremont, "The Pathfinder." Fremont, an officer in the Army Topographical Corps, explored much of the area between the Rocky Mountains and the Pacific Ocean in three major expeditions in 1842, 1843-44, and 1845. His famous scout and guide was Christopher "Kit" Carson.

Carson was born in Madison County, Ky, in 1809 and his family moved to the Missouri frontier in 1811. After his father's death, he was apprenticed to David Workman, a saddler, in Franklin, Howard County, Mo. In 1826 he ran away to join a caravan heading over the Santa Fe Trail to Taos, N.M., and this became his headquarters and home for the next several years. From 1826 to 1840 he made his living as a teamster, cook, guide, and hunter for exploring parties. He also spent time as a fur trapper and participated in several of the mountain men's rendezvous'. Among his acquaintances was the famed Jim Bridger. He became an expert in the way of the Indians and was sympathetic to their needs.

Fremont was high in his praise of all of his scouts but when his reports were published it was the adventures of Kit Carson that captured the imagination of the public. He was featured in several of the dime novels published at the time with such titles as "Kit Carson, Prince of the Gold Hunters" and "The Prairie Flower, or Adventures in the Far West."

During the Mexican War Carson initially served Fremont as a messenger. Enroute to Washington, D.C., he met Brig. Gen. Stephen Kearny at Socorro, N.M., and was ordered to guide the Army of the West to California. Kearny's forces were attacked by Mexicans at San Pasqual, Calif., and pinned down. Carson and two others were able to slip through enemy lines to seek help from American forces in San Diego, 30 miles away, and Kearny's men were rescued.

Kit Carson's commission as a second lieutenant in 1847, signed by President James Polk, was blocked by the U.S. Senate who did like his sympathy for Indians.

After the Mexican War, Carson returned to his family in New Mexico to establish a ranch. The Army called on him numerous times to lead their units in pursuit of hostile Indians. In 1853 he was appointed U.S. Indian agent, with headquarters at Taos.

When the Civil War broke out, Carson left his post as Indian agent to recruit a regiment. Regular Army troops were pulled out of frontier service to fight the Confederates in the East and volunteers were mobilized to contain hostile Indians. He was commissioned a lieutenant colonel of the 1st New Mexican Volunteers, who fought against the Apache, Navajo, and Comanche Indians. He commanded the regiment and was soon promoted to the rank of colonel. At the end of the war he was brevetted brigadier general "for gallantry and for distinguished services in New Mexico." (The brevet commission nominally promoted an officer to a higher honorary rank without higher pay.)

His regiment was involved in a number of small-scale skirmishes before Carson launched his eight-month scorched-earth campaign in 1863 against the hostile Navajos in northern New Mexico. In 1864 he commanded the forces in a bloody battle at Adobe Walls, an abandoned trading post in western Texas. His force of about 400 men was attacked by between 1,500 and 3,000 Kiowas, Comanches, and other Plains Indians. Carson and his men were able to escape with only 25 fatalities.

The 1st New Mexican Volunteers, under Carson, were stationed for a period after the war at Fort Garland in southern Colorado Territory. He served as the post commander in 1866-67. He died the following year at Fort Lyons.

Colorado has honored the scout and frontier guide in several ways. A town is named in his honor—Kit Carson is located on US 287 and US 40 in Cheyenne County in the eastern part of the state. Just north of Cheyenne County is Kit Carson County.

When the Army established their training center at Colorado Springs at the outset of World War II they named it in honor of Kit Carson—first designated as Camp Carson today the post is designated Fort Carson.

INDEX

425

427

428

Maybell 288
Mayo, Drs. William and Charles 235
McAllister, Major Henry 51, 114
McAllister House Museum 114, 115
McCandless, Cmdr. Bruce 36
McCarty, Bill and Tom 335
McCarty, Tom, gang 385
McFarlane, Ida 206
McGregor Ranch 97
McGregor Ranch Museum 94
McInnes House ("The Wedding Cake House") 89
McKee, Thomas 333, 334
McKenzie House 89
McKinley, William 395
McLain's Independent Battery 10
McLean, Evalyn Walsh 395
McLean, Ned 395
McNeill, Chris 276
Mears, Otto 333, 387
Medina, Mariano 178, 180
Meeker 278, 280-282, 284, 285
Meeker, Nathan C. 15, 15, 184-186, 279, 280
Meeker Home Museum 184-186
Meeker Massacre 14, 184, 281, 282, 332, 335, 388
Merino 170
Merritt, Col. Wesley 280, 281
Mesa College 245
Mesa Verde 5, 6, 17
Mesa Verde National Park 21, 370-375
Metropolitan State College 32
Meyer, August R. 223
Miles, Vera 321
Mill and Smeltermen's Union 103
Miller, A. J. 405
Miller, Glenn 171
Miller, Frank 401, 403
Milliken, Dr. Robert Andrews 102
"Million Dollar Highway" 387
Millman, Bird 315
Mills, Enos 98
Mills, Enos Cabin and Museum 97
Mills, Enos Cabin and Nature Trail 98
Mills, J. Warner 405, 409
Miner's Hospital 397
Miner's Museum 191, 192
Miramont Castle 119
Mitchell, Brig. Gen. Robert 158
Mix, Tom 235, 318, 321
Mizel Museum of Judaica 60
Moffat, David H. 22, 269, 170, 278
Moffat County Museum 278

Moffat Road 269, 270, 277
Moffat Tunnel 22
Moffat Tunnel District 270
Molina 253
Mollie Kathleen Gold Mine 126
Monfort Feed Lots 184
Monge, Louis Jose 313
Monte Vista 351, 353, 357
Monte Vista Historical Society Museum 351
Montrose 17, 21, 41, 330, 332-335
Montrose County Historical Museum 333
Monument Valley National Park 375
Moorman, Henry 367
Morgan, Col. Christopher A. 171
Mormon Battalion 9, 137
Mormons 131, 137
Morris, William 159
Morrison 78
Most Precious Blood Catholic Church 342
Mother Cabrini Shrine 71-73
Mt. Elbert 6
Mt. Evans 7, 211
Mount Silverheels 420
Mount Sopris Historical Museum 238
Mountain City 205
Mountain Man Gallery 422
Mountain Ute Tribe 373
Mudsill 420
Mullen, J. K. 33
Municipal Museum 184
Murphy, 2nd Lt. Raymond G. 133
Museum of Space Exploration 114
Museum of the American Cowboy 111
Museum of the Mesa Verde Cowboys 369
Museum of Western Art 50
Museum of Western Colorado 246-250

Namaqua 178
National Bureau of Standards laboratory 22
National Carvers Museum 106
National Mining Hall of Fame & Museum 223, 225
Naval Air Station-Denver 37
Navy's Man-in-the-Sea Program 85
New Castle 240, 241
New Castle Historical Museum 240, 241
New Mexico Volunteer Regiment 341